Inter/Actions/Inter/Sections

ABOUT NAEA

The National Art Education Association is the world's largest professional visual arts education association and a leader in educational research, policy, and practice for art education. NAEA's mission is to advance visual arts education to fulfill human potential and promote global understanding.

Membership includes elementary and secondary art teachers, middle school and high school students in the National Art Honor Society programs, artists, administrators, museum educators, arts council staff, university professors, and students from the United States and several foreign countries. It also includes publishers, manufacturers, and suppliers of art materials; parents; students; retired art educators; and others concerned about quality art education in our schools.

NAEA publishes *Art Education, Studies in Art Education*, and other professional papers on art education; holds an annual convention; conducts research; sponsors a teacher awards program; develops standards for student learning, school programs, and teacher preparation; and co-sponsors workshops, seminars, and institutes on art education. For further information, visit our website at www.arteducators.org.

1806 Robert Fulton Drive, Suite 300, Reston, VA 20191

To order a copy of this book or obtain additional information, contact National Art Education Association: www.arteducators.org or 800-299-8321.

Order No. 313
ISBN 978-1-890160-49-4

Inter/Actions/Inter/Sections: Art Education in a Digital Visual Culture / ROBERT W. SWEENY, EDITOR

NATIONAL ART EDUCATION ASSOCIATION

Table of Contents

Section 4: Potentialities

Critical Agency: Wired, Jacked, and Plugged-In

Some *body* is sitting in *its* room texting another *body* via cell phone... while listening to rhythmic rants of hip-hop through a headset wired to an MP3 player... while surfing the Internet on a laptop computer... while occasionally glancing at scenes from *Terminator* on a nearby DVD player as the movie's violent actions and sounds command attention. On the adjacent counter a video game console is turned on but its game left in mid-play... a high-tech titanium mountain bike leans against the wall with a GPS (Global Positioning System) navigation device attached to its handlebars... a pet dog lies on the floor, sleeping with an RFID (Radio Frequency Identification) chip imbedded in its neck... the door of a small microwave oven is open, its light illuminating an open box of processed food, its contents, cheese and meat turnovers, waiting to be "nuked"...a digital picture frame, with programmed music, loops through a series of snapshots of bodies posing alone or together at techno-geek social events... a 52-inch high-definition LCD flat-screen television mounted on the wall faces an unmade bed with five remote control devices aligned on its adjacent night stand. This techno-designed "smart bedroom" is also outfitted with its own wireless port for Internet connectivity... quadraphonic speakers of a complex sound system are tucked into each of its corners... a control panel to operate a motion detection system for turning on/off high intensity track lighting, and a security alarm for warding off burglars and unwanted intruders, is mounted on the wall adjacent to the door... in one corner of the room, an unobtrusive, stealth robotic vacuum system awaits, its timer set to go off daily and begin sweeping the floor for unwanted dust balls, food crumbs, spat fingernails—even though the real purpose for its purchase was to satisfy a desire, an obsession, a fetish with technology and, if for no other reason, than to provide the other artificial agents in the room with company.

This not-too-absurd, fictional narrative characterizes the ubiquitous presence and overwhelming consumption and naturalization of technology by the human body and the body politic. Since its industrialization in the 19th century, its mechanization in the early 20th century, and digitalization in the latter 20th and early 21st century, an exponential increase in the mechanical, analog, and electronic mediation of the cultural body has taken place. Today, television, advertising, the Internet, and other mass information systems whose academic, institutional, and corporate assumptions and practices are delivered through vast networks of electronic technology continue to manufacture the body's insatiable desire and consent for leisurely and pleasurable efficiencies.

As the cultural imperative for its connectivity has increased, so has the body's dependency on the latest and fastest hardware, the most stimulating and challenging software, and a surfeit of miscellaneous electronic gadgets and gizmos. As conspicuous consumption and facility with attached or imbedded electronic devices enhances the body's proficiency and efficiency, such obsessions impede its critical agency. In other words, when the circumstances of the body's colonization by technologically mediated culture define its raison d'être, its creative and political agency is put at risk. Connectivity at this extreme level constitutes the body as cyborg, a plug-in, ready-at-hand to function on demand.

What does it mean to be connected, connected electronically; to consume, consume indiscriminately; to multitask, multitask neurotically; to exist and find purpose solely within the parameters of technologically mediated culture? What is the saturation point, the point at which the body is overwhelmed and anesthetized by technological efficiency; the point of unrelenting pleasure at the expense of criticality; at what point should the sublime ideology of technology be held in check? Ironically, as we are experiencing an increase in the isolation of the body through the use of electronic technology, a reciprocal desire for greater socialization is taking place in the form of cyber communities such as Facebook, MySpace, and Second Life. Isolated by their preoccupation with technologies, bodies are reaching out through these same technologies to build virtual relationships and virtual communities. While learning to use new technologies is imperative to functioning in contemporary culture, equally important are emancipatory pedagogies that enable users to expose, examine, and critique the totalizing and oppressive assumptions of technology and its academic, institutional, and corporate mediations of the body.

The contributors to this volume of essays are educators and artists who use new technologies in the art studio and classroom while transgressing the academic, institutional, and corporate parameters of technology. The purpose of their transgressions is to provide themselves and their students with transformative experiences. Their critical teaching strategies are inclusive in that students are not deprived the pleasure of their various technological devices and processes. On the contrary, given that the ubiquity and necessity of these devices have been assimilated into private and public memory and cultural history, the authors have developed pedagogical strategies—exploratory, experimental, and improvisational modes of addressing technological culture—that will enable their students' creative and intellectual agency, and their development as critical citizens in a cultural democracy.

Charles Garoian
2009 / Penn State University

I ♥ Technology, Always and Forever /

ROBERT W. SWEENY

I LOVE TECHNOLOGY, NOT AS MUCH AS YOU, YOU SEE.
BUT STILL, I LOVE TECHNOLOGY, ALWAYS AND FOREVER.

–*NAPOLEON DYNAMITE* (HESS, 2004)

This anthology deals with digital technology and art education. Each of the essays found within explores some aspect of each of these overlapping areas, whether concerned with the teaching of specific aspects of a software or computer program, the analysis of the methodologies that are most appropriate when incorporating digital technologies in the art classroom, the historical underpinnings of current technological practices in a variety of art educational settings, or the general possibilities for art education in a digital visual culture.

Each essay may be considered a 'line of flight' (Deleuze & Guattari, 1977) that begins by discussing the shared territory, that of art education and digital technology, and then leaves the orbit of its categorization, forming new combinations of thoughts, words, actions, and images, sketching the outlines of a digital visual culture. Because the authors deal with the field of art education, the more appropriate phrase may be 'lines of sight' (Sweeny, 2004), as these lines of text on the printed page provide new perspectives on how images and actions are seen, interpreted, resisted, and reflected in a digital visual culture.

This phrase best suits the discussions that are contained within this volume. As compared with the many writings in the field of art education that have covered similar ground, these essays deal with a widened range of gestures, actions, and influences. This expanded field is not simply more to see, feel, and experience; it is increasingly interconnected. When compared with earlier writings dealing with art education and digital technology, the authors in this anthology are describing networked forms of creativity, collaborative models of production and distribution, and educational approaches that are digital, dynamic, and distributed.

Digital visual culture should be understood not only as forms of visual culture that are digital in nature, but also as interconnected cultural products that reflect the complexity of life in a network society (Castells, 1996). While this may seem like a simple adjustment to the now-familiar term, it is, as we will see in the essays collected herein, not as simple as looking to the means of production. While images produced through digital means are easily assimilated into this category, what of images that are produced through non-digital means, and are reproduced in a digital manner, such as compact discs that carry acronyms such as ADD (analog recording, digital mastering, digital reproduction)? Are there levels to digital forms of expression that make some more digital, while others are less digital? If so, what do these varying levels of digital-ness have to say about how digital images are made, consumed, refused, and reproduced?

In these technologically complex times, it is increasingly difficult to make distinctions between the analog and the digital. As Brian Massumi (2002) argues, these distinctions are convoluted, as with the case of the actual and the virtual, which are folded together in social interactions, personal identifications, and technical processes. Challenging as it may be, it is crucial for art educators to look more closely into these foldings, as the forms of visuality produced blur the binaries upon which much of the Modernist core of art education is based.

These essays describe complex digital visualities that are currently in the process of being formed, becoming virtualities. Oftentimes, interactions with digital technologies are framed in the language of emotions central to the human condition: hate, fear, and love. The epigram indicates such a relationship, drawn from contemporary popular culture. In the song from the popular film *Napoleon Dynamite* (Hess, 2004), Kip is serenading LaFawnduh, the woman that he met online, indicating his love for both her and the technology that brought them together. While he announces that he loves LaFawnduh, he still must reaffirm his love for technology, 'always and forever.'

Existing in an unidentified time, one where 'moon boots' and the Internet coexist, Kip's admission points to the current use of digital networks for personal expression, social interaction, and individual fulfillment. It also raises issues of sociocultural difference within these interactions; LaFawnduh comes from another town, and as an African American, is racially distinct from the homogenous European-American population represented in the film. The Internet, which has long been described as a space in which identities are malleable and shifting, allows for the physical connection between these two individuals, extending the potential for new layers of identity to be added. As a popular film, *Napoleon Dynamite* exists within and refers to the complex networks of what will be referred to throughout this text as 'digital visual culture.'

Following just one exegetic path, one can look to the production of the film for an indication of the complexities entailed by the discussion of digital visual culture. *Napoleon Dynamite* was shot on traditional film stock, and was later converted to digital format common for film distribution. Two of the main storylines of the film deal with 1) drawing as a form of subjectivity, and 2) online dating and representation. As a viewer, I have access to the DVD version of the film, which is supplemented by director commentary, subtitles, and a variety of languages. Accompanying the film is the original short film that preceded the feature length version. This inclusion allows the viewer the ability to compare scene similarities, shifts in dialogue, and cinematography, and to follow the creative process of the director and crew.

The film has led to numerous popular cultural offshoots, including 'Vote for Pedro' t-shirts, and numerous spoofs available for viewing on YouTube. *Napoleon Dynamite* is by no means the only example of this diversification. As media theorist Henry Jenkins (2006) suggests, one characteristic of contemporary media forms is that they are composed of multiple layers. It is within this layering, Jenkins suggests, that the individual has the opportunity to not only personalize content, but to generate content, and participate in these media networks in a meaningful way.

It is the responsibility of art educators living within networks of digital visual culture to determine how best to personalize, generate, and participate—to take the relevant methods and materials and make them meaningful in an age of participatory media. It is a matter of identifying forms of interaction and examples of intersection that take place within digital visual culture.

INTERACTIONS/INTERSECTIONS

The past practices, current pedagogies and potential applications of digital visual culture can be described by the terms *intersections* and *interactions*. These are both terms used when discussing digital technology, though *interactivity* may be more common. As Manovich (1999) suggests, the interactive properties of new media are actually just as confining as prior media forms. The ability to choose from numerous options merely provides more choice within parameters that are ultimately determined by the designer.

While Manovich (1999) debunks the myth of interactivity, I would rather explore the construction of the words themselves, as they may tell us much about the ways in which we use technology, and also the ways that technology uses us. The terms share the same prefix, *inter-*, meaning between, sharing common attributes. The differences in the base term will be the most instructive for the discussions of digital visual culture that follow; *action* implies movement, connection, synthesis, while *section* involves a breaking apart, a dividing. As I will suggest, these terms can be used to represent the poles of technological use, the positive and the negative. They also represent two broad categories that, if connected, might help to describe how digital visual culture is produced, consumed, destroyed, and understood.

Interaction is one of the most common terms used in discussion of digital technology. Computer menus are described as 'interactive,' as are most of the technologies that link together in contemporary digital networks. The participatory media described by Jenkins (2006) derive their strength from their interactivity, the ability for users to approach content through numerous points of access, rearrange to his or her liking, and add content that is self-generated. As mentioned earlier, much of the value placed upon interaction within new media is overrated; new media art, in particular, simply offers more choices. When presented as liberatory practice, new media work might be deceptive at best; at worst it can actually restrict or repress the user.

As one description of the influence of digital technology, interaction should be seen as representing a general feeling of optimism with regard to the impact of digital technology upon the user. As with Kip, the interaction allowed by the Internet brings him in contact with his true love (to which technology is a close second). As anyone familiar with digital technologies can attest, not all such interactions bring about such fulfillment, such passion. In fact, for every example of technology as savior, there is one that shows its dystopian potential.

If interaction represents the utopian tendencies in digital technology use, then intersections might be seen as its opposite. If interaction represents the coming together of diverse individuals, materials, or experiences, then intersection should be understood as the breaking apart of these connections. If taken from the common usage, intersections are zones that are established for rerouting. Traffic intersections allow drivers to slow down or stop, to change direction, for turns to be made, and for potential collisions to occur. Intersections can also be thought of as the combining of different materials, or directionalities, in the sense of two roads coming together. But, when compared with interaction, the intersected always produces a remainder that then allows for further expansion, redirection, and synthesis.

In *Anti-Oedipus: Capitalism and Schizophrenia* (1977), Deleuze and Guattari develop the notion of the 'body without organs,' which is a form of identification that is always partial, always in the process of formation, similar in many ways to the body described in the preface by Charles Garoian. The 'machinic assemblages' that constitute the body without organs frame the operations of the individual as one that sections off or allows for various flows: organic (blood, feces, urine), mechanical (use of technology, art, science), and social (development of morals, language). In the process, modern subjectivity is fragmented, an action that Deleuze and Guattari see as directly tied to the destabilizations inherent in capitalism; this process is potentially empowering, if one is willing to break from outdated (Oedipal) forms of identification.

When viewed through the framework of the machinic assemblage, all social interaction, and certainly all technological interaction as the term is discussed previously, involves the constant sectioning and resectioning of information and matter, the perpetual action that brings together dissimilar material only to redistribute it, in a recursive manner. If art educators were to think of the operations of digital technologies in these terms, as a continual process of combination and fracturing, deterritorialization and reterritorialization, consisting of both positive and negative, often simultaneously, then the complexities of production, distribution, and consumption in a digital visual culture might be better understood. Each digital interaction entails an intersection, each connection a limiting of alternate linkages—utopian possibility coupled with dystopian potential.

The intersections that are described in this anthology are multiform; they involve individuals, classrooms, educators, and technologies, which come together and move apart, changing all involved. The collection of essays is formally divided into four sections: Media Forms, Methodologies, Prior Practices, and Potentialities. Within these sections there are numerous examples where ideas, individuals, and images interact and intersect. These categories allow for general classifications to be made, though there are additional thematic relationships to be found between the chapters. In order to provide another organizational structure, I will now provide an overview of each chapter as determined by thematic connections; you, the reader, are of course encouraged to make your own connections, or disconnections, as you see fit.[1]

Many of the chapters deal with the development and maintenance of identity in a digital visual culture. Taylor, Ballengee-Morris, and Carpenter discuss the possibilities for the pedagogical exploration of the virtual world Second Life, in "Digital Visual Culture, Social Networking, and Virtual Worlds: Second Life and Art Education." This chapter describes how the boundaries of the real and the virtual are playfully blurred, as the authors discuss the relationship between the virtual and the physical self, and how Second Life can productively unsettle traditional teacher/student roles. Identity is also the theme of the chapter by Lián Amaris; in "Fragmented Self-Portraits: How the Historical Avant-Garde Foretold Online Identity Construction," she describes the influence of Peter Bürger's (1984) *Theory of the Avant-Garde* in the understanding of identity in networked technologies. Reading the popular social networking site Facebook through the Cubist practice of montage, Amaris suggests the educational potential of art historical theory in the understanding of current digital visual culture.

Another author looking to the identities represented by avatars in Second Life is Christine Liao. In "Avatar as Pedagogy: Critical Strategies for Visual Culture in the Virtual Environment," Liao analyzes the visual characteristics of avatars, and looks to artists who use physical representation as a form of expression and cultural critique. She proposes the notion of the 'critical avatar subject' that might allow for the questioning of identities. Mary Stokrocki and Sandra Sutton Andrews explore the possibilities for both critical reflection and constructive action in virtual worlds, in "Empowering the Disenfranchised: Explorations in Building Sites and Futures in Second Life." Through qualitative research involving three homeless youths, the authors suggest possibilities for social justice through the use of social media forms. Though their study does not focus on the development of avatars, David Darts, Juan Carlos Castro, Anita Sinner, and Kit Grauer build upon similar themes, discussing possibilities for digital art education that takes place outside of the traditional classroom setting. In their chapter, titled "New Media Arts Education: How Community-Based Programs Can Reshape Teaching and Learning in the Age of Web 2.0," the authors suggest that the education taking place in community-based arts centers might serve as an instructive model for art educators looking for creative critical models for teaching digital technologies.

Many authors discuss the relationship between digital visual culture and Constructivist learning theories. Melanie Buffington, with Kathryn R. Helms, Jan A. Johnston, and Sohhyoun Yoon, present options for art educators interested in utilizing social media in "Web 2.0 and Social Constructivism." Outlining the use of sites such as del.icio.us, Second Life, and blogs, the authors argue that the inclusion of these elements of digital visual culture supports constructivist learning principles in public schools and university settings. Nicholas Hostert also provides an overview of the educational possibilities for blogging in "Uncommon Dialogue: Digital Critique Beyond the Art Classroom." Hostert describes a qualitative research study carried out in a Chicago area high school, comparing interactions that take place online and in class, and suggesting numerous benefits generated through these forms of communication.

David Gill also addresses the principles of constructivist learning in his analysis of the teaching of 3-D Computer Graphics, in "Vertex Mode: Situated Use of 3-D Modeling and Animation Software." This qualitative study outlines the influence that digital visual culture holds on those interested in learning digital technologies in the art classroom. In a similar manner, Carleton Palmer describes the challenges and successes in teaching digital imaging technologies for incarcerated populations, in "A Digital Visual Culture Course for Incarcerated Youth." Palmer provides the reader with a useful overview of his program as he describes art educational practices in this unique site.

Building upon the work of educational psychologists such as Vygotsky (1978), Marissa McClure argues that the inclusion of digital video in the Kindergarten classroom represents a rhizomatic destabilization of traditional teacher/student roles, in "Digital Visual Childhood: Preschoolers and the New Narratives of Digital Video in the Blogosphere." Also making reference to traditional learning theories, in this case media literacy, Sheng Kuan Cheng argues for a 'critical cyberliteracy' in "Cybermedia Literacy Art Education." Where Buffington, et al. present numerous potential opportunities for educational application of social media, Chung offers a thought-engaging critique of cyberspace, one that replaces optimism with careful consideration of experiences that reflect corporate interests and capitalist manipulation.

The relationship between culture and digital technologies is discussed in many of the chapters. In "Developing ChinaVine.org: Educating Inside and Outside the Site," by Kristin Congdon and Doug Blandy, the challenges of representing Chinese folk art and culture in an online environment are outlined.

The authors present a number of useful technical, sociological, and educational suggestions for art educators who wish to explore and honor world folk art traditions. Looking to the Talmud, the ancient Hebrew religious text, Mel Alexenberg makes cross-cultural and cross-temporal comparisons, in "Space-Time Structures of Digital Visual Culture: Paradigm Shift from Hellenistic to Hebraic Roots of Western Civilization." Alexenberg asserts that Hebraic thought is more closely related to the multilayered nature of the Internet, and the understanding of this worldview might help art educators to better understand the hypertextual qualities of contemporary digital visual culture. Kevin Tavin offers a personal narrative that describes the technoculture of the preservice art educator and elementary educator, and his use of hypertext theories, in "From Story-Space to PowerPoint: Searching for an (In)Adequate Space to Make a Point." Building on the work of critical pedagogues such as Joe Kinchloe and Henry Giroux, Tavin frankly discusses the benefits as well as the constraints found within both programs, reviewing a 10-year period of exploration and frustration, and offering suggestions for those who seek to explore hypertext theory and pedagogy.

Another theme that runs through many of the essays in this anthology is the updating of traditional media and methods through digital means. Sara Wilson McKay addresses the unique challenges that digital information represents for art educators, in "In Search of the Public Domain: Addressing the Threat of Copyright Laws in Art Education." Wilson McKay outlines these challenges, while suggesting numerous constructive options for art educators reproducing digital images. Sheichau Wang describes the potential for electronic portfolios in "Digital Journals: The Past, Present, and Future of Electronic Portfolios for Visual Culture Learners." In this chapter, Wang shares the results of two studies of e-portfolio use, and also discusses the potential for networked portfolio that use the blog format, providing the reader with numerous suggestions for the successful use of these technologies. Ryan Shin also discusses the differences between traditional media and digital media, in "Four Digital Media Art Practices: Moving Beyond Drawing and Painting on the Computer." In this chapter, Shin shares his experiences with teaching digital technologies to preservice art teachers, describing their struggles and successes, and providing the teacher educator with a number of helpful pedagogical strategies. Shin also makes the argument that digital media rely upon a unique set of methods, which art educators must acknowledge if digital art is to be made a relevant part of art educational practice in the 21st century.

Along similar lines, Mara Jevera Fulmer and James W. Shurter discuss the development of podcasts and an e-zine (electronic magazine) in the teaching of graphic design, in "Thinking Big, Creating Small: Podcast Tips for Graphic Design Students." This chapter describes in detail the processes and pitfalls of utilizing developing digital technologies to provide content that builds upon and complements traditional classroom instruction. Selin Ozguzer also deals with the translation of traditional teaching methods and themes in the teaching of graphic design, proposing that the introduction of interactive Flash-based games can provide art educational content in a dynamic, educationally sound manner. In "Educational Applications of Flash in Graphic Design Education," Ozguzer suggests that the visual and interactive qualities of the program make it far more accessible than the traditional activities found in Graphic Design classrooms.

Yet another theme that runs through the text is physicality and the ephemeral in digital visual culture. Ryan Patton and Matt Kenyon discuss the potential for video games in art education in their chapter "Physical Computing and Video Game Art Education." While authors such as Taylor, et al. point out that virtual environments such as Second Life may be considered video games depending on the intent of the programmers and the participants, Patton and Kenyon clearly outline new territory for art educators interested in the physical, interactive nature of video games. Michelle Tillander presents a theoretical reading of the notion of invisibility in her chapter, "Digital Visual Culture: The Paradox of the [In] visible." In her analysis of the concept of the interface, she suggests that "...art educators and artists illuminate a range of [in]visible new media conversations for art education, which can be used in developing innovative art and technology curricula." Karen Keifer-Boyd engages the reader in a multilayered exploration of identity and digital technology, in "Masquerading the Immateriality of Materiality." In this chapter, Keifer-Boyd intertwines the narratives of future art educators and students with discussions of avatar construction and identity deconstruction, shifting between past, present, and future in a destabilizing and provocative manner.

Each chapter offers practical suggestions for those art educators who wish to add new methodologies to their teaching, or to rethink existing practices, while presenting the reader with the challenges that accompany teaching, learning, and producing in a digital visual culture. In the process, art education and digital technology are rethought, and re-viewed, through these developing notions of identity and virtuality, modifications upon traditional learning theories, reconceptualizations of culture, translations of prior practices, ludic interfaces, and the relationship between physicality and the ephemeral. Each adds a node to the expanding network that is current art educational practice, indicating the places where these practices have initialized, and pointing toward numerous possibilities for future art educators. This is a network that will continue to expand as technologies and individuals interact, cultures and communities intersect, and educators and students respond to and help to create new forms of digital visual culture: always and forever.

REFERENCES

Castells, M. (1996). *The rise of the network society.* Malden, MA: Blackwell.

Deleuze, G., & Guattari, F. (1977). *Anti-Oedipus: Capitalism and schizophrenia.* Minneapolis, MN: University of Minnesota Press

Hess, J. (Director). (2004). *Napoleon Dynamite* [Motion Picture]. United States: Access Films.

Jenkins, H. (2006). *Convergence culture: Where old and new media collide.* New York: NYU Press.

Manovich, L. (1999). *The language of new media.* Cambridge, MA: MIT Press.

Massumi, B. (2002). *Parables of the virtual. Movement, affect, sensation.* Durham, NC: Duke University Press.

Sweeny, R. (2004). Lines of sight in "The Network Society:" Simulation, art education, and a digital visual culture. *Studies in Art Education, 46*(1).

Vygotsky, L.S. (1978). *Mind in society: The development of higher psychological processes.* Cambridge, MA: Harvard University Press.

ENDNOTE

1 I have also presented the reader with yet another form of classification; the 'word clouds' that introduce each section are visual representations of word frequency within each section. This was done using the applet 'Wordle,' found at http://www.wordle.net. Wordle.net by Jonathan Feinberg is licensed under a Creative Commons Attribution-Noncommercial-No Derivative Works 3.0 United States License.

media forms
time material effects four first
technologies way ways
data teacher 3-D artists seen
part type
experience study also
group well interactivity began
classroom Educational
curriculum designed educators personal
one much
media even
learning
contemporary Podcasts tools CG
popular student
groups
art
Rather information
help text
may University making
classes web
Maya used Creative
production story people Teachers topics
many graphic
Visual
site arts
Software
school Freedman experiences
Press participants created
second games
class aesthetic Flash
like Culture
made work knowledge college
project Images
Computer children's
process game questions
teaching technology language
artwork learn
Principles documentation content different specific
Education
Context within
often image
invisible idea Internet
another Animation retrieved course
students
create
just learned
ed exercises
studies program results computers interactive example
participant new
strategies
visible development video using creating
make approach
narrative social Children
interaction
digital
materials ideas life
form thus Use York aesthetics
design three
cultural
research communication

Vertex Mode: Situated Use of 3-D Modeling and Animation Software / DAVID V. GILL[1]

INTRODUCTION: 3-D COMPUTER GRAPHICS

It is difficult to overstate the impact that 3-D computer graphic imagery has had on the character and aesthetic qualities of fine art and popular media forms of art such as video games, television, and cinema during the last 25 years. As Gardner (2002) points out, the technique of producing a 3-D digital model and subsequently applying materials, lighting, and animation to bring the model to life has revolutionized the way popular media is created and has made possible cinema that was impossible to create without 3-D computer graphics (3-D CG). Examples of this type of cinema production include entirely 3-D CG animated features such as *Finding Nemo* (2003) and *Wall-E* (2008) by Pixar, to films that rely on digital animations for spectacular special effects like those seen in the *Lord of the Rings* trilogy (2001-2003). 3-D CG also emerged in television advertisements and programs beginning in the 1980s. At the same time that cinematic 3-D CG became popular in the early 1990s, video games also were being transformed through the use of 3-D CG (Kerlow, 2000).

The first 3-D modeling and animation programs made for the personal computer first emerged during the 1980s (Gardner, 2002). Two popular programs today are Alias' Maya (recently purchased by Autodesk) and Softimage's Softimage, which evolved from digital cinema production tools used in Hollywood. A third popular software program is Autodesk's 3-DS Max (formerly 3-D Studio Max and 3-D Studio), which emerged out of the popular computer-aided design package Autocad. In the last few years, software companies marketing 3-D modeling and animation software have begun offering academic licenses that restrict the user to non-commercial activity. These licenses are widely available for less than 10% of the commercial software's purchase price and are now within the budgets of many school districts. Although space does not permit its discussion here, Spalter (1999) completely describes software-independent 3-D CG methods of creation in her book.

CONTEXT: ART EDUCATION AND COMPUTER GRAPHICS

While image projection technology (Eisenhauer, 2006) and new technologies for art materials (Efland, 1990) have been rapidly adopted by art educators, Spalter (1999) suspects that many artists have not embraced computer graphic technology because of its military origins. Despite this wariness, Johnson (1997) noted that more than 80 articles in art education journals appeared between 1987 and 1997 promoting the inclusion of computer graphics production in the art education curriculum. Recently, Stankiewicz (2004), Freedman (2003), Carpenter and Taylor (2002, 2003), Prater (2001), and Keifer-Boyd (2005), among others, have all advocated the use of computers in the art classroom for a variety of curricular purposes. Delacruz (2004) examined obstacles to computer technology adoption in art education, noting important inconsistencies in preservice art teacher preparation and daily working conditions in school districts.

Despite the number of articles in the art education literature concerning computers in the art classroom, Sakatani's (2005) article is unique in being the only one to report on a classroom employing 3-D CG. In his study of middle school art students, which took place in the mid-1990s, he found that a constructivist approach to teaching computer technology in the art classroom was useful for their exploration of virtual reality. Sakatani found that students were motivated by and learned interactive technology inductively within collaborative groups. He concluded that students were engaged by the use of technology for art learning in the situated, real-world context of the project.

CASE STUDY: LEARNING 3-D CG IN A HIGH SCHOOL CLASSROOM

The remainder of this chapter will report on dissertation research examining one high school digital art curriculum in a suburban American Midwestern city. The design selected for the research project was a thematic case study, selected because the lack of previous studies on the subject in the literature made hypothesis construction impossible.[2] The methodological model for the design of the study was two studies done by Freedman and Relan (1990, 1992) that concerned student use of digital paint software at the time when those programs were first entering the classroom. During field research for the dissertation, encounters with participants led to themes emerging in the accumulating data. The emergent themes informed grounded theory construction by the researcher and allowed for modification of the research plan when unexpected data emerged. Data gathered during the pre-study period and a pilot study completed the previous summer were used to develop preliminary themes and research questions.

The study focused on outcomes from a spring semester Advanced Digital Images course, but pre-study observations encompassed the prerequisite Introductory Digital Images course held the previous semester. In the introductory course, students were familiarized with digital studio art technology and software including Photoshop and the 3-D modeling and animation program Maya. The last half of this 16-week course was spent working in small groups to create a 10-second animation using Maya. The teacher used a minimal amount of class lecture, delivering 10-minute mini-demonstrations at the beginning of some classes, but relying on personalized instruction and discovery learning of software by students in the process of creating their animations.

In the advanced course, the entire semester was dedicated to the single objective of creating a 3- to 5-minute narrative animation using Maya. Rather than complete a series of exercises or tutorials to learn or re-learn the software (some students had taken the introductory course in previous school years), the teacher again provided only minimal amounts of lecture/demonstrations, allowing students to explore the expansive Maya program on their own terms. This situated learning approach to the course afforded students the maximum amount of time to solve particular problems that emerged from each group's individual projects and to complete their animations. Within a few weeks, groups of students were learning different functions of the software, based on the unique needs of their projects. Their research produced situated understanding in different areas of the software that was specific and deep. For this reason, the teacher resisted taking on the role of an expert Maya user, but instead acted as a coach or guide, providing strategies and suggesting resources when students encountered problems. Sakatani (2005), Prater (2001), and Perkins (1991) among others state that this type of constructivist, student-centered pedagogy is efficacious in the technology classroom.

The participants in the study were 16 males and 1 female between the ages of 15 and 18 and the male classroom art teacher. I chose not to study one group of 5 male students when 2 of them failed to return consent forms. The gender imbalance in students taking the class was not unusual for the digital art classes. In previous semesters of the introductory and advanced courses, there were typically between 3 and 6 females enrolled in an average class size of 24 students. The reasons for this gender imbalance became an important unresolved emergent theme in the study, discussed briefly in this chapter as a suggestion for future research.

The art teacher had been instructing the digital courses for 4 years and was the art department chairperson. Most students were college bound, came from affluent families, and were used to computer technology being available to them. Participants formed five collaborative working groups during the first week of the advanced class and few changes were made to the groups thereafter. Students were allowed to select their groups' members and the majority of groups were comprised of students of the same age and grade level. Within the groups, many of the students knew each other and some were friends before the class began.

The site for the study was an art department computer graphics lab with 29 workstations, a digital projector, scanners, and a printer. Each student had use of a computer with network access including Internet, Adobe Photoshop, Alias Maya 6, and Microsoft Movie Maker. The school had one full-time technical support specialist on staff.

INFLUENCE OF VISUAL CULTURE ON THE CREATIVE PROCESS

The first research question investigated how a course of study in animation using Maya utilized and informed participant perceptions and attitudes about visual culture, especially video games, cinema, and television, as was suggested by pilot study and pre-study observations. These observations were quickly confirmed in a pre-study survey where it became clear that participant enthusiasm for genres of visual culture, particularly video games, led directly to their desire to participate in the 3-D CG medium and enroll in the digital art courses. In the survey, 80% of participants reported taking the class because of an interest in computer games, movie special effects, and/or 3-D animated movies. Also in the survey, participants reported spending an average of 9.9 hours per week playing video games, more than they reported watching television or using the Internet. Furthermore, 78% wanted to explore careers in video game production. Only one participant reported not playing video games—the female in the class.

Additionally, in semi-structured interviews, data emerged that participants were paying closer critical attention to 3-D CG they encountered in their visual culture as a result of being in the class. Additionally, findings indicated that participants' admiration of the skills of commercial 3-D CG artists and designers increased as they experienced the process of creating similar work during the course. One participant commented:

> I know how much effort they're putting into it, and... I respect the movie a lot more, and I appreciate it... for how much work and time they probably put into it. That's how I look at it, and just wondering like, how they did it. (Male participant, personal communication, 6/2/06)

Here the participant expresses both the admiration for the work that goes into 3-D CG productions and the beginnings of deconstructing visual culture for production techniques.

Data emerged in the study that suggested participants' knowledge of popular visual culture was being utilized in the classroom in meaningful ways. This information was gathered from semi-structured and unstructured interviews with participants and from observing group exchanges where communications about projects were taking place. Participants usually communicated ideas through verbal exchanges filled with references to examples from popular media, including TV, cinema, and video games. Problem solving by example also was common, where students analyzed and could cite specific cinema and video game references for possible solutions to difficulties. One group leader talked about her group's inspiration to create an animation featuring a dinosaur in a modern city:

> We kind of thought of King Kong a little bit, and then they (group members) thought of some game. Was it Rampage? Something like that, with... a lizard. (Female participant, personal communication, 2/6/06)

Here the participant shows how group members' common experiences with visual culture, including cinema and video games, are used in the classroom to communicate ideas.

In the early phases of the participants' productions, the influence of popular visual culture imagery on idea formation became apparent. Once students democratically determined a loose production idea, each participant immediately began to decide on the imagery they wanted in the animation, drawing primarily on experiences from popular visual culture. Specific scenes planned for the production were previsualized, imagined, and planned before their story had been determined. This led to obvious narrative problems as groups attempted to accommodate various individual ideas and imagery from media genres such as cinema and video games into a coherent whole. Isolated previsualized scenes were sometimes storyboarded or even created digitally by the individual participant whose idea it was, while the central story was usually agreed upon during group meetings. Participant groups were reluctant to discard ideas or work from the production for a variety of personal and time management reasons.

As the study continued, it became obvious that participant groups were primarily interested in the visual appeal of their animations and much less interested in creating compelling narrative. The teacher noted that one of the groups was having particular difficulty filling in story between visually appealing scenes the students conceived at the outset of the production:

> They had so many different elements to the story that just didn't quite go together.... To come to a conclusion that any of them really cared much about narrative before they started, I would venture to say that that was not the case. (Classroom art teacher, personal communication, 5/4/06)

While this particular group had profound difficulties in coming up with a story, most other groups had minimal storylines as well. Given the length of their productions, usually between 3 and 5 minutes, creating a compelling narrative was an admittedly difficult task, but the participants' approach was uniformly to previsualize and let the story work itself out later.

The previsualization phenomenon also was related to the adoption of game-inspired themes for the groups' projects. All of the participant groups in the study were inspired by games, traditional or video, and were all interested in creating an animation entirely or partially based on one or more of them. This merging of games, particularly video games, into the 3-D CG animation genre produced many problems and inventive solutions as participants attempted to emulate the non-linear quality of the video game narrative. Interestingly, the cinematic production of *Doom* (2005) was attempted in part to capture the excitement of the popular video game in the same way, but participants did not mention being influenced by the film in interviews. The mission structure of video games, with the player's embodiment in central character development, made translation of video game playing experiences into 3-D CG animations difficult. Participants grappled with how to show the excitement of games where the dramatic outcomes are partially dependent on the player's actions. As a result, participants frequently changed point of view in their animations to simulate a video game experience, and one group included game graphics to complete the effect.

LEARNING TO COMMUNICATE VISUAL IDEAS

The second research question asked what students learned about visual art in order to communicate their ideas through Maya. Since the students had little experience with the Maya software, technical learning about the software and its demands was continuous, meaningful, and substantial. Participants were able to construct knowledge about ways to model complex objects using a variety of tools and methods for keeping animations within the limitations of their computer hardware. Participants also learned to utilize seriation (Freedman & Relan, 1990, 1992), the saving of copies or clones (Sweeny, 2005) of their models and animation data at various stages of development.

Participants demonstrated increasing ability to critically evaluate their artwork and the work of their group partners. This critical ability emerged as they subjected the group's work to spontaneous, constant, informal critique and group evaluation in their persistent demand for visual appeal (looking "cool") in their 3-D CG artwork. Sequences were rarely abandoned due to difficulties. Instead, problematic or poor quality sequences were handed off to other group members for editing. The pattern of production followed by critical judgment followed by technical adaptation and more production was repeatedly observed. One participant described this informal critique process:

> We'll just all do our own thing on whatever we're working on, and then... the group will come and take a look at it and if they'll like it... then we'll just go back to our independent selves and re-work the animation... and see if the group members like it. (Male participant, personal communication, 4/19/06)

This situated collaboration for expressive purposes is a valuable skill for any artist hoping for a career in the visual arts, and it is a skill that students gained throughout the semester.

The criteria for visual appeal came from their substantial knowledge of the visual qualities (Boughton & Freedman, in process) of preferred examples of popular visual culture, most often video games. Participants all desired and strove to create realistic imagery with Maya by directly manipulating visual qualities particular to 3-D CG such as object polygons, textures, space, time, special effects, and light. While the Advanced Digital Images course did not specifically require or reward realism in animations, all participants attempted it, with varying degrees of success. Despite the technical difficulties, time required, and their novice status with Maya, participants learned to expand differentiated and purposeful use of each visual quality as the course went on. The realism they achieved was important for expressing ideas about media genre types, humor, drama, and contextual information.

Through active production of an animation project, participants constructed meaningful knowledge about how to express themselves using popular visual culture narrative devices and humor. Some participants learned to utilize expressive narrative devices including cinematic montage to help propel their story ideas forward. In one case, a participant group used montage to abbreviate the long action sequence of a chess game. To maintain audience interest and to make the amount of production work reasonable given the time constraints of the semester, group members could cite and mimic techniques used in the wizard's chess match from *Harry Potter and the Sorcerer's Stone* (2001) and battle sequences from *Braveheart* (1995).

A few participants experimented with techniques for expressing humor in their productions. Expressing humor sometimes involved the creation of context, referencing real-world places, visual culture, and politics to enable humorous situations to develop. In other cases, participants attempted physical humor, utilizing character deformations reminiscent of traditional cel animation.

Despite the difficulties of creating with professional software, most participants learned to sustain inquiry (Gude, 2007) and even described working with Maya as "fun." The feeling of fun was reported by participants in part due to the open-ended nature of the software and its power, the collaborative group experience, and the potential for participants to create images they cared about to the limits of their imagination. Some participants experienced a feeling of flow while working with Maya. Csikszentmihalyi (1990) notes that the experience of flow is intensely pleasurable, motivating people to continue to seek out experiences that produce it. Many reported the phenomenon of time flying by in the class, and one participant commented:

> It's fun when... you know what you want to make, right, and you're just flowing. You're using the program and nothing is getting in the way, you're just flowing and you keep making, <snaps fingers a few times> and you keep progressing through your project, through what you want to make and then you finally finish it and it's like, wow. It looks cool, and you're... satisfied from it, you get a good feeling. (Emphasis added, Male Participant, personal communication, 4/17/06)

LEARNING MAYA: INDIVIDUAL AND GROUP STRATEGIES

The final research question investigated the strategies and skills participants learned or developed in order to acquire fluency with the Maya software. Data emerged that indicated participants constructed knowledge about how to learn the Maya software inductively, through interrogation of the software during creation. Findings indicated that participant experiences with a variety of graphic-laden software utilizing iconography outside of the classroom, importantly including many video games, taught them how to learn unfamiliar software. This affected their attitudes, expectations, preferences, and strategies for learning the Maya software. Given the minimal amount of traditional didactic instruction in the software by the teacher, non-constructivist learning theories cannot account for the rapidity of participant progress during the course. Sequential saved files of the participants' Maya efforts attest to their abilities to seriate their models and progress quickly.

Student participants' ability to work together on their Maya productions was essential for their success in the course. Student cooperative groups exhibited positive interdependence (Johnson & Johnson, 1991), and provided each group member with learning support, motivation, and morale. Results from the study indicate that individual group members tended to specialize in certain functions within the animation process and that diversity of participant backgrounds was beneficial to problem solving. Participants primarily turned to other group members for assistance, preferring immediate response over waiting for the teacher or researching the problem. This is not surprising considering the social constructivist (Sakatani, 2005) mode of instruction used in the class. Student technical difficulties with the software could eventually outstrip the teacher's knowledge base as students became more specialized in the use of specific functions needed for their animations. In these cases, the art teacher functions as a coach or guide, advising on strategies and suggesting specific areas for further research.

DISCUSSION AND CONCLUSION

The exploratory thematic case study described in this chapter represents a first attempt to determine the outcomes of a course in 3-D CG and determining effective pedagogical strategies for teaching digital and traditional forms of art to the Millennial Generation. Teachers wishing to implement a course of study in 3-D CG now have preliminary findings that support the value of such a course as part of a secondary education visual culture program. The findings outlined in this chapter have shown that participants constructed deep and meaningful knowledge about visual art and 3-D CG during the Advanced Digital Images course. Data emerged indicating specific ways in which participant experiences with popular visual culture gained outside of the classroom were being applied to learning and creating with the Maya software. Likewise, the ways that student perceptions of popular visual culture were being influenced by their experiences in the course were illuminated. This intersection of emerging art knowledge and visual culture was a surprising dynamic that has not been previously documented or questioned by researchers. For the first time, the process by which students collaboratively utilize their visual culture experiences in the creation of 3-D CG within the digital art classroom was shown.

Through creative interaction with software, participants learned to manipulate visual qualities (Boughton & Freedman, in process) to express ideas. Their ability to remain motivated and sustain inquiry (Gude, 2007) was due in part to their legitimate, collaborative participation in a meaningful project where they had the opportunity to express ideas through a medium they enjoyed and respected. Pedagogically, approaching the teaching of 3-D modeling and animation by providing situated, cooperative, and student-centered experiences in a constructivist, visual culture context seems to offer the best chance for success and the greatest potential benefit to students.

Additionally, this study has demonstrated that non-constructivist theories of cognition are insufficient to explain the rapid progress of student participants in learning the Maya software during the course. Participants were able to learn to use the software by inductive interrogation and collaboration based on personal, idiosyncratic experiences and strategies gained through learning to play a variety of video games. This finding poses challenging problems for attaining gender balance in the digital art classroom, if we accept demographic data that shows far fewer young females are playing video games.

The study reported on in this chapter represents an exciting first step in exploring learning outcomes and pedagogical approaches in teaching and learning with 3-D CG. Much more research remains to be done for a full appreciation and understanding of the benefits and pitfalls of student use of 3-D CG in the art classroom. Primary areas for future research must address how more diverse groups of students, including a more gender-balanced class, would approach the task of creating with Maya or other 3-D modeling and animation software. Students of different cultural and socio-economic backgrounds also need to be studied for data on how those students might approach the task. Alternatives to the situated, student-centered model of pedagogy used by the classroom art teacher should likewise be examined for comparison purposes. This study also shows the importance of finding ways to prepare preservice art teachers to become fluent in the medium of 2-D and 3-D CG, as well as ways to help them to become lifelong learners of new media software.

Finally, public school art departments can benefit from courses in digital technology as parents and administrators see the value in teaching the rudiments of the digital technologies that permeate our lives and the lives of our students. The ability to visualize and manipulate a digital three-dimensional object or environment is growing increasingly important in the context of daily life, as ubiquitous computing devices like global positioning systems and virtual reality become commonplace. In the digital visual culture, the cognitive ability to visualize and manipulate 3-D information is becoming essential to everyone. The art classroom utilizing 3-D modeling and animation software is one valuable way for students to develop the abilities needed to humanely interact in the graphic technology-mediated world.

REFERENCES

Boughton, D., & Freedman, K. (in process). *Making art meaningful: A practical approach to teaching visual culture.* New York: McGraw Hill.

Carpenter, S., & Taylor, P. (2003). Racing thoughts: Altering our ways of knowing and being in art through computer hypertext. *Studies in Art Education, 45*(1), 40-55.

Csikszentmihalyi, M. (1990). *Flow: The psychology of optimal experience.* New York: Harper Collins.

Delacruz, E. (2004). Teachers' working conditions and the unmet promise of technology. *Studies in Art Education, 46*(1), 6-19.

Efland, A. (1990). *A history of art education: Intellectual and social currents in teaching the visual arts.* New York: Teachers College Press.

Eisenhauer, J. (2006). Next slide please: The magical, scientific, and corporate discourses of visual projection technologies. *Studies in Art Education, 47*(3), 198-214.

Freedman, K. (2003). *Teaching visual culture: Curriculum, aesthetics, and the social life of art.* New York: Teachers College Press.

Freedman, K., & Relan, A. (1990). The use of applications software in school: Paint system image development processes as a model for situated learning. *Journal of Research on Computing in Education, 23*(1), 101-112.

Freedman, K., & Relan, A. (1992). Computer graphics, artistic production, and social processes. *Studies in Art Education, 33*(2), 98-109.

Gardner, G. (2002). *Computer graphics and animation: History, careers, expert advice.* Washington, DC: GGC Publishing.

Gude, O. (2007). Principles of possibility: Considerations for a 21st century art & culture curriculum. *Art Education, 60*(1), 6-17.

Johnson, M. (1997). Orientations to curriculum in computer art education. *Art Education, 50*(3), 43-47.

Johnson, D., & Johnson, R. (1991). *Learning together and alone: Cooperative, competitive, and individualistic learning.* Englewood Cliffs, NJ: Prentice Hall.

Keifer-Boyd, K. (2005). Children teaching children with their computer game creations. *Visual Arts Research, 31*(1), 117-128.

Kerlow, I. V. (2000). *The art of 3-D computer animation and imaging* (2nd ed). New York: John Wiley & Sons.

Perkins, D. N. (1991). Technology meets constructivism: Do they make a marriage? *Educational Technology, 31*(5), 18-23.

Prater, M. (2001). Constructivism and technology in art education. *Art Education, 54*(6), 43-48.

Robson, C. (2002). *Real world research* (2nd ed.). Oxford, UK: Blackwell Publishers.

Sakatani, K. (2005). Harmony quest: An interdisciplinary arts based project incorporating virtual reality. *Visual Arts Research, 31*(1), 53-62.

Spalter, A. (1999). *The computer in the visual arts.* Reading, MA: Addison Wesley Longman.

Stankiewicz, M. (2004). Notions of technology and visual literacy. *Studies in Art Education, 46*(1), 88-91.

Sweeny, R. (2005). Three funerals and a wedding: Art education, digital images, and an aesthetic of cloning. *Visual Arts Research, 31*(1), 26-37.

Taylor, P., & Carpenter, S. (2002). Inventively linking: Teaching and learning with computer hypertext. *Art Education, 55*(4), 6-12.

ENDNOTES

1 This research was supported in part by a Dissertation Completion Fellowship from Northern Illinois University.

2 Thematic case study data gathering is similar to grounded theory research where the researcher formulates some preliminary research questions that are explored and modified in an iterative fashion during field experiences. For a broader explanation of this type of research method, see Robson (2002).

Thinking Big, Creating Small: Podcast Tips for Graphic Design Students / MARA JEVERA FULMER AND JAMES W. SHURTER

Faced with growing distractions from YouTube, Facebook, MySpace, and iPod videos, our design faculty's ability to engage with students through the digital haze has been met with frustratingly inconsistent levels of success. In order to involve millennial/post-millennial students in critical and conceptual thinking related to art and design, Graphic Design faculty Mara Jevera Fulmer, Associate Professor, and James W. Shurter, Instructor, at C.S. Mott Community College in Flint, Michigan, resolved to leap into the fray with the creation of a series of educational podcasts. The expansive popularity of podcasts, a method of online broadcasting self-contained audio (and now video) material originally meant to be played on the highly popular iPod manufactured by Apple Inc., has made it possible for even the most techno newbie to share their own original audio and video programming with the rest of the world.

A 2005 study funded by the Kaiser Family Foundation, "Generation M: Media in the Lives of 8-18-year-olds" (Rideout, et al., 2005), indicates that now more than ever, youth are plugged in and multitasking in ways that seemed almost impossible in the past. One of their key findings indicated that, while the amount of time that young people spent using media has changed little, still about 6 hours per day, "they are actually exposed to the equivalent of 8 hours a day of media content" (p. 6). The challenge for us, we believe, was to find ways to overcome the distractions by the very media we were preparing our students to enter. This same media also has the power to improve lives, ease instruction and communication, and improve the exchange of information, if only we could harness it to the benefit of our students.

Having been awarded a Faculty Innovation Award from the college for our proposal, we chose to utilize the same tools of this media barrage to address basic concepts in typography, design vocabulary, and processes in graphic design in a podcast series titled "Graphic Tips for Students." The aim of creating the podcasts was to overcome the short attention spans, constant multitasking, and visual "snacking" upon different websites, social media, and messaging that seemed to undermine our students' absorption of course material. At the same time, we hoped to focus on very specific topics that were often glossed over by instructors or ignored by students, but were details important to their development as designers.

Much has been written on the positive and negative effects of media multitasking, especially among youth today and, while the debate continues in the popular press (see Lohr, 2007; Wallis, 2006; Johnson, 2006; Anderson, 2001), much research among scholarly communities has also addressed this subject. At the Institute for the Future of the Mind (IFM), Oxford University researchers hope to address the "influence of virtual technologies on attention and cognitive control in young people" (Deal & Sharples, 2008), as described on their website. In addition, a study was underway at IFM that was meant "to determine how communication technologies impact upon the ability of individuals to attend to a task" (Westwell & Sharples, 2008). Featured in an article on the front page of the *New York Times*, researcher David E. Meyer, director of the Brain, Cognition, and Action Laboratory at the University of Michigan, indicated that multitasking can increase one's chances of making mistakes (Lohr, 2007). And, while popular perception is that younger people can multitask better than older people, the researchers at IFM found in their study comparing 18- to 21-year-olds against 35- to 39-year-olds that when both groups were interrupted with media such as "by a phone call, cellphone text messages or an [online] instant message, the older group match the younger group in speed and accuracy." According to Westwell, "The older people think more slowly, but they have a faster fluid intelligence, so they are better able to block out interruptions and choose what to focus on" (Lohr, 2007).

Rather than declaring a definitive solution, we embarked upon a rather unscientific experiment. What if we joined the media haze? After all, studies indicate that more people than ever are downloading podcasts or watching video online (Lenhart, Madden, Macgill, & Smith, 2007). At the very least we could post our own content out in cyberspace that would address the little details, the basics in graphic design that our students ignored. We felt the podcasts would be a good first entry into this digital storm and so we began by creating a list of topics that we wanted to address. These included: basic typographic elements, measuring, digital file types and uses, image resolution, grid layout, and so forth. Whenever possible, comparative examples from the world around us would be used to demonstrate important concepts. For example, linespacing could be explained through its similarities to backyard fences, while other subjects could be demonstrated through direct examples from the tools of the trade such as vintage wood-block or metal type. Topics would address basic typographic subjects such as kerning, linespacing, and measurement. In the future, we would then move into more varied topics such as the use of positive and negative shapes in logo design.

THE PROCESS

Because of the nature of the topics to be discussed—for example, the nuances of letterspacing and kerning—each video podcast to be created depended upon a high visual fidelity to maintain clarity while also being succinct in its topic presentation. Technical challenges and glitches were plentiful in the early stages of development of these short 4- to 7-minute videos. After working out the kinks, a basic step-by-step process was followed in order to maintain a consistent and easy workflow:

1. Script writing and storyboard
2. Design layout (4:3 or 640x480) in InDesign, kept neat and simple
3. Export to Max Quality JPEGS from InDesign
4. Video edit in iMovie (insert QT video of pre-made Intro & Closing credits common to all and created in Flash)
5. Insert Audio music soundtrack (very low) on audio track #2
6. Record voice-over directly into iMovie (audio track #1), edit, adjust
7. Export to QuickTime full quality (expert settings) video, 640x480, 48 hz stereo

This simple process allowed us to focus on the topics being created and reduce the continuous fussing over technology that we faced earlier. It was also important to maintain a larger visual screen size in order for many of the concepts being demonstrated to be visible.

While we considered ourselves to be technically savvy, having worked for years as professional designers and still maintaining clients outside our full-time teaching, we found ourselves challenged as we tried to find the best fit and flow between software programs. Eventually, we developed an approach using a combination of Adobe's Flash, Illustrator, InDesign and Photoshop for content development. At the time of this writing we were using Adobe's Creative Suite 3. We kept it simple for final video editing, using Apple's iMovie and QuickTime Pro. Later, when a decision was made to launch it as an e-zine/blog, we used Apple's iWeb because of its quick and easy-to-use features. Creating opening and closing credits in Flash stymied us at first when we discovered some glitches with the QuickTime export features, which we eventually overcame by adjusting our approach to animating some graphics. Initial plans included the development of as many as 20 podcasts in the first year. However, the delay caused by the demands of overcoming the technical challenges of the initial workflow reduced our plans to 8 in the first year, and even that proved to be a challenge due to other heavy work demands.

THE LAUNCH

The first four podcasts were launched in early March 2008, and all dealt with the basics of measurement in typography. Uploading them to *Blackboard*, the course management software used by the college, we arranged for the podcasts to be accessible to several basic and intermediate graphic design classes. Students could view these directly on their computer desktops without moving them to a portable viewer such as an *iPod* or other mp3 player. Initial feedback from students was very good. Several even sent emails to say they found the podcasts very useful. As instructors, we were encouraged to see students viewing them in the labs when they were referred to the podcasts for a review of a relevant topic.

ACCESS ISSUES

We soon realized that there were limitations to Blackboard access that would undermine our podcast project. These included college server downtime (for maintenance, upgrades, and the like), and the fact that students were cut off from Blackboard access outside of the regular semester or if they were not enrolled in a class that used it. This would also mean making copies of the podcasts available to every course, basically creating unnecessary copies and using up precious college server space.

To overcome the problems of access, we discussed the various options available, including iTunes University, YouTube, Vimeo, and so forth. In the end, we decided to launch our own blog with the podcasts as the main content with the comments feature and RSS feed enabled, hoping to gain some student feedback. The use of RSS (Rich Site Summary) would, theoretically, allow anyone to subscribe to our podcasts providing them with automatic notification when we upload new content. We used Apple's iWeb for this, using Fulmer's dotmac account (now MobileMe). Apple's iWeb also could then feed each video to iTunes, expanding our potential audience. A domain name was also purchased and redirected to the new blog to make it an easier URL to share.

Blogs, or weblogs, have become useful tools for educators, including art instructors, for their potential to share images and writings, debate popular topics, or just float new ideas for which a print-based peer-reviewed forum might not be readily available or appropriate. Acting as the equivalent of the online water cooler, the blog allows artists and writers of all measure to post their materials for an immediate online critique. Indeed, many artists have embraced it as an artistic medium of its own (see Net-Art.org or NetArtConnexion.net). An excellent example of how the blog has been used to share information in the field of art education is the social network site Art Education 2.0 (arted20.ning.com), which features a lively discussion on all aspects of art education. In addition, Douglas Marschalek addressed the creation of a Web-based learning environment in the context of art education dealing with the basics of content, including images, text and technology (Marschalek, 2002).

Simultaneous to the creation of the blog, Fulmer was brainstorming with a group of current students about ways to reach former and potentially future students. They suggested creating a group on Facebook since they knew of many alumni who were very proud of their roots at the urban community college and wanted to help others coming up behind them. A group was created called "Graphic Design @ Mott CC" and had nearly 100 members of current and former students and faculty as of this writing.

THE E-ZINE

With a way to publicize the podcasts through Facebook, the blog idea began to grow, too. We wanted to reach a wider audience and were not necessarily concerned about limiting it to our own students. Maybe there were alumni, or students who left before graduating, or even high school instructors, all of who just wanted access to a quick review of a simple concept. In order to help make the podcasts a bit more legitimate in the public arena, we decided to turn them into an e-zine (electronic magazine), creating a serial publication from the podcasts and applying to the Library of Congress for an ISSN. While many print magazines have used the online e-zine format to expand upon their print version, it is still unclear as to how many Web-only magazines exist since not all so-called e-zines go through the trouble of being listed with the Library of Congress. Some academic e-zines, or e-journals as they would be called in the academic world, like *InterCulture* which exists only online, are beginning to have their effect on the academic tenure system (Jensen, 2007). And, according to a recent article in the *Chronicle of Higher Education*, digital scholarship is having a growing impact on the interdisciplinary aspects of research in academia (Howard, 2008).

At first the Library of Congress would not approve our application, replying that they had never done that for video podcasts. However, they were still intrigued by our proposal and were willing to discuss our counter proposal. We offered to recreate the blog as an e-zine which would primarily include a text and image version of the original podcast content. This text/image version would serve as the official e-zine with links to the video podcast versions. Yet, a third version of each article was created that was in a printer-friendly format designed to resemble a section of a magazine. In essence, we had now created three versions of each topic. The four initial podcasts were then launched in late March as Issue 2008-01 of the e-zine *Graphic Tips for Students* (ISSN 1941-5117).

The first issue's cover title is "Type and the Art of Measuring Design" with the four included articles titled with sometimes puzzling questions:

- What are points & picas?
- When is type like a fence?
- When do letter pairs act friendly?
- How is type measured?

Whenever possible, students were referred to one of the other podcasts (or corresponding text/image articles) when topics overlapped. This served to keep control of the length and complexity of a topic which could easily get out of hand. The next issue, which was planned for another four podcasts, was scheduled for launch in Fall 2008 as Issue 2008-02. Topics would include:

- Anatomy of Letterforms: Part I
- Anatomy of Letterforms: Part II
- The Page and the Grid
- When is Type Justified?

The Library of Congress contacts were pleased that we had also addressed an ADA compliance issue for the hearing impaired that would have arisen with a video podcast-only e-zine. During the development of the podcasts, Fulmer's class included one hearing-impaired student who was consulted on how these podcasts would be useful to her. The student indicated that the combination of a print and video version was an appealing option, allowing her to read along with the printed version while also viewing the video demonstrations. The ability to start, stop, and rewind the video was also indicated as useful by students who offered feedback.

In addition, slower bandwidth connections to the Internet had hampered access for some of our students who still depend upon dial-up. By not having the video podcasts load first, students would be able to go directly to print versions without having to wait an interminable amount of time. The video podcasts themselves address a different learning style for the YouTube crowd, while the print-ready downloadable versions were meant to encourage offline and longer-term referencing. Some career tech high school instructors at a local visual communications program have also begun to reference the e-zine in their classes.

The e-zine can be found at www.GraphicTips.org and even features links to t-shirt designs (through cafépress) and a short little book—*thoughts on graphic design(ers) • Ideas Book No. 1* (Fulmer, 2008)—that were created in tandem and with a humorous style in order to promote remembering the concepts being taught. So far, we do not anticipate much of a big "sale" but will continue to explore creative ways to promote the website and its content. The Facebook group has, in addition to promoting the e-zine website, also been used to promote other events on campus related to our program, such as the annual student art show and a curriculum survey of student/alumni. As for adding the podcasts to Blackboard, now all we had to do was add a link within the Blackboard course content. Regardless, we hoped that the domain name—www.GraphicTips.org—would be easy enough to remember.

THE FUTURE

Future plans are to produce the e-zine with a series of three or four related topics per "issue," at least twice a year, and making available a CD-ROM version annually for anyone who requests it. Topics, which began as fairly basic type and measurement issues, will expand into other simple demonstrations of more general design principles. Examples of topics that will be addressed in the future include relating various basic principles of two-dimensional design to graphic design/visual communications. One of our challenges program-wide has been to continue strengthening the principles addressed in the foundation art and design courses as they apply to later graphic design situations.

By breaking the topics down into small bites of demonstrated concepts, the e-zine/podcast may help fulfill the visual "snackfest" our students seem to be munching on while still feeding their intellectual and creative growth as budding designers. The experiment has been a learning experience for both faculty and we are hopeful regarding its overall success. Over the coming years, we will have the opportunity to more fully promote the use of the podcasts within the classroom environment. However, we realize that with the rapid changes in technology, we will be constantly adjusting our approach on how we go about creating and utilizing this multimedia format. Rather than this being a project that ends, we anticipate that as we build and revise material for our courses, our e-zine will also continue to evolve as an outreach tool for expanding students' learning opportunities.

REFERENCES

Anderson, P. (2001, August 5). Study: Multitasking is counterproductive. Accessed November 2008, from http://archives.cnn.com

Art Education 2.0. Accessed November 2008, from http://arted20.ning.com

Deal, D., & Sharples, J. (2008). The influence of virtual technologies on attention and cognitive control in young people. Accessed November 2008, from http://www.futuremind.ox.ac.uk

Fulmer, M. (2008). *Thoughts on graphic design(ers) • Ideas book no. 1*. Grand Blanc, MI: Author.

Howard, J. (2008, November 10). Digital scholarship embraces tradition and change, report says, *Chronicle of Higher Education*. Accessed November 2008, from http://chronicle.com

InterCulture, Department of Interdisciplinary Humanities, Florida State University. Accessed November 2008, from http://iph.fsu.edu/interculture/interculture.html

Jensen, M. (2008, June 15). The new metrics of scholarly authority, *Chronicle of Higher Education*. Accessed November 2008, from http://chronicle.com

Johnson, S. (2006, March 27). Viewpoint: Don't fear the digital. It's dumbing down our kids? Hardly. Why plugging in is good for you, *Time, 167*(13), 56.

Lenhart, A., Madden, M., Macgill, A.R., & Smith, A. (2007, December). Teens and social media: The use of social media gains a greater foothold in teen life as they embrace the conversational nature of interactive online media. Pew Internet & American Life Project Study.

Lohr, S. (2007, March 25). Slow down, brave multitasker, and don't read this in traffic, *New York Times*. Accessed November, 2008, from http://www.nytimes.com

Marschalek, D. (2002). Building Better Web-based Learning Environments: Thinking in 3s. *Art Education, 55*(4), 13-18.

Net-Art.org. Accessed November 2008, from http://net-art.org

Net.Art Connexion. Accessed November 2008, from http://www.netartconnexion.net

Rideout, V., Roberts, D. F., & Foehr, U. G. (2005, March). Generation M: Media in the lives of 8-18 Year-olds. Kaiser Family Foundation Study, Executive Summary.

Wallis, C. (2006, March 27). Are kids too wired for their own good? What science tells us about the pluses- and minuses-of doing everything at once. *Time, 167*(13), 48-55.

Westwell, M., & Sharples, J. (2008). The impact of interruptions from communications technologies upon the ability of an individual to concentrate upon the task. Accessed November, 2008, from www.futuremind.ox.ac.uk

Digital Visual Childhood: Preschoolers and the New Narratives of Digital Video in the Blogosphere /

MARISSA MCCLURE

"IT'S A SANDRO CAPER WITH 45 LEGS!" NON-LINEARITY AND A NEW NARRATIVE OF DEVELOPMENT

A blitz of hand-drawn monster footprints in our preschool classroom (Figures 1 & 2) coincided with the disappearance of a fat stack of drawing paper squares. As 5-year-old Sebastián[1] exclaimed, "I found another one," a newly 4-year-old friend crouched to the floor with a magnifying glass to verify its authenticity. "It's it!" he squealed, noticing that I was just above him with a digital video camera. As quickly as they had initiated the narrative, the boys gathered up their stack of evidence and gave them to me for safekeeping. "Put these in the project room," they demanded.

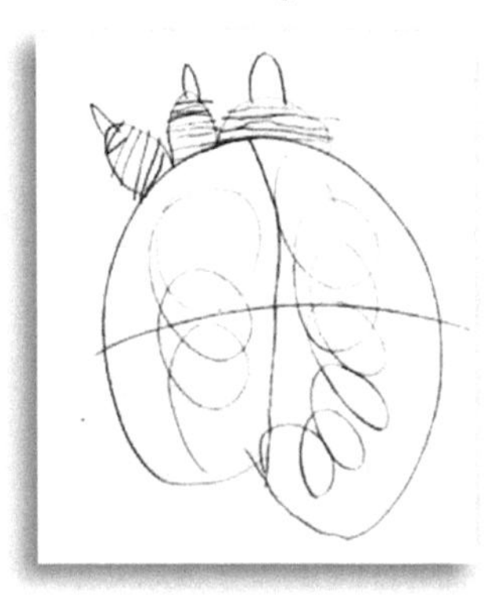

FIGURES 1 AND 2: *Sandro Caper footprints.*

Despite the boys' affectation of secrecy, my assistant teacher and I were convinced the other children would usurp this new idea of the monster footprints and weave it with haphazard eloquence into the ongoing array of spiral storylines that buoyed classroom social and intellectual life. The two friends, caught in a momentum that would betray them, spoke of "the monster" often as they ran around the room making "scaring" arms and curating footprint exhibitions. The Sandro Caper, a monster suddenly endowed with a name, became the buzz of the classroom.

Sandro gained narrative velocity as larger subgroups of the 21 three-, four-, and five-year-old children in our multi-age class succumbed as provocateurs. Playing babies became "feeding monsters" and any drawn footprints "found" were attributed to Sandro itself. A self-perpetuating, site-specific style was developing: some Sandro footprints were formally distinctive, marked by a kind of spiral fingerprint even when Sebastián didn't draw them.[2] This familiar seepage of multiple, overlapping, and contradictory stories deep into the fabric of classroom social and intellectual life fits Corsaro's (1992) idea of interpretive reproduction. Within this framework, he describes "development as productive-reproductive process of increasing density and a reorganization of knowledge that changes with children's developing cognitive and language abilities and with changes in their social worlds" (Corsaro & Eder, 1990, p. 200). He makes public and collaborative Piaget's (1945) internal concepts of accommodation and assimilation to position children's development as a publicly negotiated process through which they produce and reproduce culture, knowledges, languages, and symbols as they amass kinder-cultural capital (Bourdieu, 1984).[3] In my conjecture, this description of child development corresponds to Manovich's (1995) definition of digital cinema. He explains:

> We no longer think of the history of cinema as a linear march towards only one possible language, or as a progression towards more and more accurate verisimilitude. Rather, we have come to see its history as a succession of distinct and equally expressive languages, each with its own aesthetic variables, each new language closing off some of the possibilities of the previous one—a cultural logic not dissimilar to Kuhn's analysis of scientific paradigms. (Manovich, 1995)

Within this chapter, I use the Sandro narrative as a lens through which to discuss the educative and discursive properties of digital media as they intersect with emerging conceptions of children's multi-modal development in overlapping symbolic languages as mapped by the process of pedagogical documentation. I am interested in how qualities unique to digital media allow it to both function as a "more capable peer" in a variation of Dyson's (1993, 1997, 1999, 2003) neo-Vygotskian conception of how children learn to use language to make meaning. While Dyson's work concerns children as writers, her conclusions are apt for an understanding of how children use graphic and visual language to make meaning. Paraphrasing Vyogtsky, Dyson explains that children grow into (i.e., produce and reproduce) the intellectual life that surrounds them. Educators working in preschools in Reggio Emilia, Italy, who document children's use of the "visual" and "digital" "languages" (Reggio Children, 2004), describe Dyson's structural view of language development. In this chapter, I propose parallels between the process of children's development in writing and in visual languages that challenges still dominant ideas in art teaching practice that development is linear, individual, and internal—the residues of developmental stage theories of children's art. In conclusion, by referencing our classroom blog (a visual and aural memory of our work), I position children's development in visual symbolic language as non-linear, rhizomatic, collective, collaborative, and public. Throughout, I position pedagogical documentation[4] as a decolonizing research methodology through which adults and children co-construct narratives, meanings, and representations. In conclusion, I call for further research that investigates how children's making in digital languages contributes to new narratives of child development, early childhood art education, and young children's media literacy.

IN THE CLASSROOM: DOCUMENTATION GOES DIGITAL

Eager to build upon the children's attraction to the Sandro and influenced by both the Reggio Emilia (Edwards, Gandini, & Foreman, 1998) and project approaches (Katz & Chard, 2000) to curriculum, my assistant teacher and I developed a provocation. We would photocopy the footprints the boys had given us for safekeeping and place them throughout the classroom to surprise them the next morning. In this case, however, we arrived to the classroom the next morning to find that the Sebastián had the same idea (Figure 3).

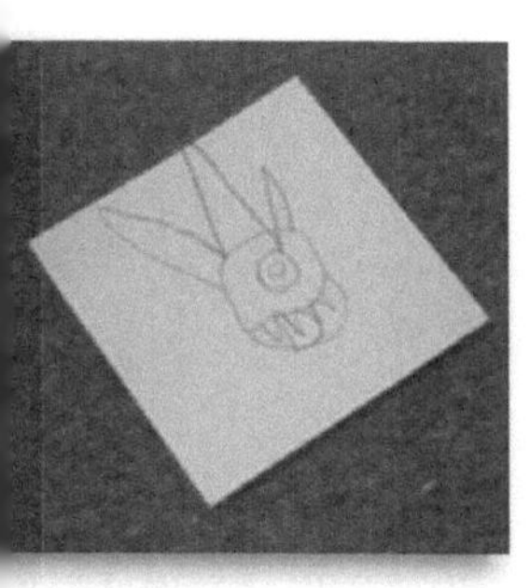

FIGURE 3: *Sebastián leaves a Sandro Caper footprint outside our classroom door.*

As was typical for our way of working, we had planned several possible outcomes as well as documentation strategies that included digitally photographing and recording the children's responses to the provocation. We were accustomed to using the process of pedagogical documentation in this relatively non-systematic way and relied on digital media as a convenient way to add to a narrative that we would re-construct from traces of children's words, actions, processes, and products. While as the lead teacher, I was committed to the decolonizing methodology of documentation with children, I did not initially think critically about the ways in which the specific attributes of digital media altered and democratized the process of documentation. The coincidental convergence of the boys' pushing the Sandro line further without our provocation and their demanding control of documentation made these attributes visible in way that I did not anticipate.

The documentation process was cyclical in our classroom: Documentation photographs were continually displayed and we revisited digital video with the children. This was an integral part of both our teaching and research process—insights the children gleaned from reviewing their previous works and words allowed us to build outward from their hypothesis in a way that was spiral and negotiated. But, when we watched digital video together, we noticed an unusual specificity and strength of memory. Four-year-old children could easily talk, in April, about something that happened in October.

We noticed that, as the children became accustomed to digital video, a shift occurred. They began to request that we document certain episodes. These episodes ranged from a fairy tale written and performed for classmates to evidence of change over time to a documentation of a rudimentary form of animation several children accidentally discovered with discarded transparencies and a rescued overhead projector. It appeared that the children viewed digital video as a muse to extend play or as an omnipotent referent that could prove or disprove their theories in addition to preserving them. As a result of this shift, my role changed from teacher/researcher to co-researcher; a partial collapse of the binary oppositions between teacher/student and adult/child.

FIGURE 4: *One view of our documentation wall.*

We began to use digital media in an inherently different way—not to selectively record a "story" of what happened (as we would use analog media) but to produce and co-construct knowledge. This knowledge did not necessarily rely upon an underlying linear narrative or referent. Rather, the children used digital loops in a non-linear, exploratory way, much like those other media readily available to them (paint, clay, graphic media, blocks, and so forth). In this way, the loops—in actuality, short clips that the children watched repeatedly—became parts of an assemblage of multi-media forms that the children used voraciously to construct knowledge through extended play episodes—nearly analogous to Manovich's positioning of digital media as a particular case of animation (Manovich, 1995, 2001, 2002) where the loop, in its repetition, functions as both an historic and new narrative form (Manovich, 2001).

We needed a place to quickly store digital video and to document children's actions and comments, so I turned to a classroom blog I had created some months earlier with the free blogging software found at blogger.com. At the time, I thought the blog could be a communication tool that made documentation accessible for curious families. However, privacy concerns limited the access I could provide and I never achieved that. We re-purposed the blog as a tool for documentation in the classroom, using it with the children. Our classroom had no computer (up until this point, children had watched the digital video of themselves on the small, camera replay screen) so I purchased an inexpensive laptop and we began to watch. I thought we would have a place to quickly upload and archive video made of children at work—a complement to the still documentation photography that was a fixture in our classroom space.

WHAT (AND HOW) WERE WE WATCHING?

Almost immediately, Frankie (a newly minted member of the Sandro group) ran into the hallway with the footprint he retrieved from his cubby—semi-public storage space for the most intriguing kindercultural contraband—and demanded

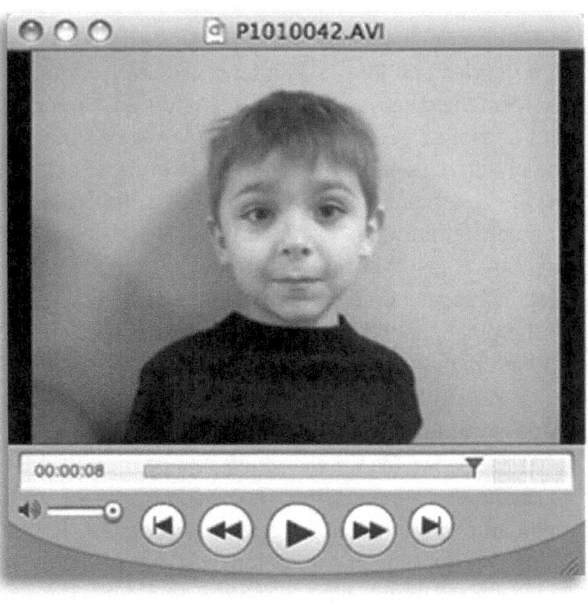

FIGURE 5 (LEFT): *Digital video still of Frankie leaving the classroom to add to the footprints outside. The boys sitting at the table continue to make footprints.*

FIGURE 6 (RIGHT): *Digital video still of Frankie describing the Sandro Caper with 45 legs.*

"Come on!" as he left the door. Five children followed him as my assistant teacher and I watched closely through our observation windows, waiting for our own tickets to play.

With nearly telepathic ease, the children unanimously decided to stack the footprints top-to-bottom to see how long they would stretch down the basement corridor (Figure 5). "Get the camera! We're making a movie!" Frankie shouted. As I pressed the "record" button Frankie deadpanned, "It's a Sandro Caper with 45 legs" (Figure 6). Immediately, he reviewed his performance and requested another take. Running down the line of 58 footprints, he commanded me to keep the camera rolling while he implored his friends that "We're doin' the rest!" and "We need tons of paper then!"

I suppressed my urge to edit and to intervene. While I watched Sandro's footprints stretch far down the basement hallway, I recorded the conflicts that arose in negotiating this new narrative movement. Tearful faces on the screen and stomped footprints on the floor made me feel as I was invading the children's most intimate moments. I was no longer documenting; creating a seamless narrative from bits cobbled together reliant on the conceit of video as documentary. We had crossed over.

BLOGGING AND BORDER-CROSSING

Digital video and blogging, with children, in the preschool classroom allows for multiple border-crossings (Giroux, 1992). In the first crossing, both media invite collaboration between adults and children: a co-construction that is rarely seen in traditional general and art classroom settings where making is either over- or under-determined (Thompson, 1995). This is what Grace and Tobin (1997), in their study of children's making videos, describe as "transgressions" "organized and authorized *within* the curriculum" (p. 161, original emphasis). Citing Bakhtin (1941), they describe these seepages as "carnivalesque" as they are intellectually vital—revealing possible connections between pleasure, motivation, and development. Second, archiving digital video loops via a classroom blog blurs boundaries between making, exhibition, and performance and challenges the dominancy of the narrative as the referent of the moving image.

It is the third border-crossing that intrigues me the most as an educator and researcher—the way in which these loops, unedited, make visible unseen and sometimes uncomfortable moments in the classroom. In this application, digital video seems to most closely approximate Benjamin's (1935) idea of the "optical unconscious" whereby video captures the slippages not evident in participants' shared memory of experience but documented through the lens.

This apparent omnipotence itself violates the idea that video presupposes either record or narrative. This breakage fundamentally altered the way in which we used digital video in the classroom. Rather than remaining a tool for documentation, digital video became a media in its own right.

DIGITAL VIDEO AS MORE CAPABLE PEER

Both Corsaro and Dyson's non-linear views of development rely partially on a metaphor of the scaffold (Wood, Bruner, & Ross, 1976). When children reach a point where they can no longer go on their own, a more competent peer "scaffolds" them to another level of development. It is my assertion that digital video both facilitates this process and reshapes the idea of the scaffold from its Modernist, linear, progressive model. In my classrooms, I have seen the process unfold more like a game of Chutes and Ladders® where the chutes are as meaningful as the ladders—not backward slides but opportunities for continuous reflection and redefinition. Loops of digital video hosted on a classroom blog seem to provide occasion for this kind of repeated, purposeful reflection in a way that teachers' or friends' reminders cannot.

These observations lead me to consider whether, as Taylor and Carpenter (2007) assert, "Digital kids think and process information fundamentally differently as a result of their complete immersion in (...) digital [media]" (p. 84). Their thoughts seem to echo Benjamin's (1935) caution that our ways of perceiving are altered by media delivery. Of course, while Benjamin was writing during the birth of analog technology, these questions are now at the forefront of emergent research—leading to new narratives of learning and knowledge construction for even the youngest of "digital natives" (Prensky, 2001).

THE NEW NARRATIVES

We know little about how young children receive and interpret information through video. We know even less about how children communicate as social actors and cultural producers using digital video or about the specific attributes of digital video used in an educational and art context. No work addresses how documentary digital video can function within a preschool classroom. Further, scholarship in early childhood education and art education rarely concerns young children's interactions with contemporary artmaking processes and with new media. Most accounts of young children's school art emphasize children's interactions with traditional media—paint and clay.

These accounts, often unintentionally, tend to reinforce the idea that children are naturally creative and attracted to open-ended exploration with materials. This position stands in stark contrast to the anxiety that surrounds young children's interactions with popular visual culture. We are all aware of the commonsense construction of young children as a "suggestible, univalent, and homogenous group" subservient to notions of "media addition and imitative violence" (Bignell, 2002). It is easy to conjure up visions of the very same children who are clad in Ariel and Power Rangers PJs clandestinely watching Saturday morning cartoons, throwing Supernanny-esque tantrums at grocery stores over Cocoa Puffs and Yogos, and peeking at explicit sites online. A fear that children unreflectively consume digital garbage simultaneously creates a seemingly autonomous kinderculture while it stokes the angst that wise families and teachers can't permeate the generational taste barrier.

In contrast, few studies interrogate the gulf between these divides. More work needs to address the process of making digital video with children—of making within a context and with a media so intimately familiar to a generation of young children with seemingly unparalleled access to television, movies, video games, and computer and digital media who live well-documented (family videos, photographs, and increasing "mommy" blogs) lives and are used to seeing themselves on film and in digital media. While significant studies and anthologies address children's video productions (Grace & Tobin, 1997; Szekely & Szekely, 2005), researchers and teachers must pay further attention to the particularities and possibilities of digital media.

These potentials include not only traditional ways of making with digital media—like the extended Sandro narrative—but also the implication of loops in relationship to development and motivation. What are the possibilities of making when children are behind the digital video camera, either on their own or with the collaboration of adults? What are the complications of adults' own lurking, border-crossing (Giroux, 1992), and trespassing the murky in-between spheres between the digital video as "record" or document as collaborative art form, or between adult as producer and child as participant and vice versa?

FIGURE 7:
Digital video still of the Sandro Caper footprints extending down our basement corridor.

In his conception of the three pedagogical sites, Wilson (2005) provides a particularly useful theoretical overlay for understanding how documentary digital video might work. In the first site, children make for and by themselves. In the second site, children's making is authorized within a more formalized educational context (for example, a classroom). In the third site, children's interests intersect with adult's interests but much of what happens in the third site is too inappropriate or too suggestive (sexual, scatological, and offensive) to be authorized within a classroom. The sites have fluid and complicated borders—borders that digital and documentary video accentuate. In just the one 4-minute loop during the Sandro narrative that I shared earlier, the children and we moved transparently through these overlapping and negotiated physical and "social worlds" (Dyson, 2003).

The intrusion of digital video media, then, provides a space where these slips can be opened and interrogated rather than residing only in the memories of both adult and child participants. Furthermore, this kind of discursive inquiry positions children as co-producers and reproducers of culture in an intergenerational interrogation, not as virtual objects (Bignell, 2002) of a discourse that is for or about and not with them (Mitchell & Reid-Walsh, 2002).

REFERENCES

Benjamin, W. (2008). *The work of art in the age of its technological reproduction and other writings on media.* Belknap Press. (Original work published 1935).

Bignell, J. (2002). Writing the child in media theory. *The Yearbook of English Studies, 32*, 127-139.

Bourdieu, P. (1984). *Distinction: A social critique of the judgment of taste.* Cambridge, MA: Harvard University Press.

Corsaro, W., & Eder, D. (1990). Children's peer cultures. *Annual Review of Sociology, 16*, 197-220.

Corsaro, W. (1992). Interpretive reproduction in children's peer cultures. *Social Psychology Quarterly, 55*(2), 160-177.

Duncum, P. (1985). The fantasy embeddedness of girls' horse drawings. *Art Education, 38*(6), 42-26.

Duncum, P. (1989). Children's unsolicited drawings of violence as a site of social contradiction. *Studies in Art Education, 30*(4), 249-256.

Dyson, A. (1993). *Social worlds of children learning to write in an urban primary school.* New York: Teachers College Press.

Dyson, A. (1997). *Writing superheroes: Contemporary childhood, popular culture, and classroom literacy.* New York: Teachers College Press.

Dyson, A. (1999). Transforming transfer: Unruly children, contrary texts, and the persistence of the pedagogical order. *Review of Research in Education, 24*, 141-171.

Dyson, A. (2003). *The brothers and sisters learn to write: Popular literacies in childhood and school cultures.* New York: Teachers College Press.

Edwards, C., Gandini, L., & Forman, G. (Eds.). (1998). *The hundred languages of children: The Reggio Emilia approach—advanced reflections* (2nd ed.). Westport, CT: Ablex.

Giroux, H. (1992). *Border crossings: Cultural workers and the politics of education.* London: Routledge.

Grace, D., & Tobin, J. (1997). Carnival in the classroom: Elementary students making videos. In J. Tobin (Ed.), *Making a place for pleasure in early childhood education* (pp. 159-187). New Haven, CT: Yale University Press.

Katz, L., & Chard, S. (2000). *Engaging children's minds: The project approach* (2nd ed.). Stamford, CT: Ablex.

Manovich, L. (1995) What is digital cinema? Retrieved September 30, 2008, from http://manovich.net/TEXT/digital-cinema.html

Manovich, L. (2001). *The language of new media.* Cambridge, MA: MIT Press.

Manovich, L. (2002). What is digital cinema? In N. Mirzoeff (Ed.), *The visual culture reader* (pp. 405-416). London: Routledge.

Mitchell, C., & Reid-Walsh, J. (2002). *Researching children's popular culture: The cultural spaces of childhood.* London: Routledge.

Piaget, J. (1945). *Play, dreams and imitation in childhood.* London: Heinemann.

Prensky, M. (2001). Digital natives, digital immigrants. *On the Horizon, 9*(5), 1-2.

Reggio Children. (2004). *Children, art, artists: The expressive languages of children, the artistic language of Alberto Burri.* Reggio Emilia: Reggio Children.

Smith, L. (1999). *Decolonizing methodologies: Research and Indigenous Peoples.* New York: Palgrave.

Szekely, G., & Szekely, I. (2005). *Video art for the classroom.* Reston, VA: National Art Education Association.

Taylor, P. G., & Carpenter, B. S. (2007). Mediating art education: Digital kids, art, and technology. *Visual Arts Research*, 92-103.

Thompson, C. & Bales, S. (1991). "Michael doesn't like my dinosaurs": Conversations in a preschool art class. *Studies in Art Education, 33*(1), 43-55.

Thompson, C. (1995). What should I draw today? Sketchbooks in early childhood. *Art Education, 48*, 6-11.

Thompson, C. (2002). Celebrating complexity: Children's talk about the media. 3/2 *International Journal of Education and the Arts.* Retrieved May 31, 2007, from www.ijea.org/v3n2/

Thompson, C. (2003). Kinderculture in the art classroom: Early childhood art and the mediation of culture. *Studies in Art Education, 44*(2), 135-146.

Thompson, C. (2004, March). The Ket aesthetic: visual culture in childhood. Paper presented at the Objects in/and Visual Culture Conference, State College, PA.

Thompson, C. (2006). The "Ket" aesthetic: Visual culture in childhood. In J. Fineberg (Ed.), *When we were young: New perspectives on the art of the child* (pp. 31-43). Berkeley, CA: University of California Press.

Wilson, B. (1974). The superheroes of JC Holz: Plus an outline of a theory of child art. *Art Education, 27*(8), 2-9.

Wilson, B. (1976). Little Julian's impure drawings: Why children make art. *Art Education, 17*(2), 45-61.

Wilson, B. (2004). Child art after modernism: Visual culture and the new narratives. In E. Eisner & M. Day (Eds.), *Handbook of research and policy in art education* (pp. 299-328). Mahwah, NJ: Lawrence Erlbaum.

Wilson, B. (2005). More lessons from the superheroes of J.C. Holz: The visual culture of childhood and the third pedagogical site. *Art Education, 58*(6), 18-34.

Wilson, B., & Wilson, M. (1977). An iconoclastic view of the imagery sources of the drawing of young people. *Art Education, 30*(1), 5-11.

Wilson, B., & Wilson, M. (1981). The use and uselessness of developmental stages. *Art Education, 34*(5), 4-5.

Wilson, B., & Wilson, M. (1982). *Teaching children to draw.* NJ: Prentice Hall.

Wood, D., Bruner, J., & Ross, G. (1976). The role of tutoring in problem solving. *Journal of Child Psychology and Psychiatry, 17*, 89-100.

ENDNOTES

1 Children's names and images are used with permission from their families.

2 Other Sandro footprints were not necessarily formally similar to those first footprints. Nevertheless, the boys welcomed these footprints and the children who made them into their play. In this way, making a footprint was a "ticket" (Dyson, 1997) to play and to reproduce this site-specific style.

3 Corsaro's conclusions challenge stage theories of development—those that continue to shape popular teaching lore about young children's art, despite more recent scholarship that emphasizes the social contexts of making (Duncum, 1985, 1989; Thompson, 1991, 1995, 2002, 2003, 2004, 2006; Wilson, 1974, 1976, 2004, 2005; Wilson & Wilson, 1977, 1981, 1982).

4 Pedagogical documentation, as conceived by educators in Reggio Emilia, is a complex process that involves documenting of children's words and actions, continuous and dynamic interpretations of classroom situations, and installation of documentation for further dialogue. Documentation takes on the forms of a variety of media, including but not limited to photographs and transcriptions of children's dialogues and increasingly, digital media including digital photograph, digital video, and scanned reproductions of children's work in multiple media. The process is decolonizing because it can be an approach to research *with* children (Smith, 1999).

Educational Applications of Flash in Graphic Design Education /

SELIN OZGUZER

In the last decade computers have become integral to the field of graphic design. Computer technology is now used in every phase of the designing process, from the creation of an initial design to the finished product. This extensive use of new technologies has significantly altered how to effectively teach graphic design at the university level.

Before the integration of computers into the classroom, in-class work and outside-class projects assigned to teach the principles of perception and design fundamentals were all done by hand. The introduction of computers into design classes necessitated the inclusion of software instruction in the graphic design curriculum as the need arose for students to be proficient in the many design programs that have emerged, such as Photoshop, Illustrator, InDesign, QuarkXpress, and the like. As a result, professors are required to teach design software concurrently with design fundamentals, thus limiting the time to be allocated to each. The inclusion of technology in design curriculum resulted in two approaches: either having individual courses that teach how to use specific software—such as Adobe Photoshop or Illustrator—or squeezing the necessary software instructions into design courses as short demonstrations, thus letting students learn the major portion of software usage on their own.[1]

Technological developments have also affected the presentations used to teach these design concepts and principles. The slide and overhead projectors of former days have given way to PowerPoint presentations, thus digitizing teaching methods further, although there are instructors who do not have access to these technologies and are left to use outdated modes that are increasingly unsupported. Even the way students research information has changed, making them much more likely to turn to the Web instead of books and periodicals.

The question, then, is how to incorporate these new technologies into instruction in order to improve student interaction with course content. As a professor of graphic design, as well as a designer who uses Flash interactivity in my creative work, I believe Flash can be used in graphic design education to develop more stimulating instructional aids that go beyond current presentational tools. While Flash has been recognized for its educational applications for some time, especially at the primary and secondary school level, it has yet rarely been used in graphic design instruction at higher education.[2] The application of Flash interactivity in graphic design education can bring forth many positive results that are otherwise hard to achieve.

ADVANTAGES OF USING FLASH IN GRAPHIC DESIGN EDUCATION

The strength of Flash lies in its interactivity, making it valuable as an enriched instructional aid. It is not a replacement for the instructor, but it can ameliorate the education given in as well as out of class. As previously mentioned, the inclusion of software instruction in the already full curriculum requires the design teacher to cover more information in less time. This creates a dilemma: How can a professor limit lectures to a given time slot, without diluting or eliminating topics deemed necessary?

The use of Flash in education provides a solution that alleviates the constraints on a teacher's in-class time. Flash makes it possible for professors to continue instruction outside the classroom through the use of its interactive qualities. The interactivity inherent to Flash supplies instant feedback, thus providing the necessary instructional guidance while also engaging the student with the course material outside of class. Thus, neither teachers nor students are restricted to only class time for covering essential topics. More material can be taught by utilizing more effectively outside-of-class time.

Extensive, recent scholarship in education points out that active,[3] discovery-based learning,[4] where students actively pursue knowledge, results in better educational outcomes. According to Conway, Cohen, and Stanhope's (1991) research,[5] one of these outcomes is long-term retention of information by students. As active participants, rather than passive spectators, students engage more in the learning process than if the information is presented In the assigned readings or lecture format. The advantages of Flash are, therefore, immense in implementation of active, discovery-based learning, due to its interactivity and instant feedback.[6]

In education, three types of interactions have been recognized: learner-teacher, learner-learner, and learner-content interaction.[7] In the classroom, students have the opportunity for immediate feedback through the interactions with the teacher and/or their peers (learner-teacher, learner-learner). These interactions and the resulting guidance represent an important part of the learning experience. But, while studying outside of class, using the traditional methods, students do not receive real-time feedback, making the absorption of certain topics quite difficult. This is where Flash comes in handy: for the learner-content interaction. A teacher's development of outside-class study materials—using Flash interactivity in games, exercises, simulations, and demonstrations—can provide the desired and necessary immediate feedback allowing for establishment of the student-content interaction.

Most broadly, Flash interactivity helps to increase student engagement in the course material at hand. Teachers everywhere, regardless of the subject they teach, experience student expectations that learning should be effortless and more fun. A problematic by-product of this attitude is the challenge professors encounter in urging students to study outside of class. With the use of interactivity, Flash can make the course material seem to be more "fun" or "worth learning" in the eyes of students. This results in students who are more engaged in working, both at home and in class, when assignments are presented as educational interactive games, exercises, and the like.[8]

EXPERIENCES IN FLASH APPLICATIONS

My experience of using Flash as an interactive teaching tool encompasses a set of instructional materials I have created for the Introduction to Typography course I regularly offer at Jacksonville University. My overall aim is to build up a set of course-content materials that will stimulate active learning. With my students interacting with, and reflecting upon the material and immediately applying the knowledge gained in varied ways, it is hoped that they will come to better understand the subject and achieve the long-term goal of retention of information.[9] As Ebner and Holzinger (2002) have noted, students do not learn by simply receiving information, but rather by constructively reflecting on material and interacting with it, creating, thus, an understanding.[10] Journell (2007) reminds that Dewey (1910) warns against using teaching techniques such as repetition of facts [rote learning] by saying "This makes the subjects mechanical and thus restrictive of intellectual power" (p. 51). The interactive instructional materials I have designed up to now consist of educational games, practice tests, and supplemental exercises that require reflection and active participation on students' part to facilitate understanding and avoid rote learning.

EDUCATIONAL GAMES

One of the means of developing the course content at which I aimed was my creation of interactive games to teach certain sub-topics and skills in my Typography course. As the younger generation finds games motivating, and research shows that this motivation improves learning outcomes, well-designed games that help students achieve the agreed-upon goals of education are good solutions for establishing student engagement.[11]

Letter Puzzle. The "Letter Puzzle" (Figure 1) is an educational game designed as a digital, interactive version of a typography assignment previously carried out using paper, scissors, and glue. It focuses on acquainting students with letterforms and the parts that compose them by making the players create the specific letters with the pieces given. In this game, a letter is divided into 16 square pieces and 15 of those pieces are arranged in a random order around a

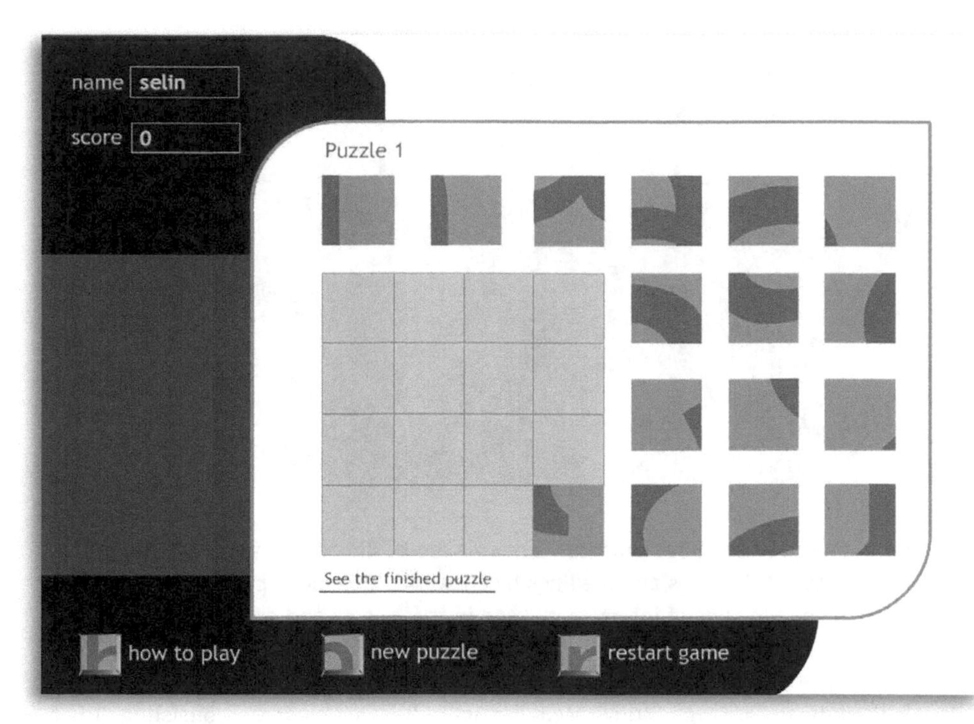

FIGURE 1: *Letter puzzle game.*

grid of four by four squares. Each piece has its own specific place and a specific drop zone on the grid and the 16th piece is already positioned in its place as the starting point of the game. The students are asked to drag and drop the pieces onto the appropriate squares of the grid using the already positioned pieces on the grid for guidance.

What makes the interactive, computer version of "Letter Puzzle" superior over the off-the-computer, paper version is that, if the pieces are dragged and dropped onto the wrong squares, they automatically return to their original places around the grid. This gives students instant feedback that their choice was wrong. To make it more competitive, fun and engaging, as well as atypical classwork for students, points are awarded for placing the right piece in the right drop zone. With each unsuccessful try, the points received by the player are reduced. The "Letter Puzzle" includes four different puzzle variations that students can attempt as many times as they want. The competitive point system encourages them to try it more than once to increase their scores and thus learn the subject better through reiteration.

PRACTICE TESTS

Another means of achieving my intended course content was my creation of interactive study materials such as tests and exercises to help students recall and test their knowledge. Practice Tests are designed to help students' study and review

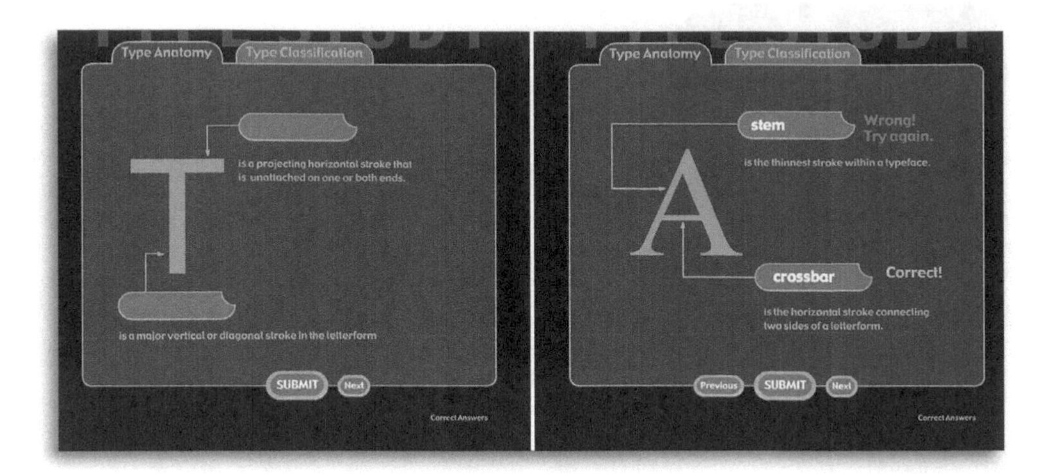

FIGURE 2: *Type Study Module.*

for exams, whereas Supplemental Exercises are designed for students to go over the subjects of lectures and readings by answering questions posed to enhance absorption. The style of interactivity used in these tests and exercises differs subject to subject, as different topics require different solutions.

Type Study Module. An example of the Practice Tests that I have designed is the interactive "Type Study" Module (Figure 2). This module—consisting of two parts, "Type Anatomy" and "Type Classification"—is a pre-exam study aid in the form of a fill-in-the-blank type test to review typographic information. In the "Type Anatomy" section, students are asked to name the indicated parts of the letters and write their answers in the text boxes provided. Under each text box, there is a description of the part to be named. The same description is repeated for other letters with the same part to instill the term firmly in memory through repetition. After filling out the boxes, students click on the "Submit" button and receive the feedback of whether their answers are right or wrong. If they cannot come up with the right answer, they can click on the "Correct Answers" button that puts the correct answer in the text box and allows them to check out the term in question.

Because a main objective for graphic design students is to become versatile in dealing with visuals, students are given not just the verbal definition and asked for the name of the term. They are shown the part of the letter in question visually as well. As Dual Coding Theory of Paivio (2006) asserts, visual and verbal information are processed differently in the brain and both have their limitations.[12] Providing them at the same time to support each other can enhance learning and make it easier for the students to recall the knowledge.

READINGS AND SUPPLEMENTAL EXERCISES

As previously mentioned, in almost all classrooms today, PowerPoint is used to deliver presentations. As instructors supplement visual and written information on each slide with more detailed oral information, it is counter-productive to make available the PowerPoints of lectures used in class to students for study purposes. These presentations, even with photographs and animations to make them more comprehensive and effective, are not means of active learning.[13] The same is true when this type of course material is converted into computer readings created with Flash if these use only the 'click-to-learn-more' kind of interactivity. This is because there is no meaningful learner-content interaction taking place to receive the learner responses and give feedback. While most of them use Flash at 'click-to-learn-more' level, there are some educational sites that use interactivity at a higher degree.[14] My work focuses on using Flash interactivity at its full capacity to create meaningful interactions of students with reading materials.

A point underscored about active learning is that having students immediately use the information they have learned in many different ways and in real-life situations increases their retention of knowledge.[15] My solution to achieve this end is preparing interactive supplemental exercises to be used with readings to complement them. My work on this type of instructional aid is at the preliminary stages, requiring more development because the content of various readings dictates the type of interactivity and exercises needed to boost the retention of knowledge. The examples presented here, "Gestalt Principles of Perception" and "History of Writing," demonstrate how differing content calls for differing approaches to interactivity for such supplemental exercises.

Gestalt Principles of Perception. In this reading, Gestalt Principles such as proximity, similarity, continuation, closure, and figure and ground are explained to show how humans perceive and organize visual information. The supplemental exercises—each demonstrating a specific principle—let students play and interact with them, thus providing the chance to observe these principles and experiment with them. For example, with the proximity principle, students can play and change the proximity of the elements one to another and observe how their perception changes. With the closure principle, students can increase or decrease the areas removed from a circle to observe how much of the circle can be eliminated before it becomes unidentifiable. They also have options of different ways to erase the parts of a circle to observe the different effects. One way is to start from one point and erase a whole section. Another way is to take numerous chunks out of the circle while increasing the areas those chunks cover (Figure 3).

History of Writing. The supplemental exercises for this type of reading require a different approach to interactivity because the subject matter is more verbally based, rather than visual as in the previous example. Various kinds of interactivity are applied in these exercises, with questions dispersed in between segments of the text for the students to answer relying upon the text they have read. Pertinent questions are phrased to urge the students to analyze the text and find the relevant points to supply answers. They have to work to find the answer, and this requires them to be more engaged with the content than simply reading it. Students who constructively reflect upon material and interact with it also understand it better. Superior learning has been found to result from material that is acted upon.[16]

Other than pertinent questions, "matching" types of exercises are also used for assigned readings. For example, students are first asked to match the words "ideograph" and "pictograph," each with its correct definition. To encourage them to reflect on the material they have learned and apply it in a present-day situation, they are then asked to match the images for modern-day ideographs and pictographs with the terms relevant. The aim is to build upon the previous knowledge to achieve profound learning by making them apply the principle to familiar things in their environment, and thus use the information actively.

FIGURE 3 (LEFT): *Interactive supplemental exercise for Closure Principle.*

FIGURE 4 (RIGHT): *Engaging Interactive exercise for Hieroglyphics.*

Another interactive exercise that I have created is linked to readings and my coverage of the differing writing systems of Egyptian hieroglyphics and the Phoenician and Greek alphabets. To engage the students in this subject, an area is created for them to drag and drop in hieroglyphic phonograms (Figure 4) or letters from other ancient alphabets to write their own names or other words they wish. This area is designed in such a way that the distinct methods of writing of each culture and alphabet is observed, such as writing from left to right, top to bottom, or in boustrophedon,[17] for example.

CONCLUSION

In this chapter, I reviewed my own experience of using Flash as an interactive teaching tool. The set of class materials I have designed for my Introduction to Typography course represent instructional aids that have helpfully alleviated some of the constraints on my in-class teaching time. As active, discovery-based learning tools, they represent assignments more stimulating and engaging for students, due to the interactivity and instant feedback. One of the problems of using the technological innovations in education is focusing on the exploitation of capabilities of technology rather than using it to meet the instructional need. Having hi-tech instructional methods are useless if their main aim is not designed to play a supportive role to the educational content. My aim has been to create materials that meet a perceived educational need by using what technology now offers.[18] I intend to gather all the instructional materials created for a course into a collective, engaging study set.

One of the demands faced during the development of this study set was facilitating interactivity in support of educational content. The use of interactivity in the set focuses on teaching the subject in the best possible way rather than just decorating it with showy, pointless elements. Each element designed by using Flash interactivity has a planned, educational purpose in the study set. Another necessity was creating short and easy-to-understand instructions for the students on how to use these materials. Up to this point, student responses to the study materials were positive and almost all of the students had no problems with understanding the instructions on how to use interactive elements. Paying extra attention to have clear instructions and a user-friendly, self-explanatory navigation helped with this, though more complex games and interactive elements may require more detailed work on instructions. The last requirement was making the materials available to students in a way that they could use it anytime. Distributing the content both by posting it on the Internet and as a CD make it possible for students to have access to the study set whenever and wherever they want, and to review it as many times as they need and, equally importantly, at their own pace. This dual-channeled distribution method alleviates the challenges students face in accessing the materials when they don't have Internet connection readily available or Flash plug-in loaded in their computer.

While at the beginning stages with this project, I am, at the same time, exploring the possibilities of implementing Flash in more complex educational games, exercises, and study materials for other Graphic Design courses to help students build upon knowledge gained through interactive participation. I believe my approach to Flash interactivity is more useful in lower-level courses that lay out the fundamental concepts of design where rules of perception, terminology, and basics of design strategies are taught. After finishing this first prototype set and mastering its problems, I plan to start developing new games and other interactive course materials with higher complexity levels, where the nature of challenges may change and new ones may arise.

REFERENCES

Active learning (2006). Suddenly Smart Inc. Retrieved May 2008, from www.suddenlysmart.com/resources_activelearning.htm

Active vs. passive learning (n.d.). Las Positas College. Retrieved May 2008, from http://lpc1.clpccd.cc.ca.us/lpc/hanna/learning/activevspassive.htm

Alavi, M., & Leidner, D. E. (2001, March). Research commentary: Technology—mediated learning—a call for greater depth and breadth of research. *Information Systems Research, 12*(1), 1-10. Retrieved May 2008, from http://infosys.highwire.org/cgi/reprint/12/1/1

Bonwell, C. C. & Eison, J. A. (1991, September). Active learning: Creating excitement in the classroom [Electronic version]. *ERIC Digest*, ED340272. Retrieved May 2008, from www.ericdigests.org/1992-4/

Chen, E. H. (2004, Fall). A review of learning theories from visual literacy. *Journal of Educational Computing, Design and Online Learning, 5.* Retrieved May 2008, from http://coe.ksu.edu/jecdol/Vol_5/html/VisualLiteracy.htm

Comparing Piaget and Vygotsky. The University of Iowa. Retrieved October 2008, from www.education.uiowa.edu/resources/tep/eportfolio/07p075folder/Piaget_Vygotsky.htm

Conway, M. A., Cohen, G. & Stanhope, N. (1991). On the very long-term retention of knowledge acquired through formal education: Twelve years of cognitive psychology. *Journal of Experimental Psychology: General, 120*(4), 395-409.

Crawford, C. (2004). *On interactive storytelling.* Berkeley: New Riders.

The culture of education in visual arts [Midterm paper]. Retrieved October 2008, from www.orgsites.com/ky/tams/culture-art-ed-midterm.doc

Designing {with} typography [Interactive educational site]. Retrieved October 2008, from http://pixelsparks.com/dwt/

Ebner, M., & Holzinger, A. (2002). E-Learning in civil engineering: The experience applied to a lecture course in structural concrete. *JAPIT Scientific Journal of Applied Information Technology, 1*(1), 1-9. Retrieved June 2008, from: www.japit.org/vol1/issue1/ebner_holzinger_02.pdf

Felder, R., & Brent, R. (2003). Learning by doing. *Chemical Engineering Education, 37*(4), 282-283. Retrieved June 2008, from www4.ncsu.edu/unity/lockers/users/f/felder/public/Columns/Active.pdf

Gee, J. P. (2003). What video games have to teach us about learning and literacy [Electronic Version]. New York: Palgrave Macmillan. Retrieved October 2008, from www.palgrave.com/products/title.aspx?is=1403965382

Ginn, W. Y. (n.d.). Jean Piaget - intellectual development. Retrieved October 2008, from www.sk.com.br/sk-piage.html

Heller, S. (Ed.) (1998). *The education of a graphic designer.* New York: Allworth Press.

Holzinger, A., & Ebner, M. (2003). Interaction and usability of simulations & animations: A case study of the flash technology. In M. Rauterberg, M. Menozzi, & J. Wesson (Eds.), *INTERACT '03: Human-computer interaction* (pp.777–780). Amsterdam, NL: IOS Press. Retrieved May 2008, from www.idemployee.id.tue.nl/g.w.m.rauterberg/conferences/INTERACT2003/INTERACT2003-p777.pdf

Journell, W. (2007, Winter). Dewey and standardization: A philosophical look at the implications for social studies. *Social Studies Research and Practice, 2*(3), 8. Retrieved October 2008, from www.socstrp.org/issues/getfile.cfm?volID=2&IssueID=6&ArticleID=69

Kearsley, G. (1995, May 30). The nature and value of interaction in distance learning. Paper prepared for the Third Distance Education Research Symposium. Retrieved May 2008, from www.mat.unb.br/ead/interac.html

Koschmann, T. D., Myers, A. C., Feltovich, P. J., & Barrows, H. S. (1994). Using technology to assist in realizing effective learning and instruction: A principled approach to the use of computers in collaborative learning. *The Journal of the Learning Sciences, 3*(3), 227-264.

Lane, D. M., & Peres, S. C. (2006). Interactive simulations in the teaching of statistics: Promise and pitfalls. In A. Rossman & B. Chance (Eds.), ICOTS 7- Seventh International Conference on Teaching Statistics: Interactive software targeting specific statistical concepts (Session 7D). University of Auckland, NZ: IASE. Retrieved May 2008, from www.stat.auckland.ac.nz/~iase/publications.php?show=17#top

Leidner, D. E., & Jarvenpaa, S. L. (1995, September). The use of information technology to enhance management school education: A theoretical view. *MIS Quarterly, 19*(3), 265- 291. Retrieved May 2008, from http://www.misq.org/archivist/home.html#award

Mayer, R. E. (2005). Cognitive theory of multimedia learning. In R. E. Mayer (Ed.), *The Cambridge handbook of multimedia learning* (pp. 31-48). New York: Cambridge University Press.

Mayes, J. T., & Fowler, C. J. (1999). Learning technology and usability: A framework for understanding courseware. *Interacting with Computers, 11*(5), 485-497. Retrieved June 2008, from www.macs.hw.ac.uk/~rjr/dolweb/docs/Mayes&Fowler1999.pdf

Meadows, M. S. (2002). *Pause & effect: The art of interactive narrative.* Indianapolis, IN: New Riders Press.

Meggs, P. B. (1998). *The history of graphic design* (3rd ed.). New York: John Wiley and Sons.

Moore, M.G. (1989). Three types of interaction. *The American Journal of Distance Education, 3*(2). Retrieved May 2008, from http://www.ajde.com/Contents/vol3_2.htm#editorial

Moursund, D.G. (2007). Introduction to using games in education: A guide for teachers and parents [Electronic Version]. Eugene, OR: Information Age Education. Retrieved May 2008, from http://uoregon.edu/~moursund/Books/Games/games.html

Norman, K. L. (1997). *Teaching in the switched-on classroom: An introduction to electronic education and hypercourseware* [online book]. College Park, MD: Human/Computer Interaction Laboratory. Retrieved May 2008, from www.lap.umd.edu/SOC/

Paivio, A. (2006). Dual coding theory and education. Paper presented at the University of Michigan Conference on Pathways to Literacy Achievement for High Poverty Children. Retrieved June 2008, from http://readytolearnresearch.org/pathwaysconference/presentations/paivio.pdf

Papert, S. (1996). *The connected family.* Marietta, GA: Longstreet Press.

Repenning, A., & Lewis, C. (2005). Playing a game: The ecology of designing, building and testing games as educational activities. In P. Kommers & G. Richards (Eds.), *ED-MEDIA 2005—World Conference on Educational Multimedia, Hypermedia and Telecommunications* (pp. 4901-4905). Chesapeake, VA: AACE. Retrieved June 2008, from www.cs.colorado.edu/~ralex/papers/PDF/PlayingaGameEDmedia05.pdf

Shaffer, D. W. (2006). *How computer games help children learn.* New York: Palgrave Macmillan.

Szabados, B. (2004). Interactive outcome-based assessment using multimedia. *IJEE International Journal of Engineering Education, 20*(2), 141-151. Retrieved May 2008, from http://power.eng.mcmaster.ca/szabados/papers/jje.pdf

Vygotsky, L.S. (1978). *Mind in society: The development of higher psychological processes.* Cambridge, MA: Harvard University Press.

ENDNOTES

1 These two approaches bring out a debate on what Papert (1996) calls technology literacy vs. technology fluency. Technology fluency in software instruction means teaching students mainly how to explore and find answers to what they do not know besides the basics of software use. As fluency does not mean knowing everything, it is necessary to teach how to use the tutorials and software help-menus to solve problems.

2 One can talk about two types of Flash use in primary and secondary school level. One use of Flash is giving students instructional games and activities to teach them math and other subjects. The other use is letting students use Flash software to play with and create basic interactive projects. Some examples of both can be seen in the website http://www.tygh.co.uk/

3 See "Active Learning." From the scholarship on active learning, one can conclude that active learning is a term popularized by Bonwell and Eison (1991) in the beginning of the '90s. There are also scholars like Richard E. Mayer (2005) who mention that strategies for active learning have their basis in discovery-based learning. In his work, Mayer also emphasizes the importance of being cognitively active more than behaviorally active.

4 See Lane and Peres (2006), "Interactive Simulations in the Teaching of Statistics: Promise and Pitfalls," pp. 3-4, for more information. In discovery learning, learners discover principles themselves rather than by direct instruction. There are studies that question the effectiveness of pure discovery learning. These suggest that guided discovery learning is much more successful because there is more structure for the learners to follow.

5 See Lane and Peres (2006), "Interactive Simulations in the Teaching of Statistics: Promise and Pitfalls," p. 3, on Conway, Cohen, and Stanhope's (1991) findings, where students retained information for more than 12 years.

6 As a medium that deploys the benefits of active and discovery-based learning, Gee (2003) and Shaffer (2006) refer to video games and claim that they lead to active learning by stimulating critical thinking about the simulation and providing knowledge through interaction.

7 See Moore (1989) for the types of interaction that occur in education. Although Moore mainly talks about types of interactions in distance education, these interactions hold true for all kinds of education. Comparing the dynamics of distance learning to the types of engagement that Flash allows, particularly those that take place outside of the traditional classroom, one sees that Flash permits continual instant feedback with its interactivity, whereas distance learning provides feedback by mail, e-mail, or teleconference, of which only teleconference is instantaneous.

8 Although the aim of university-level teaching should not be turning everything into pure entertainment, accepting the change in the new generation of students will enhance student engagement and, thus, learning.

9 See "Active Learning."

10 See Ginn (n.d.), "The culture of education in visual arts" (n.d.), "Comparing Piaget and Vygotsky" (n.d.) and Vygotsky (1978), for other studies done on how to promote active learning by important figures in education such as Piaget, Szekely, and Vygotsky.

11 See Moursund (2007), " Introduction to Using Games in Education: A Guide for Teachers and Parents," p. 25.

12 See "Dual Coding Theory" and Chen (2004), "A Review of Learning Theories from Visual Literacy."

13 See Szabados (2004), "Interactive Outcome-Based Assessment Using Multimedia." Regardless of however technologically advanced, one needs to keep in mind that PowerPoint presentations are still an equivalent to using overhead transparencies or slide shows.

14 See http://pixelsparks.com/dwt/ for "Designing {with} typography" site. At the 'Interactive Type Tool' section of this site, more in-depth interactivity than the "click-to-learn-more" kind is achieved as the user can explore and experiment with typography by changing the size of the font or the alignment of the paragraph.

15 For more insight into this subject, see "Active vs. Passive Learning"; Felder and Brent (2003), "Learning by Doing"; Ebner and Holzinger (2002), " e-Learning in Civil Engineering," p. 3; and Moursund (2007), "Introduction to Using Games in Education," p. 37.

16 See Mayes and Fowler (1999), "Learning Technology and Usability: A Framework for Understanding Courseware," p. 3.

17 *Boustrophedon* (analogous to: "plow a field with an ox") is an ancient writing method first developed by the Greeks and adopted by the Etruscans, in which every other line is read in the opposite direction (Meggs, 1998. p. 32).

18 See Koschmann, Myers, Feltovich, and Barrows (1993-1994), "Using Technology to Assist in Realizing Effective Learning and Instruction," p. 228.

Four Digital Media Art Practices: Moving Beyond Drawing and Painting on the Computer / RYAN SHIN

"This mouse sucks! I can't draw it"; "The computer can never be close to my hands"; "I don't like painting on the computer."

These are common comments and complaints students made when using the computer to make art the first time I taught an introductory technology course for preservice art teachers at the Florida State University about 8 years ago. At that time, I struggled together with my students to find the reasons why we need to use computers in art education. My teaching approach to computer technology focused on providing students with practical studio skills, such as Photoshop techniques, building GIF animation, and website design. Being preoccupied with the conviction that I should know everything about the application programs, I taught as an inexperienced teacher does, believing that I should know all the answers to the students' questions.

Since then I have continued to hear similar complaints from the students in my digital artmaking classes for preservice art educators. They ask: As art teachers, why do we need to learn about the computer? Does the computer make better art? What are the differences between digital and traditional media? These questions have become one of the most popular discussion topics in my classes.[1] In this chapter, I will discuss several common misunderstandings underlying these questions relating to art education and the recent emergence of digital art media. Then, I will describe four digital media practices designed to deal with these seemingly widespread misunderstandings or biases.

DIGITAL ART[2] MISUNDERSTANDINGS AND BIASES

As technology assumes a more dominant presence in our everyday lives, I thought that my students would eventually overcome their misunderstandings and misleading thoughts about digital art. However, in speaking with my students, I have discovered that the gap among their experiences with technology has actually grown. At times a single classroom may contain three technology generations of students, ranging from those who grew up with cassette players, to those who first experienced the CD player, and culminating with those of the current iPod generation. It is often interesting to hear about their experiences with technology. Some of their misunderstandings regarding digital media are often voiced in class.

First, students generally believe that digital art is simply an imitation of painting and drawing produced on the computer. They think that digital art takes the window screen as the canvas upon which one simply draws with a mouse, filling in colors from the provided color spectrum palettes. This is often seen as fake or artificial work that mimics traditional media while lacking the latter's characteristic expressiveness (Lu, 2005).[3]

Therefore, it is not surprising that some art educators who have not explored the full potential of the available digital media might also share this negative understanding of digital art. Occasionally, my students will share with me their first computer art experiences in high schools. As students in beginner art classes, they first attempted to draw an object with the mouse and then color it. More often than not, they expressed disappointment that the computer could not imitate what they could do with a brush or pencil in hand. As a result, they became convinced that computers still have a long way to go to catch up with traditional means of art production.

Despite what most people think, digital media are not really designed to mimic painting. Rather, they provide a different way of expressing oneself—a new form of art (Lin, 2005). For example, most digital artists who use Photoshop are not interested in simply drawing and painting on the screen, nor in correcting photos, but are more concerned with how to use the menu, tools, and related options for personal expression and creativity (Giordan, 2002). I often hear from students who have discovered that good artwork is not the result of applying one or two tools, but of combining several tools, menus, and related options. There are endless possibilities for using layers, channels, filters, color modes, image adjustment, and advanced image selection tools, which are frequently used for digital artmaking. The strength of multi-layering is that it becomes possible for one to rearrange and compose images. Thus, multi-layering has become one of the most important and popular methods of artmaking with computers that coincidently approximates those techniques that have been applied in other non-digital media, such as watercolor, collages, films, or mixed media.

Second, students think that digital art is made by the computer, not a creative individual. Luth (2001) has explained that the primary reason many people believe that artmaking using a computer is simply a series of mouse clicks and keyboard strokes is due to mass media's misrepresentation of computer art. As an example, Luth cites a segment on TV's *Entertainment Tonight* that featured how the team of computer artists created special effects for the movie *Jurassic Park*. The show documented how an artist or computer technician hitting keyboard strokes a few times was able to animate objects and images. As a result, viewers might have been led to believe that the digital art was merely the result of computer manipulation, neglecting all of the other creative processes such as character design, modeling, rendering, settings, lighting, and other special effects. Similar misunderstandings were often expressed by preservice art teachers who had come to believe that computer generated art is not controlled by humans, but rather by machines executing a designed program, and that creative thinking and energy are neglected (Lu, 2005).

Third, many believe that no concept or idea is required to make images with a computer. This belief overemphasizes the fact that we cannot always predict what artists might produce when using various computer tools and/or visual effects when creating with the computer while it also tends to undervalue the creative potential of digital art as a new art form (Lin, 2005). Such as attitude, which naturally lends itself to the development of negative perceptions and attitudes toward new media, needs to be corrected. A student who took one of my technology courses for preservice teachers, Teaching Media and Visual Culture, pointed out where people might have developed this bias against digital art. She wrote:

> I understand where the bias could have formed with 80s technology because it was limited. Remember the old program and compare it to today's, and you will see how many less options there were for computer artists. (C. Culligan, personal communication, February 4, 2008)

Those who promote the idea that digital art is made mainly by exploration or accidental discovery run the risk of contributing to the notion that it is the computer that makes the art. An art teacher who teaches technology art classes in Wisconsin has commented that his students often are fascinated by technological special effects and believe that technology makes art, not human beings. For example, Photoshop is equipped with many fascinating features and options, such as filters, layer styles, and correction and selection tools. There are many times when students come up with 'cool' images by simple application of such options. However, this does not describe the proper creative use of a computer, nor does it describe the creative process of technology experts who use digital media to create art. From my observation, students produce better art when they are able to move beyond this dependence on technological effect. Even though they might learn a lot by experimenting with and applying tools and features, or by taking advantage of available recovery or saving options that allow users to easily correct mistakes, a quality work of art requires creative use of tools beyond the accidental results of exploration. Serious digital artists must totally immerse themselves in the creative process by applying a holistic viewpoint and employing multiple approaches (Edmonds & Candy, 2002).

FOUR DIGITAL MEDIA PRACTICES

The four digital media practices I will describe here include strategies and methods to counteract students' misunderstandings about digital media and to

experience the difference between digital and traditional media. They reflect what I have learned from teaching digital media to preservice art teachers for many years. I introduce three projects that have been incorporated into my digital media classes, and a creative art project of a web artist, all of which can be easily adapted to projects for high school or college digital art classes.

A student's example of a visual-cultural autobiography collage.

1. Visual-cultural Autobiography Beyond Self-portrait Collage—When I started teaching art and technology courses for preservice teachers, I began with a self-portrait collage as the first project. It was a safe approach to introduce the power of technology to students who were less familiar with computers. However, I have often seen students who made their collage as the result of excessive exploration and application of special technological effects and completely neglected to express any personal ideas or emotions. As a result, students often present, as an artwork, a collection of too many 'cool' effects. Therefore, I wondered how I could transform a typical self-portrait collage into an introductory digital collage that would help my students focus on developing a concept or idea in artmaking.

The Visual-cultural Autobiography project was developed to help students move beyond the typical self-expressive collage popular in computer art classes. As Amburgy, Knight, and Keifer-Boyd (2006) have claimed, visual culture study can be effectively incorporated into common studio art projects, such as the self-portrait and the still-life. In this project, I began by asking students to think of visual-cultural images that had influenced their lives. As an example of how to reflect visual culture in their personal life, I shared Ulbricht's (2007) article, "Reflections on Visual and Material Culture: An Example from Southwest Chicago Experience," and invited them to write a personal narrative paper about how visual cultural images and materials have impacted their life. Their reports included how visual culture influenced their lives, art, or even choices of careers in art or art education, as well as what they learned from being involved with them.

Next, each student was asked to make a digital collage using Adobe Photoshop, applying basic tools, menus, and options. They were also asked to apply postmodern principles found in contemporary artmaking (Gude, 2004). Students found that Gude's principles reflected well the characteristics of digital art and artmaking process, and some of the popular principles they used were layering, interaction of text and image, juxtaposition, and hybridity.

This project taught two lessons. First, it helped students get away from exploring only technological effects, technology-driven artmaking. From students' presentations, I observed that they tried to focus more on the content or idea in artmaking, discussing visual-cultural images rather than a collection of fancy digital effects. This helped eliminate a student's tendency to make art that imitated drawing or painting. After this project, a student commented that digital art should not be understood in terms of fine art technique and skill because a computer is a totally new medium. Second, this project expanded upon the concept of visual culture. Students reflected upon their own past life through visual culture, enabling them to examine the impact of visual culture in the history of personal life beyond contemporary popular/media culture.

2. Visual Culture Analysis and Digital Collage—As the next project in my preservice technology course, I continued to concentrate on students' expressions of idea or content against the sole focus on technological effects. In this project, students were invited to critique contemporary visual culture, and visualize their critical responses toward it. Students were allowed to choose a popular visual cultural site: a television program, movie, music video, video game, shopping malls, restaurants, or family entertainment places. They were asked to watch or visit, respond and react, and to experience the site. In order to examine the site they chose, they were encouraged to describe and analyze multimodal characteristics (Duncum, 2004) such as visuals, sounds, music, time, motion, texts, and words, as well as including a sequence of questions that explore aesthetic, social, political, economic, and cultural issues. After criticizing their visual cultural site, they were invited to visualize their responses.

As they started working on this second project, they were getting more used to the tools and features of Photoshop. They learned advanced features of the program. One example is to create an animation sequence of their artwork using multiple layers. Students were advised to create layers for a sequence, which makes use of frame-by-frame animation on the Animation palette in the program. They learned that their art does not need to be confined to a single picture frame, helping them develop a new perspective on digital art. This is well reflected in a student remark:

> When I thought about who I was and what I liked when I was younger, I thought computer art was sort of, silly. It seemed like it was not a real art form, this naivety coming from the lack of experience I had with creating computer art. It was not really until I took this class that I began to appreciate and observe computer art! (D. Mulleneaux, personal communication, April 4, 2008)

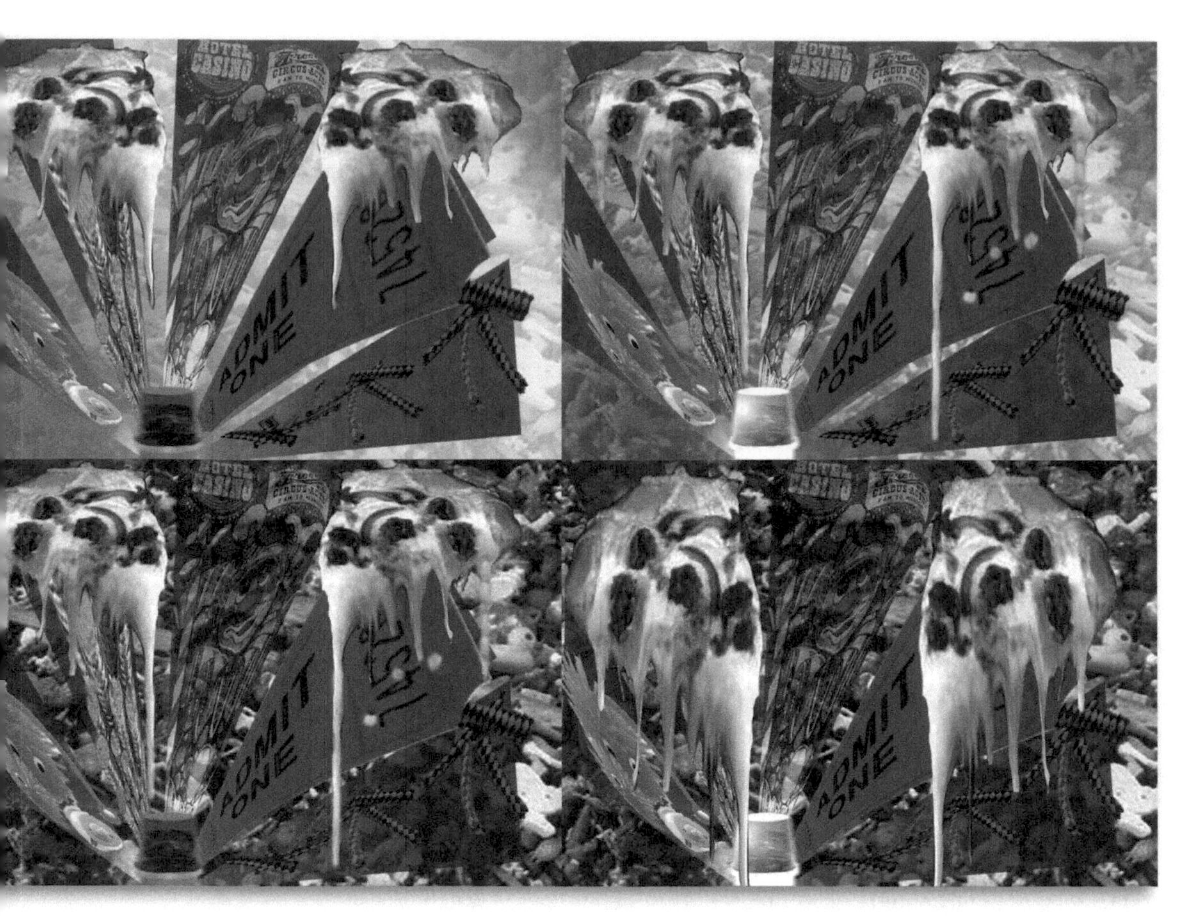

A visual culture collage. This shows a sequence of the student's artwork after criticizing Peter Piper Pizza, a family entertainment center.

Criticizing visual-cultural sites allowed students to get more used to the process of digital artmaking, using such popular methods as cutting and pasting, cropping, recombining, overlapping, and layering. In particular, it was interesting to watch students recycle pre-existing images in their computer files, rather than creating with the computer; and they commonly appropriated images using Internet search engines, participating in the practice of cloning digital images as one of the characteristics of digital visual culture (Sweeny, 2005).

3. Digital Storytelling—This next project further dispelled students' misunderstandings about digital media. Here, students are expected to use such elements as images, sounds, movie clips, and texts in their own movie project. Some of the students were scared when I introduced this project due to its seeming complexity and their lack of experience and familiarity with movie editing software. They also were concerned about not having camcorders. However, this fear for the new project declined after I gave them demonstrations on the features and functions of iMovie. I chose this movie-making software because it is freely accessible to any Mac computers, and because of the relative ease of the program for beginners, which make it applicable to K-12 art classrooms when compared to the relatively expensive Adobe Premiere or Apple Final Cut Pro. Students were also surprised to learn how easily a user can make and edit a movie with iMovie. Before beginning their own movie-making, they watched some examples from the Center for Digital Storytelling website.[4]

The process of this project is similar with what Chung (2006), who worked with graduate students, described in his digital storytelling class. Students first were asked to create a story or script that addressed a personally decisive moment in life—discrimination, gender issues, or other social justice issues, or community issues and concerns. Then, they worked with a storyboard handout and were asked to organize their story with a sequence, jotting down what media, special effects, or transitions can be used for their own story.

In developing and teaching this project, I faced certain technical and practical issues that any art teacher might face, such as recording and digitizing students' voices, incorporating music, and locating camcorders. First, I did not require students to use digital camcorders for recording because a digital story does not necessitate the inclusion of movie clips. Instead, I suggested using photos taken from digital cameras or digitized from scanning. I also advised students to take advantage of a digital camera's movie capturing feature, a common component of most any digital camera. One student commented that using a digital camera is extremely easy in downloading and importing movie clips to a computer. For the voiceover, I suggest using iMovie's voice recording feature. An alternative method I recommend would be using an iPod with a microphone or Apple GarageBand program. In the iMovie, which provides two sound channels, students used one for background music, and the other for voiceover. They were able to split sound clips, and adjust volume levels to fade in and out. Developing good editing skills in a few class sessions was challenging. However, user-friendly iMovie helped students quickly learn basic editing skills, which can make it easily applicable to the K-12 art classroom.

4. Narrative Web Art: Dimonscapes—One day one of my students sent me an e-mail informing me of an article featuring the digital artist Roz Dimon. When I looked at Dimon's works on her website,[5] my first response was how creative she has been with technology. I thought to myself that her work was an excellent example that I could use to demonstrate to my students the big difference between digital art and traditional painting and drawing. Dimon's work dynamically presents the creative use of combining and connecting technologies that most people have not yet considered. I have seen many textbooks and visited numerous website tutorials for digital art, yet Dimon's approach is very unique and creative in comparison.

Her work consists of two main components: digital imagery and textual story (or poem). Typically, the artwork is displayed in one area of the web window, and a related story is presented below or beside it. The plain and hyperlinked text for the story is differentiated by color. The viewer reads the story and as he/she clicks on the hyperlinked text, they see the image associated with the text. In so doing,

Roz Dimon. Gold Mickey, 2007. DIMONscapes® (Patent pending with all rights reserved by the artist). Reprinted here with permission from artist.

they experience interactivity and viewer participation as important characteristics of Web art (Colman, 2005). Each story features 5 to 15 or more multi-layered images. Some of her stories align with collages or collage-making processes, while others build a narrative through a sequence of hand-drawn lines or painterly brush strokes that sync with the meaning of the text. Her more recent DIMONscapes® give one the option of either using auto-play and/or interactive mode and often are accompanied by a sound track. In auto-play mode, the storied links progress automatically and build as a normal story would over time. Interactive mode takes this a step further and encourages viewers to click whatever text link they like, thus enabling them to construct and deconstruct the story and the art which relates to it in whatever sequence they desire. This use of hypertext allows a new way of looking at digital art that students can exercise in their own inventive linking (Taylor, 2000; Taylor & Carpenter, 2002) and come to appreciate their works in their own constructive way.

Dimon's artwork is made using Photoshop with a Wacom tablet and pen (for drawing and painting) and Web design editors such as Dreamweaver or Flash which add animation and interactivity to the Web page. The final images are output to high-resolution c-prints. However, her works are made to be appreciated online (Fasolino, 2008), existing virtually as hypertext with no physical form (Carpenter & Taylor, 2003). Her works can be easily adapted in college and even high school art classes, without writing highly advanced computer language and scripting for Web design. Her art will inspire students to think of creative ways to express ideas or concepts, rather than indulging in technical extravaganzas. It also helps students focus on what to say and express through poems, personal diaries, or essays.

CONCLUSION

I believe that one of the best ways to help students understand the power and value of digital media is to invite them to be actively involved with digital artmaking. I strongly suggest that preservice art teachers take digital media art classes (Colman, 2004; Galbraith,1997; Lu, 2005) and learn to overcome the aforementioned misunderstandings or biases toward digital art by examining and discussing the aesthetics of new media art (Liao, 2008; Lin, 2005; Patton, 2005; Sweeny, 2005). The four practices described in this chapter are presented to help aspiring art educators or in-service teachers understand why digital media and technology should be taught in the classroom (Dunn, 1996; Freedman, 1997, 2003; Garber, 2004; Keifer-Boyd, 2005), highlighting its strength and uniqueness as new media, as well as avoiding naïve expectations or excessive indulgence in technology. I also hope that these four digital media practices help correct the aforementioned three misunderstandings and biases on digital artmaking media and processes, allowing people to realize and appreciate the creative potential of digital media as a contemporary art form.

REFERENCES

Amburgy, P. M., Knight, W. B., & Keifer-Boyd, K. (2006). Revisioning the self-portrait and still life as visual culture. In P. Duncum (Ed.), *Visual culture in the art class: Case studies* (pp. 73-80). Reston, VA: National Art Education Association.

Carpenter, B. S., & Taylor, P. G. (2003). Racing thoughts: Altering our ways of knowing and being in art through computer hypertext. *Studies in Art Education, 45*(1), 40-55.

Colman, A. (2005). Constructing an aesthetic of Web art from a review of artists' use of the World Wide Web. *Visual Arts Research, 31*(1), 13-25.

Colman, A. (2004). Net.art and net.pedagogy: Introducing internet art to the digital art curriculum. *Studies in Art Education, 46*(1), 61-73.

Chung, S. K. (2006). Digital storytelling in integrated arts education. *The International Journal of Arts Education, 4*(1), 33-63.

Duncum, P. (2004). Visual culture isn't just visual: Multiliteracy, multimodality and meaning. *Studies in Art Education, 45*(3), 252-264.

Dunn, P. C. (1996). More power: Integrated interactive technology in art education. Art *Education, 49*(6), 6-11.

Edmonds, E., & Candy, L. (2002). Creativity, art practice, and knowledge. *Communications of the ACM, 45*(10), 91-95.

Fasolino, E. (2008, February 13). Roz Dimon's matrix: Creating multi-sensory art for the Web. *The East Hampton Star.* Retrieved May 21, 2008, from www.easthamptonstar.com/dnn/Arts/Profile/tabid/4783/Default.aspx.

Freedman, K. (1997). Visual Art/Virtual Art: Teaching technology for meaning. *Art Education, 50*(4), 6-12.

Freedman, K. (2003). *Teaching visual culture: Curriculum, aesthetics, and the social life of art.* New York: Teachers College Press.

Galbraith, L. (1997). Enhancing art teacher education with new technologies: Research possibilities and practices. *Art Education, 50*(5), 14-19.

Garber, E. (2004). MOO: Using a computer gaming environment to teach about community arts. *Art Education, 57*(4), 40-47.

Giordan, D. (2002). The art of Photoshop. Indianapolis, IN: Sams Publishing.

Gude, O. (2004). Postmodern principles: In search of a 21st-century art education. *Art Education, 57*(1), 6-14.

Keifer-Boyd, K. (2005). Children teaching children with their computer game creations. *Visual Arts Research, 31*(1), 117-128.

Liao, C. L. (2008). Avatars, Second Life,® and new media art: The challenge for contemporary art education. *Art Education, 61*(2), 87-91.

Lin, P. (2005). A dream of digital art: Beyond the myth of contemporary computer technology in visual arts. *Visual Arts Research, 31*(1), 4-12.

Lu, L. (2005). Preservice art teacher negative attitudes and perceptions of computer-generated imagery: Recommendations for preservice art education program. *Visual Arts Research, 31*(1), 89-102.

Luth, T. (2001). Some thoughts on computer art. Retrieved May 22, 2008, from www.thomasluth.com/NewFiles/ThotsPage.html.

Taylor, P. G. (2000). Madonna and hypertext: Liberatory learning in art education. *Studies in Art Education, 41*(4), 376-389.

Taylor, P. G., & Carpenter, B. S. (2002). Inventively linking: Teaching and learning with computer hypertext. *Art Education, 55*(4), 6-12.

Patton, R. (2005). "Why" project: Art in the aftermath. *Visual Arts Research, 31*(1), 76-88.

Sweeny, R. (2005). Three funerals and a wedding: Art education, digital images, and an aesthetics of cloning. *Visual Arts Research, 31*(1), 26-37.

Ulbricht, J. (2007). Reflections on vIsual and material culture: An example from Southwest Chicago experience. *Studies in Art Education, 49*(1), 59-72.

ENDNOTES

1 For further information on the aesthetical aspects of the digital media in comparison with traditional media, see Colman (2005) and Sweeny (2005); see Lin (2005) for the conceptual and philosophical exploration of the new media.

2 I define "digital art" as artworks produced as a result of a human's creative use of the computer and other new digital technologies.

3 I myself have observed some computer software vendors demonstrating these kinds of painting programs at National Conventions.

4 www.storycenter.org

5 Visit the sites, dimonscapes.com or www.artstory.net, to see her works.

Digital Visual Culture: The Paradox of the [In]visible / MICHELLE TILLANDER

THE COMPUTER SYSTEM THAT OPERATES THE STREET HAS BETTER THINGS TO DO THAN TO MONITOR EVERY SINGLE ONE OF THE MILLIONS OF PEOPLE THERE, TRYING TO PREVENT THEM FROM RUNNING INTO EACH OTHER. IT DOESN'T BOTHER TRYING TO SOLVE THIS INCREDIBLY DIFFICULT PROBLEM. ON THE STREET, AVATARS JUST WALK RIGHT THROUGH EACH OTHER. (STEPHENSON, 1992)

Digital technologies are intrinsic in our everyday activities, moving with us as an extension of ourselves. In traditional computing environments, such as those that emerged in the 1990s, educators could choose to interact with computers. Early in this era, ubiquitous technologies were described as "those that weave themselves into the fabric of everyday life until they are indistinguishable from it" (Weisner, 1991, p. 65). Today, digital visual experiences that originate from newer imaging technologies are inherently embedded in our physical environment, invisibly integrated into everyday tasks, and increasingly mobile and interactive in our visual culture. This interface is a complex contour edge as it flows into the structure of human activity. Our actions and choices are thus complicated through the interface by the mediation of both external visible tools (e.g., pencils, scissors, and iPods) and internal invisible process (heuristics, culture, concepts, cognition, and strategies). The ubiquitous nature of technology in the current Information Age subtly obscures and complicates how new media translates our social, cultural, and educational experiences.

Consequentially, new media is having a huge impact on art education—rupturing any grounding of theory about the relations between viewer and image, complicating how we produce and disseminate knowledge, and emphasizing contemporary spectatorship through "the plurality and paradoxes of many different, historically distinct viewing positions" (Williams, 1994, p. 4).

My reconceptualization about the process of teaching art and technology was stimulated by an artwork entitled *Invisible* by Giovanni Anselmo, which I saw at the Hirshhorn Museum in the exhibition Zero to Infinity: Art Povera 1962-

1972. *Invisible* was the light projection of the word visible through a slide projector. The image of the word was not visible until a gallery visitor disrupts the beam of projected light. I began to consider how technical work "is made invisible by its own successes" (Latour, 1999, p. 304). It was through the invisible experience of technology, like the artists in this exhibition who sought to expand the physical and mental boundaries of art and make transparent the divisions between art and life, that I began to re-imagine how to expand skill-driven technology teaching methods. Human-computer interaction is more than a skill; it is a social and cultural interaction between users and interfaces. This requires me to explore not only technology as tools [hardware], but as rules [software], and as a system [network] (Dusek, 2006, p. 31). This approach considers hardware, software, and system as an abstract framework, to explore new media art that translates and exposes the invisible human experiences of contemporary digital visual culture.

Lev Manovich's (2001a) theory of "human-computer-cultural-interface"—namely the boundary where technology (new digital media) and culture (beliefs, values, and assumptions) converge—has implications for how art education can conceptualize new media technology. "In short, we are no longer interfacing to a computer but to culture encoded in digital form" (p. 70). This assimilation is complicated because of how the computer layers intertwine signifiers (e.g., ideas, artifacts, and presuppositions) which bridge the "cultural layer" to the "computer layer" (p. 46). These transitions are much more complex than movement from one distinct layer to another. That is, new media conceptualized as an interface is a cultural-process bridging human, machine, and hybrid forms—resulting in a combination of sensory and semiotic relationships. Similarly, Bourriaud's (1998) notion of relational aesthetics has us consider the process of interfacing. According to Bourriaud, "the role of artworks is no longer to form imaginary and utopian realities, but to actually be ways of living and models of action within the existing real, whatever scale chosen by the artist" (p. 13). This view has broad and deep implications for art education within areas such as new media's effect on visual perception, interpretation, aesthetics, cognition styles, expression behaviors, learning patterns, and interaction in contemporary society.

Reflecting on these issues and exploring new media art conceptually, socially, and interactively offers an opportunity for art education to be a dynamic entity in preparing students for the future. These reflections evoke questions and conversations about cultural issues as related to creative and critical sensibilities to new media design and production. As a result, one approach might be for curricula to explore themes such as the "impact of cybernetic art in rendering human identity in terms of consciousness and communication," "how technologies have become part of ourselves, both in function and identity," and "how technology affects perceived boundaries among disciplines, makers/consumers, artists/viewers, and public/private" (Keifer-Boyd, 2005, p. 1). These themes expand arts and technology from solely outputs, projects, and objects—a compartmentalization often seen as a weakness of art education (Burnett, 2008).

INVISIBLE CONTOURS OF NEW MEDIA

New media artists challenge us to question the assumptions about digital visual interfaces, and consequently confront technological artifacts and processes where the social, the cultural, and the aesthetic shift (Grau 2006; Hansen 2004; Paul, 2003). Artists make visible these subtle shifts in social, cultural, and aesthetic ways of seeing that co-exist alongside one another and focus our attention visually in different ways of seeing. Likewise, art educators provide powerful strategies in the studio environment to explore these assumptions and subtleties for use in digital learning environments. These strategies include the comprehensive use of project, problem, and process-based learning, reflective journals, portfolios, case study approaches, and visual literacy competencies. As a result, art educators and artists illuminate a range of [in]visible new media conversations for art education, which can be used in developing innovative art and technology curricula. "Artists working with the Internet as a medium are concerned essentially with the creation of a new type of aesthetic that involves not only the visual representation but invisible aspects of organization, retrieval, and navigation as well" (Vesna, 2007, p. xiii). Contemporary artists reveal and process the changing relationship between technology and culture through their exploration of new media devices. Similarly, art educators' history with constructivist learning models (Simpson, 1996), where activities are interactive and student-centered, and where art students are immersed in experiences that engage in meaning-making inquiry, action, imagination, interaction, hypothesizing, invention, and personal expressions and reflections, provide responsive experiences to negotiate the changing relationship between technology and culture. McLuhan stated, "It has always been the artist who perceives that alterations in man are caused by a new medium, who recognizes that the future is present, and uses his artwork to prepare ground for it" (cited in Norden, 1969, p. 122). New media artists expose a sense of being within the digital and Internet life of contemporary times, and creatively and critically explore assumptions (Greene, 2004) and changes in cultural issues. That is to say, art educators and artists who concurrently invoke digital visual cultural dynamics and interrogate culture encoded in digital visual form make visible the invisible contours of ubiquitous technologies.

Technological consciousness often reinforces hidden hegemony as it operates at a level of process (Apple, 1982). For example, although efficiency is not directly taught in schools it invisibly penetrates the educational system. Specifically, this penetration is opaque in technological categorization of content and use in assessment and accountability.[1] Within the studio experience, art educators engage "studio thinking" within the art room (Hetland, Winner, Veenema, &

Sheridan, 2007) and as such offer an opportunity to interrupt technology models that often imperceptibly fashion common sense to conform to the necessities of production. In art education and studio thinking, the invisible patterns of efficiency and technical skills can be disrupted through pedagogy, specifically what Perkins calls the "import paradigm" (p. v), where students are engaged and learn for the future through current actions.

Like much contemporary art, an engagement with newer media art disrupts the boundaries of art categorization, questions modernist notions of aesthetics, and thus challenges models such as Discipline-Based Art Education (DBAE). As Freedman (2003) states, "high school art curriculum often includes learning objectives with a narrow focus on media skills or the elements and principles of design" (pp. 111-112). The exploration and engagement with new media is often difficult for art educators because of minimal exposure to newer media theory and art and a lack of support and infrastructure (Delacruz, 2004), and an inherent disposition about technology and art embodied in educators' beliefs, values, and assumptions (Orr, 2003). Combined, these factors create obstacles for substantive engagement.

Manovich (2001b) suggests that since the 1960s, the "rapid development of new artistic forms—assemblage, happening, installation, performance, action, conceptual art, process art, intermedia, time-based art, etc." (p. 1)—is replacing the old typology of artistic mediums (material and representational as sign and referent). He suggests that we need a new aesthetic model that shifts away from a medium-based paradigm toward a new model that bridges the old and new perspectives as one continuum. Manovich's raises questions that can be used in art education, such as, "how a cultural object organizes data and structures user's experience of this data," "what kind of user's information operations a particular medium allows for," and the impact of "information behavior" (p. 4), which describes a particular way or pattern of accessing and processing information.

While Manovich argues for a new aesthetic, Lovejoy (2004) argues for understanding the field of digital new media because of the growing impact of digital technologies on the changes occurring in the role of the artist as social communicator. Lovejoy's approach explores how digital tools catalyze new perspectives on art, and influences the way artists see, think, and work. As computers advanced, "artists began to challenge the computer to go beyond the formal tasks it had up to then performed, and found it could be used as both tool and medium" (p. 79). As new media continues to provide new worlds of design and production, we can recognize the differentiation of educational experience and interrogate questions we pose by reflecting on individual philosophies toward medium, innovation, and tools.

As Nideffer (2007) states:

> ...keeping one's own cultural practice and frames of reference "anthropologically strange" (meaning to reflect consciously to whatever degree

> possible upon one's embedded behaviors, beliefs, and values as "foreign" or "other"), enables a type of creative production that disrupts social spaces in the interest of rendering visible the invisible structures of language, meaning, and power. (p. 228)

This method engages personal reflection, moves away from cognitive transfer (Tuomi-Grohn & Engestrom, 2003), and exposes the invisible border and boundary structures of language, meaning, and power. The approach challenges us to question hidden assumptions about digital visual culture through technocultural processes and artifacts.

In the *Wizard of Oz*, when Dorothy asked the wizard, "Where are you?" The wizard responds, "I am everywhere, but to the eyes of common mortals I am invisible." Similarly, the 'hidden curriculum' as explored by Jackson (1968), Apple (1982), and Giroux and Purpel (1983) is an unseen second curricula what acts as a socialization process and influences learning by paralleling the intended and actual curriculum. The very social nature of much of digital communication requires understanding the way in which knowledge frames cultural values and social actions, and how attitudes are transmitted through structures and organizations of digital communication networks. We can interfere with the hidden curriculum to critically engage a respect for differences, increase an appreciation for diversity, as well as reveal the limitations of self-knowledge in a technological culture. As an example of the latter, Haraway (1988) describes optimistically the limitations of the self as cyborg, where vision becomes the optical device as our biological eyes and brains are interfaced with technology; and the "knowing self is partial in all its guises, never finished, whole, simply there and original: it is always constructed and stitched together imperfectly; and therefore able to join with another, to see together without claiming to be another" (p. 586). With the interface, there are always actants behind the curtain, whether it is the code language, interface designers, or curriculum specialists. Similarly, what gets hidden in the rhetoric of "The Information Age"? Do data, visualization, and virtual models obscure deeper levels of visual culture? What are the visual cultural orientations being reinforced by technology? Are these orientations part of the solution for education or do they compound the problem? These questions become imperative for art educators to consider in cooperation with rationales for art educational use of technology and need for clearly understanding the influence of technology on social change.

NEW MEDIA ART CONVERSATIONS

Digital technology plays with the notion of both tool and medium because it actively engages abstract information and concrete materials. Digital art is both a computed and experienced discourse. Artists challenge us to rethink our definitions of technology and its relationships to art through history (Grau, 2006). For example, by conceiving of the digital as part of a 'baroque event,' Munster (2006) conceives of digital media as "unfolding differential relays" (p. 6). Munster argues the digital conceived as part of a baroque flow articulates the differential relations between embodiment and technique and is not a dichotomy. This makes visible ways to disrupt the binary pairs that dominate digital culture and new media technologies (physicality and virtuality; real and hyperreal; analog and discrete states; natural and artificial; real and mythical; scientific and aesthetic). Through Munster's ideas of unfolding of digital and baroque aesthetics and the relations of connection, we can consider different associations between bodies, other materialities, affect, and the inhuman spaces of code and its flows.

For example, *i.Mirror* by artist Fei (2007) is a video about her experiences and feelings in Second Life.® Second Life, which began in 2003, is a 3-D Internet-based collective network of virtual worlds that are created, managed, and used by participants who are called Residents. *i.Mirror* introduces us to China Tracey, Fei's Second Life avatar. Fei is interested in the city as an organism, and her role as an actor and director interfacing with the city. In the main narrative, China Tracey meets a young Chinese poet avatar, Hug Yue. After several encounters in this Metaverse[2] it is gradually revealed that Hug Yue is actually a 60-year-old American. By confusing her two lives, Fei also compares them. "When you're online in a totally new world, your physical self is more invisible, and it's your inner self that's revealed" (Culp, 2008). This is a version of Baudrillard's (1994) simulacrum, where the "real" dissolves into an abstract network of signs, and the self as a social construction becomes literal. In Second Life, participants create characters from virtual market places, thus transforming identity into commodity (Heartney, 2008). Framing the main story are two shorter narratives that montage the Second Life environment and an array of avatars that inhabit this world.

In a slightly different vein, new media artists often make visible the convergence and divergence of information between the digital and material world. One example is the OneTree project by Natalie Jeremijenko (2000). The project consists of one thousand tree(s), clones of a single tree, planted into a cultural setting throughout public sites in the San Francisco Bay Area. The differences in each tree (e.g., how they grow) are the result of social and environmental forces. There are also electronic components of the project, which include Artificial Life (A-Life) trees that simulate the growth of the biological trees on a computer desktop. The growth rate of these simulated trees is controlled by a carbon dioxide meter connected to the computer. Part of this project juxtaposes the simulated (A-Life) trees and their biological counterparts. In doing so, the artist demonstrates what simulations do not represent as much as what they do. Jeremijenko explains:

> Trees are instruments to view time and environment more accurately than mere databases. The best database standards last eight years.... We ignore

> slow environmental changes unless they are crisis-driven such as hurricanes in Florida. It is more important to read and understand (that) slow change is recorded by trees. (Sardar, 2004, p. F1)

Here, Jeremijenko exemplifies artists as producer and researcher, and her work illustrates what Latour (1996, p. 183) has described as "connections, short circuits, translations, associations, and mediations that we encounter daily." In this way, the artwork restructures our relationship to technology where the aesthetic shifts so that the artwork "...no longer seeks to be a noun/object but a verb/process..." but instead acknowledges the "unfixed impermanence, to be experienced as an unrepeatable and fleeting situation" (Kwon, 2004, p. 24).

Digital media expand options for communication and provide new possibilities for information exchange and interactivity, specifically with regard to how artworks are created, seen, and distributed. This challenges many assumptions and frameworks of how information is ordered and visualized. Lagrady's (2005-2014) installation, Making Visible the Invisible, explores alternative ways to order and visualize information of a database created by the interactions of library users.[3] Lagrady's installation consists of six large LCD screens behind the main circulation desk of the Seattle Public Library. Circulating books and media are analyzed and visually mapped every hour. These real-time set of visualizations challenges the library's Dewey system for categorizing things and extends it to a visual interface that includes borrowers and the library's collection. The projections are constantly updating information through four visual modes of representation. These modes of representation are dependent on information parameters, context, and upon users' search preferences. Through the database, this artwork makes the invisible digital information visible through social and cultural context, and a network of transactions, particularly what a community of users considers interesting at any given time.

These artworks refresh our relationships to records and patterns ultimately contributing to new modes of experiencing the cultural interface of digital media. New media art confronts the declarative role of art by challenging us to discover our own cultural experiences and explore our own directions. For example, virtual reality's interactive software inscribes a kind of metadiscourse that structures a context of action. Virtual reality as a nonmaterial world constructs its own qualities while it modifies our relation of place to body, space and time, and individual and group. In *So.So.So. Somebody, Somewhere, Some Time* (Benayoun, 2002), the viewers, looking through VR binoculars, do not realize that their own story is being written as they look at elements of the banal panorama and are moved from one scene to another. Here the narrative process is inverted and for us to consider if the virtual is in the technology that defines it. Similarly, surveillance technologies' ubiquitous nature often raises interesting questions about autonomy and privacy. Artist collective Radical Software Group (RSG, 2001) creates artworks like *Carnivore* to parody surveillance technologies and monitoring information exchanges. Artist Jill Magid's (2004) *Evidence Locker* investigates how tools and processes of surveillance are ubiquitously integrated into contemporary everyday life. By engaging with *Evidence Locker*, Magid offers the viewer a unique and alternative perspective about surveillances and the digital interface. In an interview, Magid explains her performance in *Evidence Locker*,

> I have never looked at surveillance technology from the position of a civilian under its gaze... Surveillance cameras create stages, or fixed, monitored platforms. By watching an area rather than an individual, the camera in its static position seems to favor its context over the pedestrians passing through it. It seems to say: The city is permanent, the civilian ephemeral. In a positive sense, this technology offers me a way to place myself, to become visible (and potentially permanent) within the city, through a medium bigger than myself. (Lovink, 2004)

To see *Evidence Locker*, you must sign up to receive the artwork (i.e., access to an evidence locker). This participation reveals how the digital can connect and simulate any real or imagined context, thus challenging cultural institutions by confronting personal and basic relationships to context. What is the impact of digital visual culture on human cultural enterprise? Stenner's (2007) *Honeypump* engages participants in a remote location to approach a monitor and a bicycle pump resting on the floor. I approached the artwork with a bit of puzzlement as I recognized on the screen a live image of myself in the gallery; I was compelled to grab the pump handle. As I pushed on the pump and the pressure built, my image began to fade, leaving only an image of the gallery space. At that moment, my image was captured and stored, in a remote database, indefinitely. Stenner's *Honeypump* references Joseph Beuys' seminal *Honeypump in the Workplace*, which symbolized the creative energy released by the social interactions of a participatory society. The work associates Beuys' concept of "social sculpture" with the dialogic possibilities embodied in the development of digitally networked communication. The artwork reveals to us through our own participation that, as we embrace the "new" of digital media, the individual is often rendered invisible, surveilled, cataloged, marketed and processed—frequently with little awareness that his/her identity has moved indiscernibly and fluidly through digital spaces. *Honeypump* challenges participants to discover their own cultural experiences and explore their own invisible assumptions and beliefs about digital visual culture.

CONCLUSION

Experiences with new media artworks such as those described locate critical inquiry and personal actions/emotions as essential and integrated processes in questioning how we organize knowledge, form cultural practices, participate in social spaces, and understand corporeality, identity, politics, and power in the context of contemporary digital visual culture. Critical inquiry, as a type of interaction, implicates the participant in internal and external systems of epistemology. Further, interaction experienced through personal action/emotion engages an aesthetic realm of the digital interface that shapes cultural signs, beliefs, and practices (Cubitt, 1998).

Through conceptual, social, political, and interactive experiences, new media artists critically expose the subtleties of the contour edge of digital visual culture interfaces as they invisibly structure human activity. Artists and art educators offer insight as they play off of software design, promote teaching strategies that facilitate active learning and critical thinking, or engage in creative disruption, "to peel off that ideological wrapper"—a process that exploits technology's potential, as well as reveals hidden issues (Ippolito, 2002, p. 287). Just as new media artists blur the boundaries of art and life, art educators might consider the characteristics reflective of new media art and technology experiences of their students as possibilities for critically exploring technology in an art curriculum. Through these critical explorations, art educators can guide collaborative exploration of new media artwork with their students as works-in-progress to co-construct art and technology as digital visual learning experiences within art education.

REFERENCES

Apple, M. (1982). *Cultural and economic reproduction in education.* New York: Routledge.

Baudrillard J. (1994). *Simulacra and simulation.* (Tr. Sheila Faria Glaser.) Ann Arbor: University of Michigan.

Benayoun, M. (2002). *So.so.so. Somebody, somewhere, some time.* Retrieved October 31, 2008, from http://www.benayoun.com/sososo/demo/

Bourriaud N. (1998). *Relational aesthetics.* Paris: Presses du reel.

Burnett, R. (2008). Learning, education, and the arts in a digital world. In M. Alexenberg (Ed.). *Educating artists for the future: Learning at the intersections of art, science, and technology* (pp. 115-126). Chicago: Intellect.

Cubitt, S. (1998). *Digital aesthetics.* Thousand Oaks, CA: Sage.

Culp, S. (2008, February 20). [Interview with Cao Fei aka China Tracy]. *Artkrush, 78,* ¶14. Retrieved June 2, 2008, from http://artkrush.com/160442

Delacruz, E. (2004). Teachers' working conditions and the unmet promise of technology. *Studies in Art Education, 46*(1), 6-19.

Dusek, V. (2006). *Philosophy of technology.* Boston: Blackwell Publishing.

Fei, C. (2007). *i.mirror.* Retrieved, June 12, 2008, from http://youtube.com/chinatracy

Freedman, K. (2003). *Teaching visual culture: Curriculum, aesthetics, and the social life of art.* New York: Teachers College Press.

Giroux, H., & Purpel, D. (1983). *The hidden curriculum and moral education.* Richmond, CA: McCutchan Publishing.

Grau, O. (2006). *MediaArtHistories.* Cambridge, MA: MIT Press.

Greene, R. (2004). *Internet art.* London: Thames & Hudson.

Hansen, M. (2004). *New philosophy of new media.* Cambridge, MA: MIT Press.

Haraway, D. (1988). Situated knowledges: The science question in feminism and the privilege of partial perspective. *Feminist Studies, 14*(3), 575-599.

Heartney, E. (2008). Like life: as seen through the work of Chinese artist Cao Fei, the virtual universe of Second Life is more glamorous and seductive, and no less melancholy, than the world from which it offers escape. *Art in America, 96*(5), 164-167.

Hetland, L., Winner, E., Veenema, S., & Sheridan, K. S. (2007) *Studio thinking*. New York: Teachers College Press.

Ippolito, J. (2002). Ten myths of Internet art. *Leonardo: Journal of the International Society for the Arts, Science and Technology, 35*(5), 485-498.

Jackson, P. (1968). *Life in classrooms*. New York: Holt, Rinehart & Winston.

Jeremijenko, N. (2000). OneTree. Retrieved May 9, 2008, from http://www.nyu.edu/projects/xdesign/onetrees/

Keifer-Boyd, K. (2005). Technology interfaces with art education. *Visual Arts Research, 31*(1), 1-3.

Kwon, M. (2004). *One place after another: site specific art and locational identity*. Cambridge, MA: MIT Press.

Lagrady, G. (2005-2014). Making visible the invisible. Retrieved May 14, 2008, from http://www.georgelagrady.com

Latour, B. (1999). *Pandora's hope*. Boston, MA: Harvard University Press.

Latour, B. (1996). *Aramis or the love of technology*. Boston, MA: Harvard University Press.

Lovejoy, M. (2004). *Digital currents: Art in the electronic age*. New York: Routledge.

Lovink, G. (2004, October 30). [Surveillance, Performance, Self-Surveillance Interview with Jill Magid]. Retrieved May 21, 2008, from http://www.evidencelocker.net/img/artistTalk.pdf

Magid, J. (2004). *Evidence locker*. Retrieved January 19, 2005, from http://www.evidencelocker.net/story.php

Manovich, L. (2001a). *The language of new media*. Cambridge, MA: MIT Press.

Manovich, L. (2001b). *Lev Manovich analyzes the post-media age*, Retrieved June 10, 2006, from www.artmargins.com/index.php/featured-articles/412-lev-manovich-analyzes-the-post-media-age

Munster, A. (2006). *Materializing new media: Embodiment in information aesthetics*. Dartmouth, NH: Dartmouth College Press.

Nideffer, R. (2007). Game engines as embedded systems. In V. Vesna (Ed.), *Database aesthetics: Art in the age of information overflow* (pp. 211-231). Minneapolis: University of Minnesota Press.

Norden, E. (1969, 1989). [Marshall McLuhan: A candid conversation with the high priest of popcult and metaphysician of the media]. *The Canadian Journal of Communication 14*(4 & 5), 101-137. (Reprinted from *Playboy 16*(3), (1969, March), 26-27, 45, 55-56, 61, 63).

Orr, P. (2003). A hollow god: Technology's effects on paradigms and practices in secondary art education. Unpublished doctoral dissertation, Purdue University, West Lafayette, Indiana.

Paul, C. (2003). *Digital art*. London: Thames and Hudson.

Radical Software Group. (2001). *Carnivore*. Retrieved March 2005, from http://r-s-g.org/carnivor

Sardar, Z. (2004, October 23). [Natalie Jeremijenko's trees aren't simply decorative they can be read like a social register]. *San Francisco Chronicle*. p F1. Retrieved May 9, 2008, from http://www.sfgate.com/cgibin/article.cgi?file=/c/a/2004/10/23/HOGCQ9DH301.DTL&type=printable

Simpson, J. (1996). Constructivism and connection making in art education. *Art Education 49*(1), 53-59.

Stenner, J. (2007). *Honeypump*. Retrieved March 10, 2008, from http://www.jigglingwhisker.com

Stephenson, N. (1992). *Snow crash*. New York: Bantam Books.

Tuomi-Grohn, T., & Engestrom, Y. (Eds.). (2003). *Between work and school: New perspectives on transfer and boundary-crossing*. London: Pergamon.

Vesna, V. (Ed.) (2007). *Database aesthetics: Art in the age of information overflow*. Minneapolis: University of Minnesota Press.

Weisner, M. (1991). The computer for the 21st century. *Scientific American, 265*(3), 66-75.

Williams, L. (Ed.). (1994). *Viewing positions: Ways of seeing film*. Piscataway, NJ: Rutgers University Press.

ENDNOTES

1 For example, Florida has recently made the Florida Teacher Certification Exams, General Knowledge Test's Essay section available as a computer-based test. That means all sections of the GK for admission, the Subject Area Exam (Art K-12, Music K-12, and Agriculture 6-12), and the Professional Education Test required for graduation can be taken on a computer by appointment or via the regular or supplemental paper administrations.

2 Metaverse as a term first appeared in 1992 in *Snow Crash* by Neal Stephenson.

3 In *Database Aesthetic*, a database is defined by Vesna (2007, p. 156) as "a picture, and image of a system of meaning organized from a social perspective."

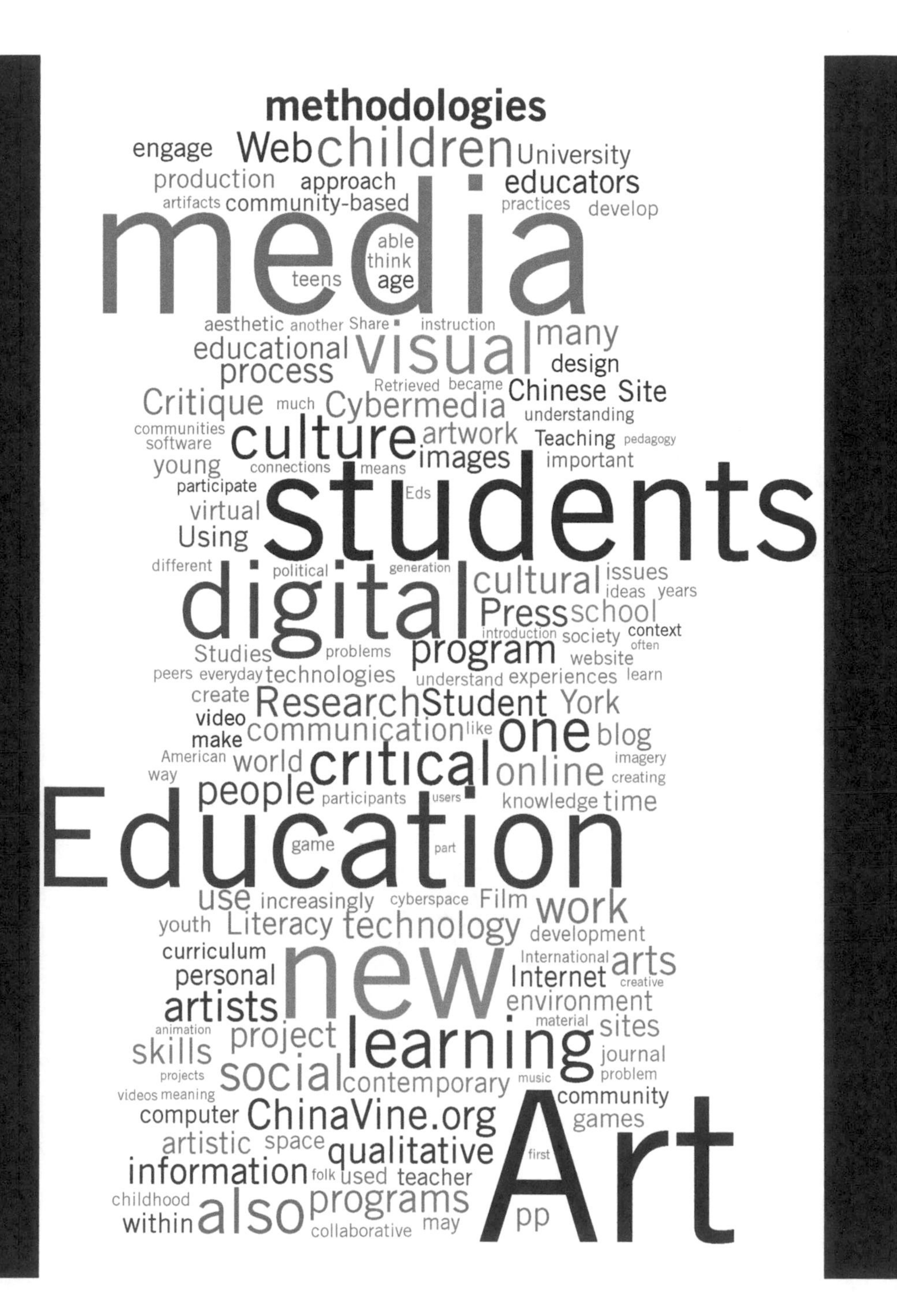
methodologies
engage Web children University
production approach educators
artifacts community-based practices develop
media
able
think
teens age
aesthetic another Share instruction
many
educational visual
process design
Retrieved became
Critique much Cybermedia Chinese Site
understanding
communities
software culture artwork Teaching pedagogy
young connections means images important
participate
Eds
students
virtual
Using
different political generation
digital cultural issues
ideas years
Press school
introduction society context
Studies problems program website often
peers everyday technologies understand experiences learn
create Research Student York
video
make communication like one blog
American imagery
world critical online
way creating
people participants users knowledge time
Education
game part
use increasingly cyberspace Film
youth Literacy technology work
development
curriculum
new International arts
personal Internet creative
artists environment
animation material sites
skills project learning
journal
projects problem
social contemporary music
videos meaning community
computer ChinaVine.org
games
artistic space
qualitative first
information folk used teacher
childhood
programs
within also collaborative may pp
Art

Cybermedia Literacy Art Education /

SHENG KUAN CHUNG

Technological innovations have helped create a virtual terrain of aesthetic production, dissemination, and consumption. The integration of technology and capitalism (namely, technocapitalism) is changing the ways we as citizens of the digital age consume, entertain, and obtain information. Noticeably, American children are immersing themselves in a mediated culture of consumption manufactured and controlled by megacorporations (e.g., Disney, Sony, and MTV). Widely disseminated online media programs/artifacts, such as video games and advertisements, not only sway children into purchasing and consuming, but also serve as pedagogical sites that shape their perceptions of reality as they formulate their own attitudes, beliefs, and values, as well as learn about themselves and the outside world (Duncum, 2002). Giroux (1999), for instance, has accused Disney of targeting young consumers and creating a fantasy world based on childhood innocence while its media images, products, and narratives grossly perpetuate gender and racial stereotypes.

To function in a technoeconomy and rapidly changing society, students need to engage in critical media literacy activities in order to become more informed consumers of cyberaesthetics. I use the term cyberaesthetics in a site-specific, ordinary language sense (Duncum, 2007), to refer to the wide range of sensory experiences—heightened awareness, radiance of mind, or moving disposition (Tavin, 2007) mediated by virtual technologies of commercially driven cybermedia sites. These sensory experiences may include the sublime, the beautiful, the pleasurable, and/or the morally deplorable. The cybermediascape is a commodified cultural jungle saturated with pleasurable, and even violent or sexual, visual spectacles. Art education must prepare the digital generation for the expanding cybersociety, equipping them with the critical knowledge and skills necessary to process the vast number of visual spectacles. This chapter thus illuminates the importance of fostering cybermedia literacy in the tech-savvy digital generation and proposes a critical approach to art education that fosters cybermedia literacy.

CYBERLITERACY: CYBERMEDIA AS A PEDAGOGICAL SITE

Unlike conventional media literacy that emphasizes analysis and evaluation of media artifacts, cyberliteracy involves understanding of the characteristics of Internet communication—speed, reach, anonymity, and interactivity—in relation to ourselves, our communities, and our cultures (Gurak, 2001). Critical cyberliteracy acknowledges the political nature of technologies and the power of users in shaping future technologies and cybercultures. Critical cyberliteracy allows users to critically engage in computer-mediated experiences and use cyberspace as a tool for social action.

The commodification of aesthetics driven by technocapitalism is in full operation in cyberspace, offering children sensory-stimulating aesthetic experiences. With a computer connected to the Internet, children have access to the cybermedia arena, where they participate in social networking (e.g., MySpace), gather information, download music, watch on-demand videos, purchase items, play virtual games (e.g., Second Life), visit multimedia websites, browse censored materials, and construct their own communities. Unsurprisingly, the tech-savvy digital generation is immersing itself in these types of activities as its everyday aesthetic sites/sights. As children participate in these types of cyberactivities, they automatically subject themselves to a virtual jungle saturated with many forms of deception (e.g., advertising masquerades as information, e-mail spam, compromising their privacy by joining a social networking site, or violating copyrights for downloading music). Because of its immense prevalence and multimedia interactivity, cybermedia may be one of the most persuasive educational forces in techno-societies. Through the imagery and message of product desirability, different beliefs and values are offered to children, either intentionally or unintentionally, and become sites of ideological struggle.

Youths are devoted users of computer technologies. Studies have consistently revealed that American school-age children use home computers mostly to play games (Roberts, Foehr, & Rideout, 2005). A recent study confirmed that 83% of American teens have a video game console at home and that 41% play console video games every day (Roberts, Foehr, & Rideout, 2005). Specifically, 65% have played the explicitly violent Grand Theft Auto video game (Roberts, Foehr, & Rideout, 2005). It is no surprise that the interactivity of video games, escalated by virtual technology, has also drawn youths to online game sites such as World of Warcraft and Naughty America Games featuring explicit violent and sexual imagery. Noticeably, children learn a different, if not conflicting, set of values from cybermedia than from what they learn in school. For instance, most school curriculums censor violent imagery, whereas corporate America transforms violence into a computer-mediated visual spectacle that can be aesthetically pleasing and visually breathtaking. Interestingly yet unsettlingly, the aesthetic elements found in a work of art also exist in the imagery of destruction (Allen & Greenberger, 1978). Destructive violent scenes impress viewers with mixed emotions—horror yet also pleasure. McLaren and Morris (1997) argued that media violence now functions much the same way as nature, as children are trained to view violence as necessary to "bring the world back to a state of happy equilibrium" (p. 116). They caution that "choreographed techno-violence is now part of the perpetual pedagogy of TV shows and subsequently participates informally in the act of child rearing" (McLaren & Morris, 1997, p. 116).

Additionally, the Internet is becoming a notorious playground for pornography exposure and child sexual solicitation. Sexualized images are increasingly prevalent in cyberspace through various channels such as websites, unsolicited e-mail, Web cameras, and chat rooms. It is estimated that 70% of American children have viewed Internet pornography (The Henry J. Kaiser Family Foundation, 2001). Alarmingly, 31% of children have pretended to be older to get into an adult website (Roberts, Foehr, & Rideout, 2005). One in four American youth has also reported an unwanted exposure to sexual material (Ybarra & Mitchell, 2005). Cyberpornography teaches children a distorted picture of human sexuality, as most pornographic scenarios perpetuate gender stereotypes that subordinate women to a role as an object of transient sexual gratification. Additionally, Internet-based interactions with strangers can lead to transmitting sexually explicit material, and further to face-to-face contact. Nearly 30% of teens contacted online by a complete stranger respond to find out more about that person (Lenhart & Madden, 2007). Many online American teens use social networking sites to make friends, and most of these users post photos to their personal profiles, such as on MySpace and Facebook. Alarmingly, teens publicize actual personal information in their profiles, which subjects them to becoming the target of online sexual predators.

Cyberspace allows children to escape real-world norms and expectations and to engage in a variety of interactive activities away from adult supervision; however, it is also more a site of technocapitalism than of entertainment. Given the fact that most online media sites are sponsored by Corporate America as promotional tools to sell its commercial products (Scherer, 2007), to participate in them users must first sign up for a free membership and create a profile disclosing their personal information. Corporate-sponsored websites not only engage young consumers in interactive games/activities, but more importantly transform their cyberexperiences into an essential part of their everyday identities (Scherer, 2007). Corporate America shapes, controls, and manipulates patterns of consumption through innovative multimedia programs and less-known but widespread unethical data mining practices to gather personal information on consumer habits, preferences, and online activities.

Access to the electronic popular media may be the dominant way in which American children learn about themselves and others and internalize social norms, values, and beliefs conveyed in the media. As the teacher of the new millennium, corporate America has replaced traditional learning institutions such as family, church, and school with engaging TV shows, movies, multimedia websites, video games, and advertisements in educating/miseducating children (Croteau & Hoynes, 1997). Through cultural pedagogy, corporate America imposes its products and ideologies on all aspects of children's everyday lives (Steinberg & Kincheloe, 1997). According to Steinberg and Kincheloe (1997), cultural pedagogy refers to the notion that learning takes place through a variety of pedagogical venues such as schooling, TV shows, movies, websites, magazines, video games, and advertisements. Instead of giving dreary classroom lectures and seatwork, cultural pedagogy emphasizes innovative, sensory-stimulating learning adventures such as fantasy kingdoms, animated toy stories, multimedia games, and interactive real-time social networking (Gaimster, 2008; Liao, 2008; Parks, 2008).

The images and messages in the cybermediascape resonate with the society in which we live and should be used accordingly as pedagogical sites for cultivating critical literacy and human agency. Cybermedia artifacts can serve as sites of critical inquiry where educational participants collectively investigate the sites' cultural and political meanings, struggle with dominant discourses, and create alternative artistic expressions to make sense of and better their everyday visual surroundings. Unfortunately, most techno-societies uphold protectionist attitudes toward children's cybermedia consumption and restrict their access to controversial online material.

CHILDHOOD PROTECTIONISM AND MEDIA CENSORSHIP

The controversy over harmful images in cyberspace has triggered calls for greater parental control, censorship, and surveillance. Children are often the target over concerns about media censorship. In 1998, the National Research Council recommended several protectionist initiatives, including new public policies, media campaigns, adult supervision, and Internet safety education to eliminate children's exposure to inappropriate cybermaterials (Thornburgh & Lin, 2002). Overwhelmingly, most if not all technologically rich societies uphold protectionist approaches and attitudes toward children's media consumption, which raises many serious questions about its effectiveness in educating the media-savvy e-generation.

Childhood protectionists assume the myth of "childhood innocence" and deploy media censorship to preserve the child's purity. This myth presumes children to be merely passive receptacles, easily seduced by media artifacts and in need of adult protection. The innocent child is an imagined child existing outside the real-world conflicts of race, class, gender, and sexuality (Rose, 1984). Such myths "empty children of any thoughts of their own, stripping them of their own political agency and social agendas" (Jenkins, 1997, p. 31). The myth of childhood innocence robs children of their ability to think analytically on their own, and of their ability to process media materials themselves (Jenkins, 1997). Expressions of media censorship project children as powerless victims incapable of shaping their own fate and speaking in their own defense. Childhood is not simply a biological stage; rather, it is a social construction shaped by interwoven cultural, political, and economic dynamics.

Modern children define their cultures in opposition to adult supervision, values, and taste hierarchies (Jenkins, 1997). Oftentimes, children are excluded from participating in mainstream media. Cyberspace is a location of agency where children can empower themselves to construct their identities, create and disseminate their cultural artifacts, and engage in public discourse and social activism (Best & Kellner, 2003). As educators, we cannot engage children in critical thought or equip them with a critical faculty if we police them from accessing real-world material. Protectionist approaches that impose adult moral authority on children are questionable because children do not see themselves as victims of media programs featuring extreme sex, violence, or other controversial ideologies (Buckingham, 2000; Chung, 2007a). Implementing censorship devices threatens the very existence of the Internet as a means of creative expression, education, and political discourse, and is bound to silence youth from democratic participation in society. To survive the postmodern adventure and the rapidly changing cybersociety, children need critical media and technoliteracy to become informed consumers of cyberaesthetics. Cybermedia literacy allows children to function in cybersociety, counter corporate domination of cultural consumption, and engage in technopolitics[1] for cultural emancipation and democratization (see Kellner, 2000).

ART EDUCATION FOR CYBERMEDIA LITERACY

Cyberspace creates a condition of hyperreality or simulations of reality that provide children with heightened aesthetic gratifications, a situation forcing educators to redefine the notion of literacy. Because visual images and messages are omnipresent in an increasingly media-saturated environment, art educators (Chung, 2005; Duncum, 2001) have strongly advocated a visual culture approach to art education that fosters media literacy. Art education can help students develop critical literacy to function in cybersociety and participate in social transformation by approaching cybermedia as a pedagogical site. Art education can also foster cyberliteracy by introducing students to the work of contemporary artists that addresses various issues of cyberculture. For example, inspired by a popular virtual game called World of Warcraft (WOW), Berlin-based artist Aram Bartholl transforms the cyberspace WOW environment into the physical world in his series of street performances. In the online WOW environment, each player is able to create a virtual character (an avatar) with a chosen outfit, race, and capabilities. Bartholl's series appropriates game scenes and characters from WOW and transforms them into a series of street performances that features common people (volunteers) doing their routine activities on the street. As each performer goes on with his/her activities walking around in the street, another person follows right behind the performer, holding a signage of the performer's name so that it looks as if floating above his/her head. Bartholl's work questions how the digital data literally embody themselves in our physical world and illuminates how cyberspace has played a central role in our everyday interactions.

A critical approach to fostering cybermedia literacy in art education first validates and utilizes children's real-world knowledge and experiences as media users by further empowering them to examine media artifacts and critically reflect upon their everyday cultural consumption and cyberaesthetic experiences. It then positions children as active agents within the cybermedia arena in deconstructing and making sense of the pleasures and troubles of visual spectacles in cyberspace and analyzing how these visual spectacles are created, shaped, and embedded with specific values and points of view. It guides children to analyze their cybermedia experiences and consider how they themselves are a part of the forces contributing to the cybermedia enterprise.

To reach this end, an unpoliced media terrain is necessary for children to learn to think for themselves, develop autonomy from their caretakers, and participate in political discourse/activism via cyberspace (Jenkins, 1997). Art education for cybermedia literacy teaches children to appreciate the aesthetic qualities of cybermedia, critically negotiate meanings and analyze cybermedia culture as a site of ideological struggle, engage with problems of visual representation and misrepresentation, and use digital technologies as instruments for creative expression and social activism (Kellner & Share, 2005). For instance, students can deconstruct a cyberadvertisement in terms of its formal design and implicit and explicit meanings, and explore the surrounding issues of manipulation, consumerism, and product desirability (Chung, 2005). They can also analyze how an informational Web search leads to commercial ads and the relationship between those ads and Web content. Studio production is an important avenue for students to understand media culture, experiencing it from the process of analyzing and deconstructing media to formulating ideas and techniques associated with media production. The process translates what they have learned into an artistic expression that deepens their understanding of the construction of cybermedia.

Critical cybermedia education should move students beyond media examination and self-analysis to exploring conditions of social injustice manifested or perpetuated in cybermedia, such as sexism in hip-hop music videos, media violence, and gay stereotyping (Chung, 2007a, 2007b, 2007c). It should encourage students to react to and talk back to mainstream politics "in the process of deconstructing injustices, expressing their own voices, and struggling to create a better society" (Kellner & Share, 2005, p. 382). Cybernetworking is a powerful tool for youth to participate in cultural production and develop a collective agency for social activism. Online social networking sites (e.g., MySpace and Facebook) offer a globally networked environment in which users have the opportunity to create their own artistic creations for cross-cultural exchange and political discourse. For example, Art Action Union (artactionunion.org), a Facebook group of artists, is working together to raise awareness of various issues of social justice by utilizing their creative skills to educate the larger Internet audience. Students can use their technology skills and media knowledge to participate in cultural jamming/reconstruction by creating and disseminating their alternative cyber-media artifacts, such as Web videos, to address issues of social injustice for the collective well-being of humanity.

CONCLUSION

American children are living in an age of computer technologies where digital devices are indispensable for their everyday functioning. A personal cell phone is now all one needs to gain access to the media jungle of the World Wide Web. For the digital generation, cyberspace is their primary playground where they consume products, acquire knowledge and aesthetic experiences, communicate with one another, and entertain themselves. It is crucial that children understand that the image-saturated cyberarena not only markets products, ideas, values, and world-views, but also influences their constructions of reality. Additionally, the expansion of the cybermediascape is largely dependent on sponsorship by commercial advertising and innovative, even questionable, corporate-sponsored programs that sustain users' interest and curiosity. The blooming of the cybermedia enterprise highlights the importance of fostering a critical faculty in children to process and utilize the vast amount of media artifacts in cyberspace. Steinberg and Kincheloe (1997) warn that American teachers who reject the necessity of a media literacy curriculum are the ones that have to cope with the effects of the popular media.

Conventional approaches to media education are questionable because they prevent children from developing/using their critical faculties to analyze real-world materials. Children need a critical faculty and cybermedia literacy to deconstruct the hyperreality constructed and manipulated by corporate America. A critical approach to fostering cybermedia literacy in art education validates children as media users by further empowering them to critically reflect upon their everyday cyberaesthetic experiences and cultural consumption. It teaches children to critically negotiate media artifacts as products of ideological struggle and to use media technologies as instruments for creative expression and social activism (Kellner & Share, 2005). The importance of such pedagogy lies in its goals of preparing children to function in a predominantly "mediated" cybersociety filled with manufactured media constructs, and equipping them with the fundamental skills and knowledge needed to understand, resist, problematize, and reconstruct the corporate construction of cyberculture for the well-being of society and its citizenry.

REFERENCES

Allen, V., & Greenberger, D. (1978). An aesthetic theory of vandalism. *Crime and Delinquency, 24*(3), 309-21.

Best, S., & Kellner, D. (2003). Contemporary youth and the postmodern adventure. *The Review of Education/Pedagogy/Cultural Studies, 25*(2), 75-93.

Buckingham, D. (2000). *After the death of childhood: Growing up in the age of electronic media.* Leicester, UK: Leicester University Press.

Chung, S. K. (2005). Media/visual literacy art education: Cigarette ad deconstruction. *Art Education, 58*(3), 19-24.

Chung, S. K. (2007a). An exploration of media violence in a junior high art classroom. *International Journal of Education Through Art, 3*(1), 57-68.

Chung, S. K. (2007b). Media literacy art education: Deconstructing lesbian and gay stereotypes in the media. *The International Journal of Art & Design Education, 26*(1), 98-107.

Chung, S. K. (2007c). Media/visual literacy art education: Sexism in hip-hop music videos. *Art Education, 60*(3), 33-38.

Croteau, D., & Hoynes, W. (1997). *Media/society: Industries, images, and audiences.* Thousand Oaks, CA: Pine Forge Press.

Duncum, P. (2001). Visual culture: Developments, definitions, and directions for art education. *Studies in Art Education, 42*(2), 101-102.

Duncum, P. (2002). Children never were what they were: Perspectives on childhood. In Y. Gaudelius & P. Speirs (Eds.), *Contemporary issues in art education* (pp. 97-107). Upper Saddle River, NJ: Prentice Hall.

Duncum, P. (2007). Nine reasons for the continuing use of an aesthetic discourse in art education. *Art Education, 60*(2), 46-51.

Gaimster, J. (2008). Reflections on interactions in virtual worlds and their implication for learning art and design. *Art Design and Communication in Higher Education, 6*(3), 187-199.

Giroux, H. (1999). *The mouse that roared: Disney and the end of innocence.* Lanham, MD: Rowman and Littlefield.

Gurak, L. (2001). *Cyberliteracy: Navigating the Internet with awareness.* New Haven, CT: Yale University Press.

Jenkins, H. (1997). Empowering children in the digital age: Towards a radical media pedagogy. *Radical Teacher, 50*, 30-35.

Kellner, D. (2000). Globalization and new social movements: Lessons for critical theory and pedagogy. In N. Burbules & C. Torres (Eds.), *Globalization and education: Critical perspectives* (pp. 299-321). New York & London: Routledge.

Kellner, D., & Share, J. (2005). Toward critical media literacy: Core concepts, debates, organizations, and policy. *Discourse: Studies in the Cultural Politics of Education, 26*(3), 369-386.

Lenhart, A., & Madden, M. (2007). Teens, privacy & online social networks. Retrieved from Pew Internet & American Life Project: www.pewinternet.org/pdfs/PIP_Teens_Privacy_SNS_Report_Final.pdf

Liao, C. L. (2008). Avatars, Second Life, and new media art: The challenge for contemporary art education. *Art Education, 61*(2), 87-91.

McLaren, P., & Morris, J. (1997). Mighty Morphin Power Rangers: The aesthetics of phallo-militaristic justice. In S. R. Steinberg & J. L. Kincheloe (Eds.), *Kinderculture: The corporate construction of childhood* (pp. 115-127). Boulder, CO: Westview Press.

Parks, N. S. (2008). Video games as reconstructionist sites of learning in art education. *Studies in Art Education*, 49(3), 235-250.

Roberts, D., Foehr, U., & Rideout, V. (2005). Generation M: Media in the lives of 8-18 year-olds (Report No.7251). Retrieved from The Henry J. Kaiser Family Foundation: www.kff.org/entmedia/upload/Generation-M-Media-in-the-Lives-of-8-18-Year-olds-Report.pdf

Rose, J. (1984). *The case of Peter Pan: The impossibility of children's fiction.* London: Macmillan.

Scherer, J. (2007). Globalization, promotional culture and the production/consumption of online games: Engaging Adidas's 'Beat Rugby' campaign. *New Media & Society*, 9(3), 475-496.

Steinberg, S. R., & Kincheloe, J. L. (1997). Introduction: No more secrets—kinderculture, information saturation, and the postmodern childhood. In S. R. Steinberg & J. L. Kincheloe (Eds.), *Kinderculture: The corporate construction of childhood* (pp. 1-30). Boulder, CO: Westview Press.

Tavin, K. (2007). Eyes wide shut: The use and uselessness of the discourse of aesthetics in art education. *Art Education, 60*(2), 40-45.

The Henry J. Kaiser Family Foundation. (2001). Generation RX.com: Teens and young adults surfing the Web for health info. Retrieved from www.kaisernetwork.org/health_cast/uploaded_files/kff121101.pdf

Thornburgh, D., & Lin, H. (Eds.) (2002). *Youth, pornography, and the internet.* Washington, DC: National Academies Press.

Ybarra, M., & Mitchell, K. (2005). Exposure to internet pornography among children and adolescents: A national survey. *Cyberpsychology & Behavior, 8*(5), 473-486.

ENDNOTE

1 For example, involving students in using media technologies to illuminate issues of violence in video games or to explore how Internet pornography exploits human bodies and sexuality. Their work can be then disseminated to cybersociety to activate social changes.

Developing ChinaVine.org: Educating Inside and Outside the Site /

KRISTIN G. CONGDON AND DOUG BLANDY

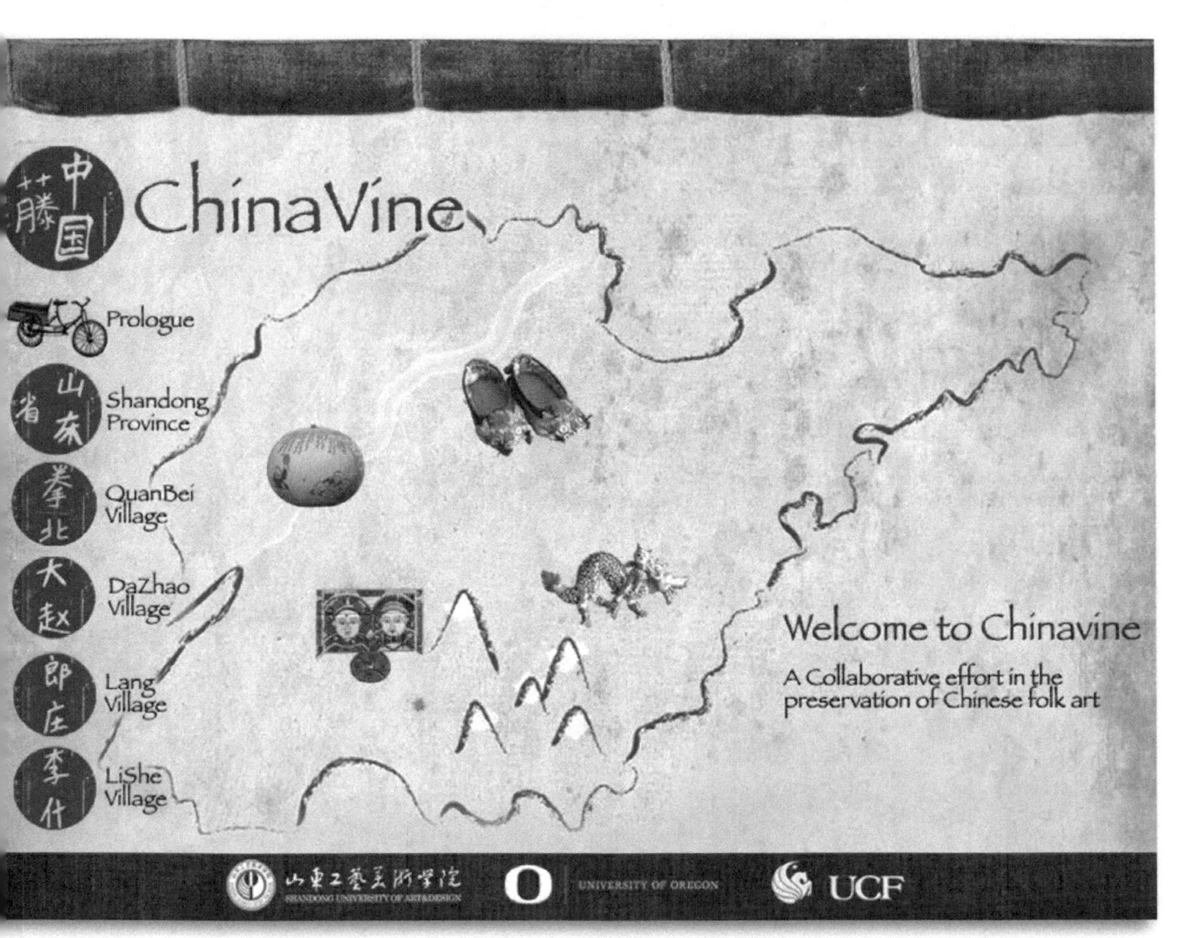

Screenshot of ChinaVine.org

Begun in May 2007, ChinaVine.org is an ongoing interactive website project that aims to educate English-speaking audiences about Chinese folk art and culture. ChinaVine.org is a partnership project that includes faculty and students at the University of Central Florida (UCF); the University of Oregon (UO); Shandong University of Art and Design in Jinan, China (SUAD); and, most recently, Beijing Normal University (BNU) and the Beijing Folk Literature and Art Association (BFLAA). ChinaVine.org includes animation, video, photographs, and written text. An interdisciplinary team of faculty and students at each of the original three universities (UCF, UO, and SUAD) has been working on various parts of the website since Spring 2007. The teams associated with ChinaVine.org share all documentary material and communicate through listservs and individual e-mail accounts. Partnership goals with BNU and BFLAA are currently being developed. As of this writing both have already hosted UCF and UO faculty and students and participated in fieldwork and documentary work with folk artists living in Beijing.

Our involvement with ChinaVine.org is motivated by our long-term commitment to working with communities for an art education purpose. The precedent for moving some of this work to an online environment was Congdon's (2006) association with the Cultural Heritage Alliance at UCF, where over a period of 4 years, a website on Florida folk artists that has been used all over the country as an educational site (www.folkvine.org) was conceptualized and implemented. Also motivating this project was Blandy's introduction to the Folk Art Research Institute at SUAD during a 2005 visit to that institution. SUAD President Pan oriented Blandy to Chinese policy for documenting and preserving the country's Intangible Cultural Heritage (ICH) and the ways in which folk arts are considered within this policy. Motivating us also is recognizing that news and information coming out of most countries is generally from a single standpoint (Gans, 2003). During our travels in China, our experiences with the Chinese people are often very different from what most people in the United States read, hear, and see through mainstream media. We are also aware that there is a keen interest in China from people in the US as a result of its rising economic standing and the 2008 Beijing Summer Olympics. We aim to diversify the understanding outsiders have about Chinese culture as we simultaneously respond to the public desire for more information about China. Because of our previous work in various communities, we know that these motivations are best addressed by working with others who share our mutual concerns and interests. Throughout the process we have had to ask fundamental questions about our responsibility to the mission of the project and all of the partners associated with ChinaVine.org. These are the questions anyone working in a community-based art project needs to address (Stimpson, 1994).

ChinaVine.org poses many complex issues and challenges, many of which have been addressed in research on technology and cross-cultural practices in education. For example, we have labored over translation problems, compatibility issues with technology, and ADA guidelines that mandate that websites be assessable to people with disabilities. This chapter will focus on the two main goals of the ChinaVine.org project: (1) Inside meaning-making: To produce a website that educates English-speaking audiences about Chinese folk art and culture; and (2) Outside meaning-making: To construct collaborate teams at UCF, UO, and SUAD. Issues, challenges, and lessons learned regarding each of these goals is discussed.

ChinaVine team member Erika Rydell in Shadong province market. (Photo by Tomas Valladares)

FOUNDATIONAL RESEARCH

Research for ChinaVine.org has been interdisciplinary and broadly oriented. As research is often done in the humanities, it has been collaborative, as opposed to individualistic (Davidson & Goldberg, 2004). No one person could possibly know Chinese history, Chinese folk art, Chinese languages, linguistics, ethnographic skills, Web design, ADA guidelines, organizational and administrative theory regarding cross-cultural work, and new ideas about the educational processes related to the Web.

As educators, we know that English-speaking societies, as well as many other cultures around the world, are increasingly being saturated with visual images. This ubiquity is due in part to the placement of advertising in increasingly new places from tee-shirts and cars to billboards and the Internet. There is also an increase in DIY (Do-It-Yourself) culture, which makes it easy for more people to create and self-publish videos and zines. Freedman (2000) notes that because of this fact, art educators are in an excellent position to teach about the complexities of learning that takes place through visual images. Knowing that our knowledge increasingly comes from visual rather than text-based information, ChinaVine.org is heavily dependent on visual images. We also recognize the value of folklore theory in our work. From this disciplinary approach we focus on the traditional practices of artistic expression in culture and we acknowledge that "our challenge is to understand how context imbues expression with meaning" (Feintuch, 1995, p. 393).
For ChinaVine.org, this means that we must understand not only the context of the artists, folklore, and art theory in China, but also the context of the Web. Scholars such as Lisa Nakamura (2007) are increasingly recognizing that depictions of people of color by outside group members are often passive and stereotypical. In

order to avoid this problem, we work closely with our Chinese partners so that they are fully engaged in the kinds of messages that are communicated.

MEANING-MAKING INSIDE THE WEBSITE

Meaning-making inside ChinaVine.org is accomplished through computer programming and the presentation layer or "skin" of the site. The site is programmed in such a way that current and future site managers can easily access and add to the site. Files are placed into categories and subcategories with naming conventions for files and directories that are easily identifiable. Page templates were created so that content can be added or refreshed regularly and easily. Style sheets associated with the color and format of the presentation are used in such a way so that updates will not compromise the overall code for the website. ChinaVine.org's programming is validated through W3C, the World Wide Consortium, permitting the site to be standardized across Web browsers. PHP: Hypertext Preprocessor was used to code the templates and to support the interactivity of the site. Using PHP permits for a dynamic administration of the site by people not knowing how to do advanced programming.

The design of the presentation layer or skin of ChinaVine.org was heavily influenced by several factors. Best practices for interactive websites were considered for a site that is meant for children, youth, and adults with an overall goal of eliminating the need for any guessing on the part of users. Design elements reinforce ease of use and navigation. Primary and secondary navigation cues are consistent throughout the site. Title and other hierarchical elements are also consistent throughout, and hotlinks are obvious. Adobe Flash, standard to most computers, is used to stream the videos. Video controls are available to give visitors more power over the viewing experience. The presentation layer also needed to be consistent and congruent with both the cultural material being presented and the visual conventions and rhetoric of our Chinese partners at SUAD and in Beijing. Since the programming and design of the site was accomplished by personnel at UCF and UO, feedback from SUAD was continuously invited. To some extent the overall look of the site was kept simple so that it could be enhanced in the future as appropriate to the addition of new material.

Important to all of those associated with ChinaVine.org is that the website be accessible to as many visitors as possible. As a consequence accessibility to users with disabilities was assumed from the very beginning. Programming and presentation was combined in a website that is 'Section 508 valid,' meaning that ChinaVine.org is consistent with requirements of the Americans with Disabilities Act and priority level 1 and most of priority level 2 of Web Content Accessibility Guidelines (WCAG) (W3C World Wide Web Consortium, 2009). Plans exist for moving the site to priority level 3, the highest level of accessibility associated with WCAG. This will require the development of text equivalents for image map links, assessment/change of foreground /background colors for text so that it offers sufficient contrast for people with color deficits, and the development of keyboard shortcuts for important links.

MEANING-MAKING OUTSIDE THE WEBSITE

All of those associated with ChinaVine.org understand that the artworks we present on the Web should be analyzed for their functions within the human context, rather than solely for their surface qualities (Anderson, 1995). When dealing with tradition in China, we recognize that it is dynamic, not fixed. As Glassie (1995) says, "tradition is a temporal concept" that is intertwined with the past and the future (p. 399). We have worked to portray the site this way. Adding Beijing artists to the site has helped with this process. Their work and the context in which they are working is different from the material on the website associated with Shandong province. Our Beijing contacts immediately informed us that we could not represent Beijing folk artists in the same way we have done with the Shandong artists. In Shandong it makes sense to ground the work in the village context because the artists are participating in the day-to-day activities of the village. In Beijing, the context is the culture and history of the artistic tradition within an immense urban environment. As a result the Beijing portion of ChinaVine.org is not organized by neighborhood, but by the traditions documented: kite-making, Manchu bow and arrow, and dough figures.

Mud doll artist in Huobali village market. (Photo by Tomas Valladares)

ChinaVine.org is as much about what is experienced on the website as the model we developed for doing work across universities, languages, and cultures. According to Davenport (2000), art educators in Europe and Latin America use the term "intercultural" to describe "educational challenges often equated with multicultural issues in the US, but with more emphasis on communication between cultural groups" (p. 379). Intercultural work recognizes that ethnographic credit needs to go to our Chinese partners and "the indigenous collaborators for whom the term informants is no longer adequate, if it ever was" (Clifford, 1988, p. 51). Our collaborative research model, across universities, cultures, and disciplinary roles, addresses the postmodern idea of networks of authors forming a collective voice, rather than the autonomous author (Plagens, 1997). To date, dozens of faculty and students have worked on the website from numerous disciplines across the universities. According to Ashford, a collaborative project such as ChinaVine.org is never one-dimensional, but is instead one that includes varying ideas of juxtaposition and montage. While ChinaVine documents Chinese artists, it is also a work of art as a website. Collaborative artwork produces a complex aesthetic that is embedded in the work. Felshin claims that collaborative projects are more socially and politically progressive if they involve different kinds of people with different areas of expertise (Ashford, Ewald, Felshin, & Phillips, 2006) as is the case with ChinaVine.org.

Our collaborative research model also includes those who visit ChinaVine.org and interact with its contents. To maximize the usefulness of ChinaVine.org for educational purposes it is licensed with Creative Commons (CC). A CC license permits maintaining copyright while allowing other uses of the work. Visitors to ChinaVine.org are free to share, copy, distribute, and display ChinaVine.org under the following conditions: ChinaVine.org must be attributed in the manner specified by UCF, UO, SUAD, and other project partners; ChinaVine.org cannot be used for commercial purposes; ChinaVine.org may not be altered, transformed, or built upon; and use of ChinaVine.org must make clear that it is licensed for use as described above.

While the collaborative process yields myriad rewards such as increased learning, more expertise to draw from, and the ability to tackle huge projects, it also poses numerous challenges. For example, as is true with any project that involves communities of people, we continually have to ask to whom we are ultimately responsible (Stimpson, 1994). Are we responsible to the artists we docu-

ChinaVine team in China, March 2008. (Photo by Ian Hernand)

ment, our Chinese academic partners, our U.S. partners, our English-speaking audience, or our own sets of values, rooted in Western or Chinese academic practices? Questions and issues that have been raised in the course of ChinaVine.org's development have related to how much tradition makes something folk art, how much violence should we portray in the killing of animals within the presentation of folktale, and what are the implications of asking Chinese artists to sign Institutional Review Board Release (IRB) forms, when the process is so out-of-context and incongruent with personal relationships to them? Each question and issue is carefully debated and deliberated. Often the responses to the issues and questions change as each situation changes. Trust and comfort with the fluidity of opinions has been necessary. However, it is in these spaces of deliberation where much of our learning takes place and through which the project is able to move forward.

CONCLUDING THOUGHTS

We recognize that one of the problems with building websites on art is that, as jagodzinski (1998) points out, the line between the actual artworks and the artificial reproduction (seen on the Web) has disappeared. "Consequently," he claims, "there is no need to 'travel' to the art gallery to view the 'genuine' articles" (p. 9). He goes on to claim that there is a "longing to bring art back into its ritualistic function where it is embodied in community" (p. 16). The artistic practices we experienced when visiting the Chinese artists were far more powerful than anything we can reproduce on the Web. Furthermore, the artistic practices as experienced by the Chinese in-group are far more powerful and meaningful than anything we experienced in a short visit. Therefore, we understand that ChinaVine.org's meaning-making is something different from the artistic expressions we aim to document and educate about. jagodzinski builds on the work of Benjamin (1969), recognizing that that reproductions cause the original artwork to lose its aura, which is what gives art its uniqueness. Once an artwork loses its aura, it no longer has ritual value. It is reduced to a commodity. We have worked to keep this reductive view of Chinese folk art from happening by creating a website that maximizes process and that is full of contextual information as primarily conveyed in video.

Baudrillard's (1994) ideas about the real and the copy could encourage a view of ChinaVine.org not as a copy referring to the work of the Chinese artists, but as something that displaces them and the contexts in which they work and renders obsolete the idea of the real. We recognize this danger and we continue to work with our Chinese partners to find ways not to have the focus on us as Web designers, but on the Chinese artists, as artists who create ritualistic processes with their artwork and make significant contributions to forming the communities of which they are a part. We also recognize that our presence is important and our opinions about our experiences matter. Consequently, balancing the many objectives of ChinaVine.org is both complicated and compelling as a research project. On the other hand, we also acknowledge Baudrillard's notion that the destruction of the original work can be seen as a political gesture that can hold great power. By working together, we may have destroyed, or at least changed, the original meaning of the cultural traditions and what is portrayed by placing information in another context and art form, but we have also created a collective of people who have formed friendships and have worked hard to understand each other's culture. The collective aesthetic evident on the website communicates this new meaning.

Building ChinaVine.org has not been easy. We have had problems with finding and using the right software and identifying a good approach to the design. We have struggled to keep all team members involved in decision-making opportunities. We sometimes have trouble communicating across languages and, at times, we labor over the right choice of words or images to convey a message. But the struggles are minor in relationship to the rewards. We have all learned a tremendous amount about websites, Chinese culture, communication patterns, folk art, and collaborative projects. And so the project continues.

REFERENCES

Anderson, T. (1995). Toward a cross-cultural approach to art criticism. *Studies in Art Education, 36*(4), 198-209.

Ashford, D., Ewald, W., Felshin, N., & Phillips, P. C. (2006). A conversation on social collaboration. *Art Journal, 65*(2), 58-82.

Baudrillard, J. (1994). *Simulacra and simulation* (S. F. Glaser, Trans.). Ann Arbor: University of Michigan Press.

Benjamin, W. (1969). *Illuminations.* New York: Schocken Books.

Clifford, J. (1988). *The predicament of culture: Twentieth-century ethnography, literature, and art.* Cambridge, MA: Harvard University Press.

Congdon, K. G. (2006). Folkvine.org: Arts-based research on the web. *Studies in Art Education, 48*(1), 36-51.

Davenport, M. (2000). Culture and education: Polishing the lenses. *Studies in Art Education, 41*(4), 361-375.

Davidson, C. N., & Goldberg, D. T. (2004, February 13). A manifesto for the humanities in a technological age. *The Chronicle of Higher Education*, pp. B7-B9.

Feintuch, B. (1995). Introduction: Words in common. *Journal of American Folklore, 108*(430), 391-394.

Freedman, K. (2000). Social perspectives on art education in the U.S.: Teaching visual culture in a democracy. *Studies in Art Education, 41*(4), 314-327.

Gans, H. J. (2003, April 11). Toward a new journalism. *The Chronicle of Higher Education*, pp. B16-B17.

Glassie, H. (1995). Tradition. *Journal of American Folklore, 108*(430), 395-412.

jagodzinski, j. (1998). Editor's introduction: Deconstructing the master signifier of community. *Journal of Social Theory in Art Education, 18*, 4-20.

Nakamura, L. (2007). *Digitizing race: Visual cultures of the internet.* Minneapolis: University of Minnesota Press.

Plagens, P. (1997, June 6). In a 'bureaucratic mode': The Lilliputian universe of postmodern art. *The Chronicle of Higher Education*, pp. B6-B7.

Stimpson, C. (1994). Introduction. In J. Kramer, *Whose art is it?* (pp. 1-35). Durham, NC: Duke University Press.

W3C World Wide Web consortium. (2009). Web content accessibility guidelines (WAG) 2.0. Retrieved January 9, 2009 from http://www.w3.org/TR/2008/REC-WCAG20-20081211/

New Media Arts Education: How Community-Based Programs Can Reshape Teaching and Learning in the Age of Web 2.0 / DAVID DARTS, JUAN CARLOS CASTRO, ANITA SINNER, AND KIT GRAUER

ACKNOWLEDGMENT: WE GRATEFULLY ACKNOWLEDGE FINANCIAL SUPPORT OF THIS RESEARCH THROUGH THE SOCIAL SCIENCES AND HUMANITIES GRANT (KIT GRAUER, PRINCIPAL INVESTIGATOR; SANDRA WEBER; DAVID DARTS; AND ANITA SINNER).

We live in a digital culture. New media and digital technology are increasingly embedded within the routines and textures of everyday life and the daily flow of mediated ideas, images and representations contribute to our changing and evolving perceptions of ourselves and the world around us (Hayles, 2000). These cultural materials have come to provide many of the symbolic resources we use to interpret our relationships and construct and represent our identities (Darts, 2007). The widespread introduction and adoption of new media technologies—including computers, mobile phones, and global communications networks—has transformed what it means to speak, to create, to think, and to have agency (Goldfarb, 2002). Combined with recent convergences between digital information, communication, and entertainment technologies and platforms, the relationships between young people, education, and new media continue to evolve and complexify. Digital communication networks and technologies are significantly lowering the barriers to cultural participation and co-creation. As a result, contemporary teens are spending almost as much time online as watching television and their activity is described as highly creative and participatory in social network environments (de Boor & Halpern, 2007).

How students and teachers experience the convergence of entertainment, computing and telecommunications, and the impact new media has on the communities in which students and teachers live, reveals new patterns of communication are underway through traditional forms of media and new media. These new patterns of interactions between artifacts, images and productions are not only converging, they are also forming new media ecologies (Fuller, 2005;

Jenkins, 2006). These new media ecologies are dynamic, evolving, and interdependent synergies of technologies and cultural practices. They are characterized by communities of practice brought together by common interests and participatory communication technologies and can be understood as a phenomenon of Web 2.0. Coined as a marketing phrase by Tim O'Reily (2005), Web 2.0 marks an important shift in Internet patterns and activities by emphasizing the Web as a place for collaboration, sharing, and interaction—rather than solely as a platform for presenting information.

According to a recent survey, over 70% of Canadian teens between 13-17 years of age regularly use social networking sites like Facebook or MySpace (TNS, 2007). Of those teens using the Internet, over half are creating and distributing new media content (Lenhart & Madden, 2005). Much of this engagement can be characterized as engaging in a participatory culture—one that is described as having low barriers to artistic expression, civic engagement, and collaborative learning (Jenkins, Clinton, Purushotma, Robison, & Weigel, 2007). At the same time, however, a majority of teens report that there is a significant disconnect between new technology and school (Levin & Arafeh, 2002).

THE ROLE OF COMMUNITY-BASED MEDIA ARTS CENTERS

Coinciding with the rise of digital media as a central and ubiquitous component of everyday life, there has been a growing acknowledgement that schools are not the only preserve of education (Buckingham, 2003). The varied media ecologies in which young people participate, for instance, have been regarded as both compelling modes of entertainment and powerful means of education. Such forms of cultural pedagogy have intensified in recent years with the global expansion and convergence of digital media, a burgeoning visual culture, and the corresponding confluence of the political and cultural spheres (Darts, 2007). Community new media arts education programs have been one response to this phenomenon by offering young people the critical and technical skills required to interpret, understand, and participate in an increasingly mediated and complex world (Prensky, 2001; Murray, 2006).

Existing largely outside of formal school settings, these community-based initiatives approach media education from creative, artistic/aesthetic skill sets and are grounded in curricula that foster self-expression, creativity, critical analysis, and the development of identity and voice. As alternate learning environments, they offer important pedagogical dimensions to evolving contemporary media ecologies. Whereas teens are regularly participating in and through virtual Web 2.0 environments, it is also apparent that embodied participation, gathering together in "real time," to engage in new media production, can also be an important aspect of the expanding new media ecologies. Community-based new media centers provide spaces for meaningful face-to-face encounters to happen.

Occurring after school, within the parameters of nonprofit organizations or museum settings, or as part of artist-in-residency and artists-in-schools programs, these community-based new media programs have become increasingly common (Goldfarb, 2002; Goodman, 2003; Tyner, 1998). A number of recent studies suggest that engaging young people as active participants in their community through participatory arts projects, community cultural development programs, artist-community collaborations, and community-based arts projects is key to youth development and learning (Darts, 2006). Policymakers, practitioners, and community members often see such programs as an effective way to accomplish a variety of objectives, including meeting children's needs for safe environments and supervision from caring adults while their parents are working; boosting academic achievement; supporting overall youth development; and encouraging youth engagement in community development (Goodman, 2003). McLaughlin and Heath (1993) have drawn attention to the role of community-based organizations in building self-esteem among disenfranchised groups of young people.

These community-based programs can be seen to occupy a 'third arena,' between school and family where young people can learn and develop (Kangisser, 1999). Working inside this alternative space offers pedagogical opportunities not immediately present within school-based settings. Richards (1998), for instance, has pointed to the more flexible and democratic styles of teaching and learning that often apply to the context of community-based settings. The artists and educators who facilitate these projects can thus take advantage of their relatively autonomous position at the intersection of larger institutions to facilitate expression of personal and political issues (Goldfarb, 2002). Many community arts-based programs report their overall aim as transmitting particular arts-related skills while helping to develop critical thinking and establishing a clear link between the two capabilities (Felshin, 1995; Holloway & Krensky, 2001; Lowe, 2001; Mancillas, 1998; Trend, 1997).

AN EXPOSÉ OF TWO NEW MEDIA EDUCATION SITES

The issues shaping new media education and the potential impact of participating in community-based new media arts programs on learners and the communities in which they live brought our research team to investigate teaching and learning at two community-based new media arts centers: The Gulf Island Film School, Galiano Island, British Columbia; and Eyebeam Atelier, New York, New York. Through these sites, we are examining how community-based media arts educational spaces can support knowledge creation and cultural production for a new generation of learners. In the following passages, we provide a brief snapshot of these two media arts centers as a point of entry for arts educators considering how new media might be integrated into their curricula and pedagogical practices.

Exploring community-based new media arts teachers' beliefs and practices in alternate learning environments can help to bring transparency to the cultural and spatial interfaces employed by teachers and students as they conceptualize, implement, and assess learning, teaching, and creating with new media (Manovich, 2001).Community arts centers deliver learning opportunities to a wide range of learners, engendering a discussion that situates new media arts and learning within the complement of research now exploring alternate learning environments as well as arts and learning studies generally. The impact of new media on the learners who participate in, and communities who possess community-based new media arts education programs represents an emergent area of research. Our goal is to understand the diverse ways arts and learning can emerge and shift our conceptions of contemporary arts educational curriculum and pedagogy.

The methodological underpinnings of this research is constructivist and interpretive in nature. We apply qualitative case study methods (observations, field notes, document analysis, open-ended and semi-structured interviews) to describe and interpret each new media arts center. However, one important feature for our methodology is that we use image-based methods as prompts in our analytical process to make meaningful links between different research experiences and materials such as photography, video, field notes, and other objects (Grauer, Irwin, de Cosson, & Wilson, 2001; Prosser, 1998). Part of the rigor of image-based methods is an emphasis on rethinking traditional notions of learning and teaching through new media production of videos, narratives, and art installations.

GULF ISLAND FILM AND TELEVISION SCHOOL: HTTP://WWW.GIFTSFILMS.COM

> It's hard to work as a group, learning to make a film is learning a range of skills all at the same time—if there is frustration in one area of a group, it's good to find out where this is coming from... most frustration comes from poor communication. These are really communication devices which help people get together to help find out what one another is saying to each other and also being able to say something effectively to the people you're working with, building a sense of community to move forward and to help tell the story, and then the sense of accomplishment as an individual and as a group is very exciting to experience and to witness. (Warren, Student mentor, Personal Communication, Spring 2008)

In a simple wood cottage nestled in the middle of Galiano Island, a class of teens is gathered around a newsprint note board listening to Warren as he draws out a simple overhead diagram of camera locations. It is day three of the Gulf Island Film School's "Teen Media Intensive Week" and participants are expected to have scripts finished by the end of the day. Over the next 6½ days, the participants, working in teams of three to four teens, will brainstorm their idea, write scripts, develop shot diagrams, perform, shoot, sound mix, and edit an entire film. From establishing wide-angle shots to maintaining the illusion of dialog through lines of axis, Warren patiently walks his class through the initial process of

Student mentor at Gulf Island Film and Television School.

establishing a coherent and emotionally powerful film. He discusses the value of good storyboards and planning, eventually emphasizing that planning is ultimately about communication. Participants are learning the technical skills to make a film and, as illustrated in Warren's final comments before setting the group off to plan their shot lists, they are learning how to work together.

Gulf Island Film and Television School (GIFTS), located on Galiano Island on Canada's west coast, is an independent new media training organization that facilitates student goals as artists through self-directed learning within intensive "film boot camp" programs. With nominal fees and no prerequisites, learners are invited to a range of course offerings from novice to expert. Programs are organized by age (12-14, 14-18, and adults) and by genre, including documentary, drama, and animation. As a residency-based model consisting of day-long workshops to month-long programs, GIFTS provides learners with the opportunity to be mentored by award-winning media professionals who help students develop concepts and videos to add to their portfolios. GIFTS' pedagogical approach invokes action-learning strategies based on tactile and oral instruction. Through hands-on collaborative work, learners are guided through all aspects of digital film production with a special emphasis placed on quality storytelling, communication, and teamwork. The instructors and administrators at GIFTS are on the leading edge of shifts in new media production, utilizing high-end desktop video editing and digital recording equipment. They also integrate social media, like YouTube, to create and extend learning spaces where past, present, and potential participants can collaborate and interact.

A central focus of the GIFTS program is the creation of independent media artists who can manipulate digital media technologies, troubleshoot on a tight schedule, and successfully negotiate the dynamics of team production. The program is thus designed to provide an open and democratic learning space where participants are offered skills and experiences to give voice to their ideas and collaborate. Emphasis is placed on creating a synergistic environment where participants work intensely together weaving story, design, and technique. The open and participatory qualities of the GIFTS curriculum resembles and utilizes emerging social media spaces by emphasizing peer-collaboration and digital dissemination of creative works.

EYEBEAM ATELIER: HTTP://EYEBEAM.ORG/

Eyebeam Atelier is a not-for-profit arts and technology center based in New York City. It provides young artists with a collaborative workspace and state-of-the-art tools for digital research and experimentation. It is a lively center of creativity and thought that encourages shared knowledge and the free exchange of ideas—a place where artists and technologists actively engage with culture, addressing the issues and concerns of our time.

The Education Studio at Eyebeam generates new and unique learning opportunities for students, artists, educators, and the general public, in addition to researching and developing new models for education within the field of art and technology. The programming includes an After-School Atelier that provides NYC public high school and middle school students the opportunity to work in a studio environment and to develop new media art projects under the guidance of Eyebeam's Teaching Artists. The program aims to help students better analyze and deconstruct media messages using imaging techniques, introducing them to guest-lecturing new media professionals, and engaging them with art and design issues. Students are offered opportunities to work on projects cooperatively with the Artists-in Residence, professional mentors, ASA staff, and their peers.

Eyebeam's Girls-Eye View (GEV) program focuses specifically on NYC middle school girls. It offers young female artists opportunities to work on art and technology projects cooperatively alongside the Artists-in-Residence and professional mentors and teachers. Students regularly work on innovative projects using digital video or sound, robotics, circuitry, and/or Web programming. Digital Day Camp (DDC), meanwhile, is an annual digital arts summer program that teaches students about new art and technology tools via an arts-based curriculum framed around a relevant social topic. Eyebeam also hosts a series of Interactive Workshops and Discussion Groups where artists and educators from institutions around New York City develop new models for education within the realm of art and technology.

NEW MEDIA AND CONTEMPORARY ART EDUCATION

Programs like the Gulf Island Film School and Eyebeam Atelier offer important insights as to how new media art might be successfully integrated into contemporary art educational practice. By examining such programs, we can begin to understand how these alternative educational spaces support and help redefine knowledge creation for a new generation of learners. Our preliminary research indicates these non-school based learning sites can serve as powerful locations of transformation and learning that effectively meet the challenges of interpreting, understanding, and participating in an increasingly mediated and complex world. The need for such transformational spaces will only continue to increase as new media ecologies become more central to the social, cultural, political, and economic dimensions of our contemporary lives.

While new media culture is generally understood for young people as a site of entertainment and social interaction, many of their experiences within these spaces can also be described as educational. Jenkins et al. (2007), for instance, characterize much of the participatory collaboration happening online as "informal mentorship" and explain how, through these interactions, knowledge and skills are passed along from the most experienced to novices (p. 3). This reinforces the notion that new media is not simply determined by technology but instead enables new relationships and opportunities for the co-production of culture and meaning. Such phenomena are challenging and upsetting many of the dominant cultural and educational paradigms upon which traditional art education is based. Community-based programs have been one approach to supplementing and supporting the learning occurring via digital technologies and social media.

There is little question that as increasing numbers of young people participate in the creation, distribution, and redistribution of culture and knowledge, art educators will be pressed to find meaningful ways to integrate digital technology and social media into the curriculum. Digital media can be a great entry point for examining our culture and exploring complex issues using references and materials students are already familiar with. This approach can successfully engage students by linking school-based curriculum to issues and materials they already care and know about. Our preliminary research indicates this is part of the formula that makes community-based media arts centers successful.

At the same time, however, it is also important to consider that young people's intimacy with digital culture and new media does not necessarily lead to critical analysis. Whereas acknowledging students' knowledge about and skills within and through digital culture is important, educators must also recognize there are many aspects about the technical, political and artistic dimensions of new media that students don't know. In this regard, young people's familiarity with and understandings of digital culture can be significantly enhanced through the introduction of formal strategies and frameworks of investigation and interpretation that are already common within traditional art educational practice (Darts, 2007). Accordingly, combining students' digital knowledge and experiences with art educators' training in the interpretation, evaluation, and production of images and texts can serve as an important approach to integrating digital media into traditional school-based art education programs. Doing so can engage students in the curriculum through topics and materials they already care about. It can also help educators learn about contemporary youth culture while inspiring students to see their everyday digital experiences as worthy of critical examination.

Another important strategy for engaging young people is through focusing directly on media arts production. This is a key component of both the Gulf Island Film School and Eyebeam Atelier programs. Studio-based approaches can be an important way to facilitate learning, particularly because young people are so enthusiastic about participating. This is not to say that critical thinking and thoughtful engagement with social issues are left out of the process. Instead, as the programs at both media arts centers demonstrate, critical engagement can happen informally throughout the media production process. Such experiential models where students actively design and produce their own media can provide numerous opportunities for media arts educators to unite media analysis with artistic practice. In such cases, learning 'through doing' takes on an added signifance.

Again, this approach meshes well with current school-based art educational settings as they are predominantly studio-based. And whereas historically, the high cost of digital equipment has hindered the integration of new media production into the art education curriculum, the ever-lowering price of digital technologies and the ever-increasing ubiquity of computers and other digital technologies within schools, when linked with curriculum that builds the cultural skills and competencies required to use digital technologies, may be helping to remove those barriers (Buckingham, 2003). Combined with the introduction of a new generation of art educators who are increasingly comfortable manipulating digital technology and new media, the movement towards media arts based approaches to art education is very likely to accelerate.

Based on our preliminary research, it is apparent that community-based programs can serve as models for designing and implementing new media art instruction into school-based programs. This in turn can lead to a better understanding of the role digital new media education in general might play in the development of young people. We are hopeful that translating the pedagogical practices and curricular approaches used in these spaces to school-based settings can directly benefit educators wishing to create intellectually rich connections and critiques through media arts curriculum. Ultimately, learning how to integrate digital technologies and new media ecologies into the curriculum will become increasingly important as teacher educators, curriculum developers, and policy makers attempt to guide educators toward affording students with the literacies and creative skills required to negotiate and actively participate in an increasingly global and mediated culture.

REFERENCES

Berwick, C. (2001, March/April). Voyeurschism. *Artbyte*, 42-51.

Buckingham, D. (2003). *Media education: Literacy, learning and contemporary culture.* Cambridge, UK: Polity Press.

Buhl, M. (2005). Visual culture as a strategic approach to art production in education. *International Journal of Education through Art, 1*(2), 103-114.

Carter, M., & Geczy, A. (2006). *Reframing art.* Oxford, UK: Berg.

Chaptal, A. (1998). New and traditional educational media: How to choose between them—teachers' choices. *Educational Media International, 35*(4), 241-246.

Darts, D. (2006). Art education for a change: Contemporary issues and the visual arts. *Art Education, 59*(5), 6-12.

Darts, D. (2007). Learning through new eyes: Media, visual culture and art education. In R. Irwin, K. Grauer, & M. Emme (Eds.), *ReVisions: Readings in Canadian art education* (pp. 80-89). Toronto, ON: Canadian Society for Education Through Art.

de Boor, T., & Halpern, L. K. (2007). Creating & connecting//Research and guidelines on online social-and educational-networking. Retrieved October 2, 2007, from http://www.nsba.org/SecondaryMenu/TLN/CreatingandConnecting.aspx

De Castell, S., & Jenson, J. (2003). Serious play: Curriculum for a post-talk era. *Journal of the Canadian Association for Curriculum Studies, 1*(1), 47-52.

Everett, A., & Caldwell, J. (2003). *New media: Theories and practices of digitextuality.* New York: Routledge.

Felshin, N. (1995). Introduction. In N. Felshin (Ed.), *But is it art? The spirit of art as activism.* (pp. 9-29). Seattle: Bay Press.

Flack, J. (2004). Phones, games and virtual worlds: New media in the classroom. Australian Screen. *Education Online, 37*, 74-79.

Fox, G.T., & Geichman, J. (2001). Creating research questions from strategies and perspectives of contemporary art. *Curriculum Inquiry, 31*(1), 33-49.

Fuller, M. (2005). *Media ecologies: Materialist energies in art and technoculture.* Cambridge, MA: The MIT Press.

Goldfarb, B. (2002). *Visual pedagogy: Media cultures in and beyond the classroom.* Durham and London: Duke University Press.

Goodman, S. (2003). *Teaching youth media: A critical guide to literacy, video production, and social change.* New York: Teachers College Press.

Grauer, K., Irwin R. L., de Cosson, A., & Wilson, S. (2001). Images for understanding: Snapshots of learning through the arts. *International Journal of Education & the Arts,* http://ijea.asu.edu/v2n9/, 18 pgs.

Hansen, M. (2004). *New philosophy for new media.* Cambridge, MA: The MIT Press.

Hayles, N. K. (2000). Visualizing the posthuman. *Art Journal, 59*(3), 50-54.

Heidegger, M. (1953/1977). The question concerning technology (W. Lovitt, Trans.). In M. Heidegger (Ed.), *The question concerning technology and other essays.* New York: Harper & Row.

Holloway, D.L. & Krensky, B. (2001). Introduction: The arts, urban education, and social change. *Education and Urban Society, 33*(4), 354-365.

Jacucci, G., & Wanger, I. (2005). Exploring relationships between learning, artifacts, physical space and computing. *Digital Creativity, 16*(1), 19-30.

Jenkins, H. (2006). *Convergence culture: Where old and new media collide.* New York: New York University Press.

Jenkins, H., Clinton, K., Purushotma, R., Robison, A. J., & Weigel, M. (2007). Confronting the challenges of participatory culture: Media education for the 21st century. Retrieved July 2, 2007, from http://www.digitallearning.macfound.org/atf/cf/%7B7E45C7E0-A3E0-4B89-AC9C-E807E1B0AE4E%7D/JENKINS_WHITE_PAPER.PDF

Kangisser, D. (1999). *The third arena: After school youth literacy programs.* New York: Robert Browne Foundation.

Keifer-Boyd, K. (2004). CyberArt pedagogies. In C. Crawford et al. (Eds.), *Proceedings of Society for Information Technology and Teacher Education International Conference 2004* (pp. 3830-3842). Chesapeake, VA: AACE.

Kraidy, U. (2002). Digital media and education: Cognitive impact of information visualization. *Journal of Educational Media, 27*(3), 95-107.

Lenhart, A., & Madden, M. (2005). Teen Content Creators and Consumers [Electronic Version]. Retrieved June 28, 2007 from http://www.pewinternet.org/pdfs/PIP_Teens_Content_Creation.pdf

Levin, D., & Arafeh, S. (2002). The digital disconnect: The widening gap between internet-savvy students and their schools [Electronic Version]. Retrieved June 10, 2007, from http://www.pewinternet.org/report_display.asp?r=67.

Lind, L. (1998). Media education—Learning to reshape the world. *Educational Media International, 35*(1), 4-8.

Lowe, S.S. (2001). The art of community transformation. *Education and Urban Society, 33*(4), 457-471.

Mancillas, A. (1998). The citizen artist. In L. F. Burnham and S. Dorland (Eds.), *The citizen artist: 20 years of art in the public arena*, (pp. 335-340). New York: Critical Press.

Manovich, L. (2001). *The language of new media.* Cambridge, MA: MIT Press.

McLaughlin, M., & Heath, S. (Eds.). (1993). *Identity and inner-city youth: Beyond gender and ethnicity.* New York: Teachers College Press.

Murray, T (2006). Contact zones: The art of CD-Rom. Retrieved on December 5, 2008, from http://contactzones.cit.cornell.edu/why.html

Neto, A. (2001). Communication in the virtual teaching and learning space. In P. Kommers & G. Richards (Eds.), *Proceedings of World Conference on Educational Multimedia, Hypermedia and Telecommunications 2001* (pp. 1731-1732). Chesapeake, VA: AACE.

O'Reily, T. (2005). What is Web 2.0: Design patterns and business models for the next generation. Retrieved May 7, 2007, from http://www.oreillynet.com/pub/a/oreilly/tim/news/2005/09/30/what-is-web-20.html

Paik, W., Lee, J., & McMahon, E. (2004). Facilitating collaborative learning in virtual (and sometimes mobile) environments. In C. Bussler, S. Hong, W. Jun, R. Kaschek, Kinshuk, S. Krishnaswamy et al. (Eds.), *Lecture Notes in Computer Science, 3307, Web information systems: WISE 2004 International Workshops Proceedings* (pp. 161-166). Berlin: Springer.

Paul, C. (2002). Renderings of digital art. *Leonardo, 35*(5), 471-478.

Prensky, M. (2001). Digital natives, Digital immigrants. *On the horizon, 9*(5).

Prosser, J. (Ed.). (1998). *Image-based research: A sourcebook for qualitative researchers.* London: Falmer Press.

Richards, C. (1998). Beyond classroom culture. In D. Buckingham (Ed.), *Teaching popular culture: Beyond radical pedagogy.* London: UCL Press.

Schenck, C. (2003). Development pedagogies. *Signs: Journal of Women in Culture and Society, 29*(2), 569-573.

Strauss, W., & Fleishmann, M. (2004). Artistic practice as construction and cultivation of knowledge space. *Leonardo, 37*(2), 141-146.

TNS. (2007). Social networking: Not just for teens. Retrieved August, 15, 2007, from http://marketnews.ca/news_detail.asp?nid=2862

Trend, D. (1997). *Cultural democracy: Politics, media, new technology.* State University of New York Press: New York.

Tyner, K. (1998). *Literacy in a digital age: Teaching and learning in the age of information.* Mahwah, NJ: Lawrence Erlbaum Associates.

Voithofer, R. J. (2005). Designing new media education research: The materiality of data, representation, and dissemination. *Educational Researcher, 34*(9), 3-14.

Willett, R., Burn, A., & Buckingham, D. (2005). New media, production practices, learning spaces. *Education, Communication & Information, 5*(1), 1-3.

Uncommon Dialogue: Digital Critique Beyond the Art Classroom / NICHOLAS HOSTERT

Students engage intensely with their media-laced digital visual culture, building digital relationships as they share text and photo messages, post images and information to websites, and explore ideas and opinions via digital discussions. In a study of the use of media among 2,032 students, age 8-18, the Henry J. Kaiser Family Foundation (2005) concluded that young people spend over 6 hours a day using media, and, compared with a similar study conducted 6 years earlier by the same foundation, they are spending 10% more time using multiple types of media simultaneously. Given these conditions, it becomes increasingly clear that the 21st-century art educator needs to not only infuse the art curriculum with media-rich experiences, but also to guide students' use of these digital tools and promote their critical understanding of the world through learning activities that develop interpersonal communication and problem-solving skills (Partnership for 21st Century Skills, 2002; Dunn, 1996). In order to do so, it is necessary to examine the potential benefits of integrating digital classroom methodologies into an art curriculum.

I conducted a research project over 18 weeks during the 2007-2008 school year exploring how high school students could use technology in meaningful, critical, and socially relevant ways via an online student blog. My study focused on how the use of the blog impacted students' artwork, critique process, and developing critical faculties; how participating in the blog promoted connections between students, their artwork, and popular culture; how participating in the blog helped students develop a sense of community; and how the use of the online critique format heightened students' awareness of the importance of this type of technology in art, education, and society. This investigative case study included 14 high school students enrolled in a second-year photography course at a large high school in the greater Chicago area. The ethnic makeup of the students in the case study was 71.4% White, 14.3% Black, 7.1% Asian, and 7.1% Hispanic. Of the participants, 28.6% were classified as special needs students with

Individualized Education Plans, and 21.4% were classified as low-income. All students had access to computers and the Internet during the school day, and all but three students had access at home.

These students used the communal blog to post their artwork, critique one another's artwork, share personal images and comments, post and embed links to online media, and critique mainstream films. The use of a blog for this type of interaction has several benefits: Blogs are free, easy to establish, allow full student authorship, and enable users to share both self-generated and popular visual media. The blog environment supports a constructivist approach to education, allowing students to construct meaning based on their own experiences as they perceive, create, and modify connections between their artworks and interests (Roberts, 2004; Prater, 2001). Students used the blog space primarily to post images for their peers to view, with other students then responding to the posted images with comments, posts of their own imagery, or Internet links to information or visual media. As students posted and responded to one another, they created an intertextual, rhizomatically connected space. *Intertextuality*, a term first outlined by poststructuralist Julia Kristeva (1980), refers to the process by which a text (word, image, etc.) derives meaning from its given context and through its relationship to other texts. The hypertextual blog environment necessarily incorporates this concept through its constitution of continually changing images, texts, and videos posted by authors and readers in a newly contextualized environment. Taylor and Carpenter (2002) found that students who used hypertext to link information and imagery achieved more complex understanding and multi-faceted interpretations of the material. Navigating intertextual relationships in this student-directed, nonlinear fashion reinforces students' understanding of the relationships between informational sources (Smolin & Lawless, 2003) and promotes critical thinking skills by "enhanc[ing] one's ability to examine the richness of disparate data, to discover relationships, [and] to synthesize ideas to form new understandings" (Keifer-Boyd, 1996, p. 40).

Students' active posting of and responding to these multiple texts may be understood as creating nodes of a rhizome, collectively building an expanding and ever-changing network of information similar to the information structure of the Internet that students navigate daily. The rhizome may be conceived as a loosely structured map of continually fluctuating points, defined in part by the ability to connect any point of the rhizome to any other point and at any point being able to restart or form new connections (Deleuze & Guattari, 1987). Digital visual culture compels art educators to explore strategies that expand pedagogy into the contemporary spaces of student interest, and the Internet is a prime location for this expansion:

> The Internet is the ultimate rhizome. It simultaneously compresses (in the sense of making easily available) and through one portal expands access

> to enormous portions of the visual cultural realm—both the art world and the popular media dimensions. Through digital means they are all collected into one space. (Wilson, 2003, pp. 227-228)

Using a rhizomatic Internet blog space, students can create connections to visual culture interests beyond the classroom, produce and publish their own texts and images, and connect their actions to other peer-generated texts and images. In many art classrooms, students typically present their artwork in a critique format, during which fellow students examine the work and respond verbally or perhaps through writing. I video-recorded every "typical" critique of this type with my group of research participants, the analysis of which revealed two noticeable characteristics that became even more apparent when compared with the digital online critiques. The videos showed that students often began their discussion of an artwork with unsupported "I like" statements that I presume are common in the first few critiques of many art classes. In these instances I directed the students to reinforce such statements, leading them through a series of questions until they were able to defend their statements by discussing how the visual and conceptual strengths of the photographs informed their initial "I like" statements. The videos also showed that nearly one-third of the students did not participate at all in the class discussions unless specifically queried or directed by me; these students had valid points to make, but were reluctant to volunteer their comments.

These two trends—of inadequate student-directed responses and reluctance to respond—changed dramatically in the online digital critique environment. Students who rarely spoke in class offered detailed, insightful comments on their peers' artwork; posted additional links to artworks, popular media, and information; and communicated with students with whom they rarely conversed in class. Students indicated that one reason they were able to more fully participate in the virtual critique space was the increased time they had to compose their thoughts. While students may respond more rapidly during an in-class critique, they are able to respond at their own pace in an online critique space, which allows them to review and revise their comments before submitting them for their peers to view. Granted, students could be given the opportunity to write down thoughts or brainstorm their critical comments in a conventional critique setting, but the online space heightens the efficiency of such tools while transferring these skills to a locale of greater student interest.

After using the digital critique space for 18 weeks, the students responded to questions about this new format via isolated video interviews. Most students confirmed that using the blog allowed them to more fully critique their peers' artwork: "I think it was better to work on [the blog] because you had as much time as you needed to write ... when you critique in person you have to think of everything to say right away" (N. Sadowski, personal communication, January

14, 2008). Similarly, students reported that it was valuable to revisit their peers' artwork at their own pace: "I really liked the fact that I could go and look at other people's pictures whenever I wanted, cause if there was a memorable picture that I wanted to see again I can just go to the blog and access [their work] from there" (R. McArtor, personal communication, January 14, 2008). Not only did students think that using the blog extended their learning into their personal environment, but they also confirmed that the blog allowed them to be more honest, critical, and willing to share their opinions while building valid connections with their peers: "I think it did help [make connections with other students] ... I'm really shy and it helped me talk and get to know other people" (A. Demma, personal communication, January 14, 2008). Another student stated, "Talking in front of your peers, like face-to-face, can be a little intimidating, but when you're, like, talking to them, but it's not so much face-to-face, it might be a little bit easier to say what's on your mind about their pictures" (A. Price, personal communication, January 14, 2008).

As students continued to use the space, their comments became more critical and the connections they made between their artwork, their peers' artwork, and outside visual media became more specific. This was most evident in their online critiques of student artwork: What began as simple, unsupported "I like" statements similar to students' initial statements in the early classroom critiques became well-supported statements that focused on how the student artists used photography techniques to convey specific concepts. Whereas only two students supported their claims in the first online critique, all 14 students' responses for the third online critique incorporated at least some discussion of specific visual characteristics and perceived conceptual goals of the artworks. Students' insights became more comprehensive, to the point that they started to examine arrangement, sequence, and titles of the photographs for meaning. For example, in a critique of another student's artwork that used orange to symbolize increased obsession, one student commented:

> I noticed that you titled your last photo *Orange Fulfillment*. If your concept was to illustrate a person becoming more and more engulfed by orange, one idea to make that concept clearer would be to make the first picture not be so saturated, the next picture more saturated, and the last the way it is. (R. McArtor, personal communication, January 14, 2008)

Students' attention to detail and critical analysis of deliberate choices in visual media was not limited to student artworks; students demonstrated similar growth in their online critiques of mainstream films. In both their first and second film critiques (spaced 12 weeks apart), students were asked to critique how the filmmakers used visual elements and techniques to convey universal themes and specific concepts. Over three-fourths of the students showed significant growth in the depth and critical insight in their critiques of the second film. For example, in her first film critique of *The Prestige* (Nolan, 2006), one student stated, "This movie is basically about how far [a] person can go to satisfy their ambition, dream, and selfish desires. And how ugly [it] can get when somebody is there [in] your way" (P. Tsybrovska, personal communication, January 14, 2008). In comparison, her second film critique of *The Fountain* (Wechsler & Aronofsky, 2006) shows that she constructed specific connections between the themes in the film and the film-makers' deliberate use of visual elements to convey those themes:

> There are [a] few dominating universal themes in this movie, such as life and death, light and dark, religion and hope. They are incorporated using rich visual language, symbols, shapes and clothes of the characters. I think the main theme of the movie is a journey of a man, trying to reach his goal or simply moving towards death. Golden color is a symbol of his goal, his final destination. For example when the guy is walking down the hallway in the hospital, he is passing lamps, that repeatedly pour light on him and then he moves into darkness again for a second. This is such an amazing image of life path for any person: dark stripe, light stripe. (P. Tsybrovska, personal communication, January 14, 2008)

This degree of analytical development in analyzing popular media indicates that students' participation in the digital critiques provided them with the opportunity to transfer the skills already being taught in many art courses to a student-centered space similar to those they encounter daily. As students provided critical insights and commentary on artworks and popular media via the blog, they were able to effortlessly view and respond to one another's contributions. This collaboration allowed increased exposure to different viewpoints and ideas as students essentially developed into critical, supportive members of a small student artist community. Using the blog allowed students to meaningfully connect via active discussions with other students that might never have occurred using traditional learning tools. Students were able to gain a better understanding of each other through engaging with one another's artwork, a benefit that was increased by the fact that the blog archived all student posts, thereby allowing students to revisit artworks and discussions indefinitely. Students confirmed this strengthening of interpersonal relationships as a result of using the blog in their post-interviews: "I can honestly say that I, like, in this class, I got to know people the most than in any other of my classes" (J. Contreras, personal communication, January 14, 2008).

As in any community, students who participated in the blog were conscious of how they might be perceived by their peers. The knowledge that their artwork would be posted online for all to view increased their awareness of viewers' responses, opinions, and social perceptions. It became clear that students were more conscious of their digital "selves" than I had initially anticipated; they spent significant amounts of time deciding how to post and write about their artwork. This social awareness was also clearly present when students shared links or information from popular media sources. For instance, as a preliminary task for a project dealing with sound and imagery, students were asked to post a music video that they thought successfully paired imagery with music for discussion on the blog. I allotted half of a class period (25 minutes) for students to accomplish this task, but they took nearly three class periods. The amount of care and effort the students demonstrated as they posted their music videos and then responded to the posts indicates that they were highly aware of how their posts would reflect personal taste, which reinforced their desire to make socially approved choices.

Students' desire to gain approval from their peers while contributing to this communal space illuminates one of the principal benefits of implementing this type of digital learning environment. Students are making many similar posts in their personal lives as they communicate and share imagery with virtual friends. I propose that my research participants now have a better awareness of digital authorship and digital representation of self; students' insight regarding the manipulation of digital tools to represent themselves and their artwork translates into an awareness of how media is generated and implemented for commercial and social uses on a daily basis in an increasingly digital world. The myth is now exposed: There is no mystery behind the choice of specific imagery in creating meaning. Students not only had the opportunity to engage in the process of imagery creating meaning; they also were able to witness their peers' direct responses to their efforts and engage in critical dialogue concerning their visual world.

As our digital visual culture becomes increasingly intertextual, it is imperative that students learn how to navigate their virtual environment in order to critically understand, evaluate, and relevantly contribute to their world. Educators and students have immense opportunities to build transformative connections that assist in developing a critical understanding of our interconnected global society. Stressing the importance for art educators to investigate visual culture in contemporary networked society, Sweeny (2004) warns, "the simplicity and the seductiveness of digital technologies may distract educators from questioning the potential for critical application and creative response" (p. 81). The research presented here indicates that incorporating a virtual critique space into the art classroom allows students to develop their critical thinking skills using increasingly accessible digital tools, resulting in more transformative, student-centered growth and insight than might be achieved through traditional methodologies. The immediacy of the online learning environment—in this instance a blog—provides an increased sense of comfort and safety, which in turn increases students' willingness to communicate openly (Watson, 1999). This self-paced environment allows unlimited time to examine visual media ranging from student artwork, to snapshots taken on a cell phone, to recent film trailers, thereby enabling the normally reluctant student to engage fully in critiques. Through their critical engagement in a digital critique space, students can form stronger connections with one another as they construct a student-directed learning community that encourages its participants to develop insightful understanding of the visual media they view while exchanging ideas in a fluid, decentered, easily accessible, and rhizomatically expandable space. The potential benefits for students' increased understanding of themselves, their peers, and their academic and social worlds through participation in this highly visual and dynamic virtual environment cannot be overlooked. In the words of one student research participant, "because, you know, we learn how to get to know people through pictures" (P. Tsybrovska, personal communication, January 14, 2008).

REFERENCES

Deleuze, G. & Guattari, F. (1987). *A thousand plateaus: Capitalism and schizophrenia* (B. Massumi, Trans.). Minneapolis: University of Minnesota Press.

Dunn, P. (1996). More power: Integrated interactive technology and art education. *Art Education, 49*(6), 6-11.

The Henry J. Kaiser Family Foundation. (2005). Generation M: Media in the lives of 8-18 year-olds. Retrieved May 7, 2008, from www.kff.org/entmedia/upload/Generation-M-Media-in-the-Lives-of-8-18-Year-olds-Report.pdf

Keifer-Boyd, K. T. (1996). Interfacing hypermedia and the internet with critical inquiry in the arts: Preservice training. *Art Education, 49*(6), 33-41.

Kristeva, J. (1980). *Desire in language: A semiotic approach to literature and art* (A. Jardine, T. Gora, & L. Roudiez, Trans.). New York: Columbia University Press.

Nolan, C. (Producer). (2006). *The prestige* [Motion picture]. United States: Warner Brothers Pictures.

Partnership for 21st Century Skills. (2002). Learning for the 21st century: A report and mile guide for 21st century skills. Retrieved March 7, 2007, from www.21stcenturyskills.org/images/stories/otherdocs/p21up_Report.pdf

Prater, M. (2001). Constructivism and technology in art education. *Art Education, 54*(6), 43-48.

Roberts, T. S. (Ed.). (2004). *Online collaborative learning: Theory and practice.* Hershey, PA: Information Science.

Smolin, I. S., & Lawless, K. A. (2003). Becoming literate in the technological age: New responsibilities and tools for teachers. *The Reading Teacher, 56*(6), 570-577.

Sweeny, R. (2004). Lines of sight in the 'network society': Simulation, art education, and digital visual culture. *Studies in Art Education, 46*(1), 74-87.

Taylor, P., & Carpenter, S. (2002). Inventively linking: Teaching and learning with computer hypertext. *Art Education, 55*(4), 6-12.

Watson, K. (1999). Evolution of a revolution in language learning: A new paradigm for the mind online. Paper presented online at the Teaching in the Community Colleges Online Conference. (ERIC Document Reproduction Service No. ED471311)

Wechsler, N. (Producer), & Aronofsky, D. (Director). (2006). *The fountain* [Motion picture]. United States: Warner Brothers Pictures.

Wilson, B. (2003). Of diagrams and rhizomes: Visual culture, contemporary art and the impossibility of mapping the content of art education. *Studies in Art Education, 44*(3), 214-229.

A Digital Visual Culture Course for Incarcerated Youth / CARLETON PALMER

Time in jail is usually not voluntary, but that is where I spent the 5 academic years from 2000 to 2005—not as an inmate but as an art teacher. Possessed of a social conscience that sometimes backfires, I took an opportunity offered by circumstance to create an art program for incarcerated youth at the Nassau County Correctional Center, a Long Island, New York, jail.

Early in my teaching career, when dinosaurs roamed the land, I was employed in a 5-year New York State experimental education project in therapeutic communities for drug addiction such as Phoenix House, so I supposed that I had a handle on what was coming my way. No one actually grasps this context until the heavy steel gates close. An adequate picture of the circumstances would take too long to paint, and a summary of my errors in getting to the point described here would be embarrassing and long, but the end result was a successful program that creatively employed digital technology in the service of youths' development of an awareness of visual qualitative problem-solving abilities; in short, that which can be argued as the process of making art.

CONTEXT

Some stellar individuals stand out in memory from the collection of personalities that made up my classes. Their boundless creativity in finding ways to do mischief to themselves and everyone else with the simplest materials such as pencils, paper clips, soap, and so on is more a testament to their limitless free time than to intellectual efficiency, but it meant that the program was not to be permitted one single conventional art material. Law enforcement organizations document, retain, and exhibit collections of inmate ephemeral martial artifacts in order to demonstrate this inventive, and sometimes diabolical, turn of mind. The Hollywood image of the prisoner painting away in oils like Van Gogh in his yellow house comes from other contexts such as are documented by Kornfeld (1997). Szekely (1982) also offers a good account of problems and practices of teaching visual art in prisons. My youngsters would have made siege engines from the canvas, easel, and brushes in a conventional art studio, cried havoc, and launched the palettes of war. A more sinister truth is that one CD can shatter into 100 splinters, suitable for literal murder, bloodshed, and mayhem.

As a solution to these problems and to provide a satisfactory art experience in this environment, I built an eight-workstation computer laboratory managed by a server under my control and taught multimedia, 3-D modeling, animation, and digital sound. A virtual CD program, Alcohol 120%, removed the problem of distributing potentially lethal physical CDs, and the simple extraction of the games included with Windows removed them as distractions. Headphones replaced speakers when it became obvious that one objective of almost every client was to annoy everyone else in as many ways possible. Cable ties secured every wire, and in those 5 years no computer parts were removed, nor was any part of the studio used feloniously.

POPULATION

Located in a jail, not a prison, males 16-21 awaited trial, sentencing, or prison-placement. The State of New York requires persons of this age to receive instruction, and a program consisting of general academic educational development, life skills, and high school equivalency preparation had been in existence for some time. An enlightened faculty requested an art teacher when a position became available.

The program had to be tailored to a clientele whose stay at the institution ranged from 1 day to 1½ years. A sequence of studies moved from a lesson in 2-D face construction using forensic software and Photoshop through more lengthy tasks using relatively easy programs such as Poser and Bryce, and professional software such as 3DSMax. Music programs like FruityLoops interested some students who provided the sound backgrounds for extended animations assembled with the multimedia program Adobe Premiere. Each of 4 of those 5 years students produced an animated movie that was burned to a CD as a portfolio documenting this digital visual art program. Since they could not be given these portfolios, many requested that copies be mailed home to their families. Motivation was often achieved with lessons that began with playing computer games, and continued with the production of images, models, effects, and animations inspired by them. The later addition of an Epson 4000 inkjet printer permitted students to produce portfolios and holiday cards that were also mailed home, and a digital keyboard let some explore music, if they had the skill, or sound effects if they did not.

Computers were networked, but no outside Internet was permitted on student machines. This networking, in addition to permitting the teacher to remotely interact, allowed students to collaborate.

OBJECTIVES

Each student's instruction required continuous modification of individual objectives, but the following are those which directed the program:

> *Qualitative problem solving:* To learn to employ qualitative means to solve qualitative problems.

Cognitive: To know how to operate computers and computer programs.

Affective: To develop confidence in the act of creation; To become comfortable with a collaborative studio and office environment.

RESOURCES AND CONSTRAINTS

"We must do more with less." Having heard this mantra repeatedly over decades of public-school teaching, and having continuously over the years kicked in materials, equipment, and salary to achieve the educational objectives I set for my students, it was a genuine pleasure to have an adequate budget for this program. In the second year I was able to design my own Dell computers with satisfactory graphics cards and RAM for the demanding graphics programs and networking of the laboratory. Although the overall project was managed by the local East Meadow Union Free School District, the budget came from New York State.

The greatest resource, however, was not material, but collegial. No amount of money would have made this project fly without an extraordinary support system of highly experienced educators united in a mission to make a success of the entire program of which this was an element. The level of trust and expertise of this group unified the program. Without that kind of support the pathos of such a situation could have become overwhelming. In addition, the moral support of colleagues within the professional organization, The New York State Association for Incarcerated Education Programs, was also welcome.

Among the generally agreed-upon factors important to learning is consistency. In order to advance understanding or develop skill it is generally agreed that a consistent time for particular learning activities must be set aside on a regular basis. This is not achievable in jail. Scheduling is a constraint. Aside from the fact that clients might be available for as little as a single day or as much as a year and a half, schedules varied from hour to hour, sometimes from minute to minute. In order to work with as many people as possible, schedules were written such that a teacher might see a student alternating days, or alternating Thursdays, or 3 days in a row, and then not for 2 weeks. A dormitory change would result in a student never being seen by a particular teacher again. Some teachers were asked to teach students on the cellblock unaccompanied by an officer and surrounded by dozens of other inmates going about their business of doing push-ups or posturing in such a way as to distract even the most attentive learner or stalwart educator. The only control the teacher had in those circumstances was good judgment about what to agree to, and what not to agree to.

Beyond the constraints already mentioned, the structural constraint inherent in the difference between the missions of educators determined to awaken and inspire the same people that the host organization, the jail, was responsible for controlling, and suppressing if necessary, dominated. Daily, I would watch youngsters' anxieties, hostility, and resistance slip away and be overtaken by engagement with the fascinating visual world coming into being at their hands, and then observe those negative effects shocked back into the forefront when it was time for them to return to the cellblock. In 5 years I witnessed many kindnesses, and not one instance of abuse of a prisoner by an officer, but a jail is about constraint and some of us are permitted to think that education is about liberation.

TECHNOLOGY

Starting cold, in 1 hour of instruction students can learn to create, texture, and animate a three-dimensional model with the computer software mentioned here, and immediately begin asking and solving qualitative visual problems that would ordinarily take many weeks of manual practice and instruction to arise. The positive factor of near-immediate feedback for a population that is characterized by a limited ability to defer gratification should not be minimized, nor should the attraction of the technology be disregarded. This is an evolution of the observations of the prescient Stanley S. Madeja (1983, 1993) concerning the direction of technology in art education.

Like the whalers and their scrimshaw, prisoners produce art without instruction, from the body art of tribal tattoos through elaborately penciled, sometimes polychrome, kerchiefs. It is common that such artifacts celebrate thug-life, pornography, and other less than savory themes that rarely appear in their realistically modeled, computer-generated products. There was little leeway or tolerance for overt protest or even the most sub-cultural self-expression in jail because such behavior is regarded as a challenge to the authority of the host organization. The classroom did not have autonomy in these matters, as it represented an aspect of that authority. Prisoners resorted to covert means of self-expression that were tolerated until they became too evident, and were then suppressed. Tattoos, handkerchiefs, soap-sculptures, and graffiti happened up to the point where they became so visible that they could not be ignored, and were then suppressed by "sweeps" of cells and other means.

HARDWARE

A personal preference for the Macintosh as an art platform had to be set aside in favor of the PC because of the prevalence of the latter. There was a greater difference between the platforms and respective software than has since developed, particularly with the current adoption by Macintosh of the Intel rather than the previous Motorola CPU, and if students were to become comfortable with one system it was thought that it should be that which is used by businesses and more than 80% of the market. On my arrival there were machines using the Windows 95, 98, and ME operating systems. Converting to Windows 2000 the first year was not a picnic given the variety of CPUs, varying amounts and kinds of RAM, different sound and video cards, and numerous broken bits, but it was accomplished. Once the studio had nine identical machines of adequate power, the hardware problems were solved.

SOFTWARE

Throughout this experience I acquired, studied, selected, tested, and rejected hundreds of pieces of software for the project. Some projects, such as training for the A+ exam, and the use of architectural, CAD, landscape, and interior design software were short-lived, but the following software programs proved durable and useful in supporting the directions of the project.

2-D

- *Photoshop*: This Adobe program is meat and potatoes for two-dimensional digital imaging and printing. Having begun to study digital imaging in the Pre-Cambrian with Aldus Digital Darkroom, I found the current CS3 Suite and enormous number of plug-ins to be a dream come true. At the time of this writing, the CS4 Suite has been released.
- *Faces*: This is professional forensic two-dimensional facial composite software.
- *Kai's SuperGoo*: SuperGoo is an animating digital image distortion tool that seems to be discontinued, but still appears in catalogs at the time of this writing.
- *Kai's Power Tools*: KPT is a series of special effects plug-ins now bundled under the title "The KPT Collection."

3-D

3-D modeling, animation, and Computer-Assisted-Design (CAD) software features often overlap, and there are many multi- and special-purpose programs. Details of the software and much more can be found on the CG Society website Wiki at http://wiki.cgsociety.org/. These are the main programs used in this project:

- *Bryce*: This 3-D modeling program concentrates on developing landscapes is easy and fun, and extremely flexible. It is now owned by Daz3D, a division of Daz Productions.
- *Poser*: This 3-D modeling program concentrates on figures. It is often used with professional applications for content production, pre-visualization, gaming, and movie production. There are many models available for the program.
- *Rhinoceros*: A 3-D modeling program that has developed greatly over the years. Basically a spline-modeling program (NURBS), it has many advanced features, but remains easy to use in its basics.
- *3DSMax*: This Autodesk product is a high-end professional program, as is Maya. Fortunately, some of its basic elements are reasonably easy to learn, and the results of its renders are spectacular. To learn to fully use this program requires a large commitment, but it is superb as a demonstrator.

Game Authoring

- *3D Game Studio*: A true game-authoring environment with enough templates and accessible features to permit students to actually make their own walk-through events.

Multimedia

- *Premiere*: An Adobe multimedia authoring product where the bits and pieces of 2-D/3-D art and animation of teams come together with music to make a movie.

Audio

- *Mixman*: DJ mix and remix software with a large body of samples, and an easily mastered interface.
- *FruityLoops*: A deceptively simple program that accepts VST plug-ins to become a huge digital audio workstation.
- *Sibelius*: Professional music software. MIDI-capable, one can write scores on virtual music paper and hear them played, or play with a capable keyboard and watch the autograph appear.
- *Wavelab*: Sound software. Made by Steinberg, Wavelab permits one to operate on waveforms, add effects, and edit sound.
- *Cubase*: Also by Steinberg, Cubase is a complete professional digital audio workstation. One can combine MIDI and Wave information for composition, recording, editing, and mixing.

GAMES

Games were selected that advanced the educational program, and a number of them worked superbly out-of-the-box as instruction, motivation, and subject matter for modeling and animating after rejecting those that were violent, irrelevant, or otherwise objectionable. Every game had to be tested before inclusion in the program, because even an otherwise useful game like The Sims had to be rejected after it was realized that one of the possible career paths within the game play was that of a burglar.[1]

- *Health-Related Games*: Laser Surgeon, Life and Death I and II, Microsurgeon, Virtual Surgeon, Combat Medic, Theme Hospital, Sim Health, Epidemic, Microcosm, Alter Ego, Mind Mirror, Emergency Room, Emergency, and Emergency EMT.
- *History Games*: Civilization III, Cleopatra, Pharaoh, Caesar III, Viking Invasion, Medieval Total War, Rampage Across Britain, Stronghold Crusader, The Age of Kings, The New World, The Age of Empires, Austerlitz, Gettysburg, Waterloo, Antietam, The Rise of Nations, and Qin.

- *Job Simulation Games*: Emergency Room, Emergency, Emergency EMT, and Vet Emergency.
- *Resources Management Simulation Games*: Airport Tycoon, Casino Tycoon, Cruise Ship Tycoon, Big Biz Tycoon, Roller Coaster Tycoon, Mall Tycoon, Railroad Tycoon, School Tycoon, Startup, Theme Park Tycoon, Zoo Tycoon, and Restaurant Empire.
- *Others*: Oregon Trail, Sim City, Rise of Nations, etc.

While other games were rotated, the following became standard:
- *Pandora's Box*: Created by the inventor of Tetris, Alexey Pajitnov, skill dealing with fundamental elements of design like line, shape, form, etc. is developed over time by playing more than 400 incrementally demanding puzzles within the framework of a mythological chase. It is huge fun, and provokes concrete conversations about making visual discriminations.
- *Myst*: This first in a series of groundbreaking, astonishingly beautiful, complex, and profoundly important games demands memory, attention, and problem-solving skills as one navigates worlds that pose visual, auditory, numerical, and other puzzles in realistic simulations toward the solution of a mystery. Students are motivated by the game to create their own 3-D worlds and artifacts.
- *Chessmaster*: Students at networked workstations can play against one another; an individual can play against the program or receive instruction. One can choose from among many custom chess sets, motivating students to design their own, which is a good introduction to 3-D lathing and Boolians.
- *The Typing of the Dead*: This is the only worthwhile "first-person-shooter" I found. Zombies and other monsters with name balloons assault the game-player(s) who destroy them messily by typing their names. The game characters inspire figure modeling and animation.

MOVIES

The rich contemporary motion picture environment of 3-D modeling and animation provided motivating and entertaining subject matter for this project. Each new blockbuster production is a move in a chess game to outdo all previous efforts, and Cinefex, a quarterly magazine devoted to motion picture visual effects, is a good resource that follows those moves. After viewing and discussing a movie, students were asked to model a character or animate a sequence inspired by a current film. Sequences then became scenes in longer pieces demanding digital movie editing decisions and skills.

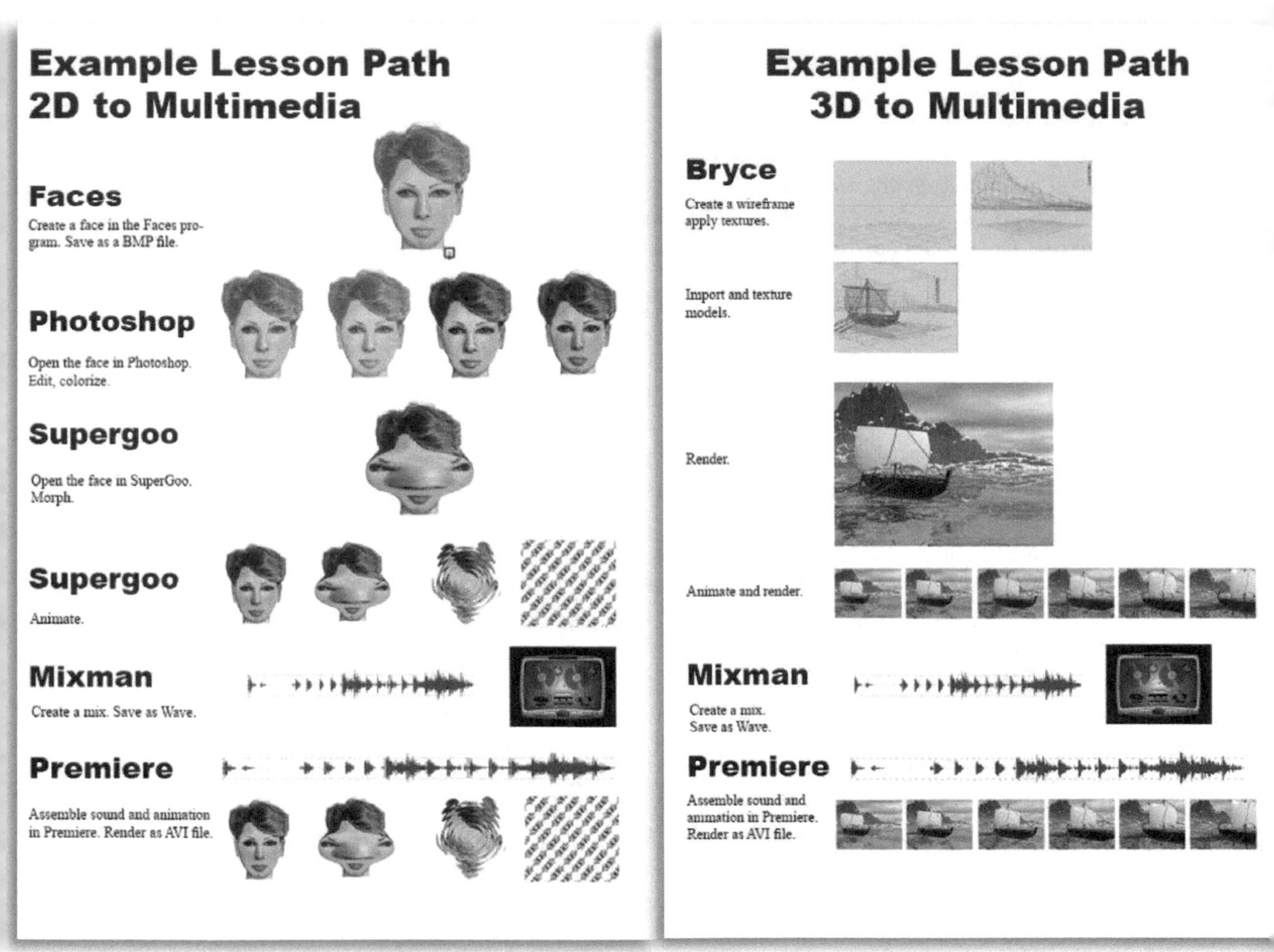

Above: Example lessons. Images courtesy of author.

SAMPLE INSTRUCTIONAL SEQUENCES

Lessons and stages of lessons were always posted for reference as an aid to individual instruction, and the walls were covered with print-outs of student work for both motivation and reference. With each student always at a different point on a different topic it was convenient to walk people through a sequence by pointing and demonstrating. Above are two among many.

PRINCIPLES AND DEFINITIONS

This program was not a formal research project, nor was it formally evaluated. Yearly visits by the East Meadow Board of Education and SuperIntendent and widely distributed student CD portfolios received positive reviews throughout the life of the program.[2] Pupil satisfaction might be inferred by the high degree of student cooperation and productivity.

Both the State and the school district would have been satisfied that students were becoming acquainted with the use of computers by whatever means, and this program far exceeded those expectations. It did, however, develop as an outgrowth of what I have found to be a useful set of art educational principles, presumptions, and operational definitions with which to guide instruction while navigating the digital visual culture.

OPERATIONAL DEFINITION OF ARTISTIC PROCESS

Aesthetic education and qualitative inquiry entered the standard vocabulary of art and art education during the second half of the 20th century partly through the Discipline-Based Art Education (DBAE) movement spearheaded by the Getty Foundation, the history of which can be recovered in a bibliography by Smith (1998), and partly by the independent efforts of major players such as Ecker (1961), who traced the maneuver, observing "artistic process as qualitative problem solving" from Dewey's (1934) thoughts on qualitative intelligence through the research of Villemain (1952) and Champlin (1952) through his own later contributions. More recent thinking has served to enrich the implicit underlying idea of multiple intelligences, as reported by Gardner (1983, 1993, 2000).

Operational definitions permit us to explore the implications of premises. If they prove useful, we test their limitations and improve them. If they fail, we look for others. A benefit of the operational definition of artistic process as "qualitative problem solving" is that the definition separates the artistic process from its possible problems and mediums. "The artistic process is qualitative problem solving; it is the controlled procedure of instituting qualitative relationships as means to the achievement of a qualitative end or total" (Ecker, 1961/1966, p. 67). This remains a useful observation whether pursuing the Nicolaides drawing exercises (with or without split-brain arguments) or critiquing a film.

The computer does the heavy lifting for animation, and therefore permits people to arrive at the point of making aesthetic judgments about qualities concerning motion, gesture, and time as creators that would otherwise be inaccessible to them without literally months or years of tedium, and then to make changes to those qualities as a result of their own problem solving. "Tweening" permits a computer animator to set the beginning and end states of a sequence which is automatically completed. At 30 frames per second the animator is relieved of 28 frames of labor on a 1-second project. A change to a variable in the end frame and rapid re-rendering permits the comparison and contrast of a time-based event along that variable. The huge number of pre-made three-dimensional models available permits the computer user to work with more complex material than the animator could build, enhancing the richness of the animating experience to include meanings that would be inaccessible otherwise. These, and many other factors beyond the scope of this chapter, characterize the potential differences between traditional and digital processes that influence aesthetic decision-making in the instructional context.

The observation is inclusive if all acts of qualitative problem solving toward qualitative ends are seen as artistic processes. It only describes the artistic process. It does not describe the problem or medium, or offer any way to judge the success or failure of any artistic effort. It is a beneficial tool in that it separates these from one another for individual consideration. Ideas of "high" art, "low" art, "fine" art, or "crafts" are not implicit in the definition, and no medium has priority, digital or otherwise.

Although artists are rarely accused of an excess of common sense, artists' process takes the form of self-reflective and iterative low-detail overview of a problem described by Ecker (1961/1966): "Artists at their work think in terms of relations of qualities, think with qualities; their thought, in a word, is qualitative" (p. 62).

Conversely, it is not unknown for artists to employ quantitative means to achieve their qualitative purposes, from the computational automata of the ancient Greek theater to 3-D modeling, animation, manipulation of computational rules, and employment of the generative properties of complex systems.

SCIENCE AND ART

If the problems to be resolved are either quantitative or qualitative, and their processes of solution are also either quantitative or qualitative, then an emphasis on qualitative problems resolved with qualitative strategies may be said to characterize artistic process, and an emphasis on quantitative problems resolved with quantitative strategies may be said to characterize scientific process. In my opinion, a purpose of any form of problem solving is to better understand the world by whatever means are appropriate.

One would probably have been ill-advised to seek out Salvador Dali for psychiatric counseling, but his painted remarks on the unconscious are iconic. Braque and Picasso did not pretend to be mathematical physicists, but their visual strategies for representing simultaneity access quantum concepts. Conversely, some scientists cite imaginative literary speculations as exciting their interest in science to begin with, and as provoking lines of inquiry pursued professionally. John W. Campbell, author and editor of *Astounding* from 1937, insisted that the art of creative Science Fiction writing be grounded in science, whether it was extrapolation of the implications of existing science, or speculation about scientific directions. That appears to imply a first step in scientific inquiry itself.

COGNITIVE STYLE

It is an unusually rarefied problem-solving atmosphere in which only one kind of thinking prevails, but it explains why dissertations in mathematics can be very few pages of symbols, while MFA exhibitions and performances can be large participatory events. The quantitative/qualitative distinction implies preferential ways of reasoning conforming to the literature of cognitive styles. The cognitive style concept moves from Bertalanffy (1968) and Werner (1948) to Witkin (1981, 1962). Among the problems of cognitive style research are thinking in terms of paired opposites, and defining one characteristic as the failure to perform successfully on a test of the other. It is a common error to suppose that poor performance on quantitative tasks implies a qualitative cognitive style, explaining the instances when a child failing out of math gets a double dose of art. If one accepts this form of dyadic reasoning for the sake of argument, it would probably be more productive to observe lability between cognitive styles, the ability to move between assumedly polarized cognitive styles as tasks demand as a form of mental efficiency.

IMPLEMENTATION AND USEFULNESS OF CONCEPTS

Instructional strategy consisted mostly of demonstration and directed dialogue, and students were encouraged to discuss why they believed one solution to a visual problem was superior to another. This was most effective in the cases where students remained in the program long enough to make and discuss enough artwork to repeatedly ascend a ladder of discourse from description absent opinion through critical reflection assessing and establishing informed opinion. At no time did the conversations ascend to meta-criticism or theory. The most difficult hurdles, after the development of technique, were to separate description from opinion, and then communicate the idea that value judgment arguments required grounds.

A typical condensed conversation of the following sort would have been repeated in various ways many times a day. (The visual event is a short animation of a green figure against a foliage background. The figure and background were created separately and judged adequate for the overall project.)

Teacher: "What do you think of the animation?"

Student: "It sucks."

Teacher: "Describe what you see."

Student: "Just green and flickers of light.

Teacher: "Is that what you wanted?"

Student: "No, I wanted to see the figure dancing."

Teacher: "Why can't you see the figure dancing."

Student: "It disappears in the trees."

Teacher: "That's called camouflage. If you wanted to separate the figure from the trees how would you do it?"

The discussion and demonstration would proceed to color, lighting, and other strategies to solve the problem. Operational definitions are advantageous in that they don't claim to be true or false, but useful. This operational definition of artistic process as qualitative problem solving has demonstrated its usefulness in a sizable body of research and practice of which Dernini's (2008) chronicle of a 25-year exploration in community art is a recent example. This concept grounded the ongoing critique that, aside from the merely technical aspects of using the medium, was the program's instructional method.

CONCLUSION

Some hundreds of incarcerated youths have therefore had a miniature Pixar or Industrial Light and Magic experience, and spent some productive hours of otherwise unproductive days immersed creatively in the contemporary digital visual culture by making visual art using the continuously evolving digital technology. This report has sketched a successful art education program for incarcerated youth within the contemporary digital visual culture, outlined the general technology and methodology employed, and attempted to situate the effort within the larger framework of art education.

REFERENCES

Bertalanffy, L. V. (1968). *General system theory: Foundations, development, applications.* New York: George Braziller.

Champlin, N. (1952). Controls in qualitative thought. Unpublished doctoral dissertation, Columbia University. ADD 1952, p. 171.

Dernini, S. (2008). *Plexus black box: A multicultural aesthetic inquiry into an international community based art project.* Academic Press of the University of Rome "La Sapienza."

Dewey, J. (1934). *Art as experience.* New York: Capricorn Books. (Ninth impression, 1958.)

Ecker, D. W. (1961). The artistic process as qualitative problem solving. Paper read at the annual meeting of the ASA, held at Wayne State University on October 28, 1961. It was subsequently published as follows:

(1963) *The Journal of Aesthetics and Art Criticism, 21*(3), pp. 283-290.

(1966) In E. Eisner & D. Ecker (Eds.), *Readings in art education* (p. 468). Waltham, MA: Blaisdell.

(1973) In M. Lippman (Ed.), *Contemporary Aesthetics* (pp. 407-15). Boston: Allyn and Bacon.

Gardner, H. (1983). *Frames of mind: The theory of multiple intelligences.* New York: Basic.

Gardner, H. (1993). *Multiple intelligences: The theory in practice.* New York: Basic.

Gardner, H. (2000). *Intelligence reframed: Multiple intelligences for the 21st century.* New York: Basic.

Kornfeld, P. (1997). *Cellblock visions: Prison art in America.* Princeton, NJ: Princeton University Press.

Kuipers, B. (1994). *Qualitative reasoning: Modeling and simulation with incomplete knowledge.* Cambridge, MA: The MIT Press.

Madeja, S. S. (1983). Computer graphics: the new subject matter for the art curriculum. *Art Education, 36*(3), 15-17.

Madeja, S. S. (1993). The age of the electronic image: the effect on art education. *Art Education, 46*(6), 8-14.

Sebeok, T. A. (1983). One, two, three spells UBERTY. In U. Eco & T. A. Sebeok (Eds.), *Dupin, Holmes, Peirce: The sign of three* (pp. 1-10). Bloomington: Indiana University Press.

Smith, R. A. (1998). The DBAE literature project. [Online], University of Illinois at Urbana-Champaign: www.naea-reston.org/pdf/DBAEBibl1.pdf

Sprott, J. C. (2001). Can a computer produce and critique art? *Leonardo, 34*(4), 369.

Szekely, G. (1982). Art education in correctional settings. *Studies in Art Education, 24*(1), 33-42.

Werner, H. (1948/1973). *Comparative psychology of mental development.* New York: International Universities Press.

Witkin, H. A., et al. (1962/1974). *Psychological differentiation: Studies of development.* New York: John Wiley and Sons.

Witkin, H. A., & Goodenough, D. R. (1981). *Cognitive styles: Essence and origins.* New York: International Universities Press.

Villemain, F. T. (1952). The qualitative character of intelligence. Unpublished doctoral dissertation, Columbia University. ADD 1952, p. 175.

ENDNOTES

1 The movement to engage the learner with digital games and simulations has made us aware of the value of many games which were examined for this project. Some hundreds of pieces of game software with such positive educational uses are categorized on the website of Social Impact Games: http://www.socialimpactgames.com/index.php

2 The four yearly portfolios and other supplements are available as Internet downloads at http://www.cpalmer.biz/DVC.htm

prior practices

artwork information portfolio Facebook required
Alexenberg
forms dynamic
studies social Digital study College
much
montage
Aesthetic software contemporary Storyspace meaning
Lessig make
original York development may also
students
shift used help Web
way
technology architecture Internet popular
arts concepts
art
PowerPoint rather case form works
spaces media see pp creative
Making
Hebraic words student
sense
Culture
center e-portfolio
curriculum
Online course
Domain Identity
Talmud knowledge
ideas Vaidhyanathan
program within process project
Laws University purpose critical environment
corporate educators another
e-portfolios
Chapter many public Thought example
structure
Copyright texts books
Portfolios
final self must content
originality cultural space multiple
created
law use images thinking
text assessment hypertextual
page create pedagogy Creativity
Press using one Like creating ways
two construction work world However
new
Even often time without
Teachers different
free
hypertext people
Avant-Garde
consciousness artists
learning Visual fair
life act future
electronic Retrieved copyrighted age collage computer
classroom
education experience
nature

Space-Time Structures of Digital Visual Culture: Paradigm Shift from Hellenistic to Hebraic Roots of Western Civilization / MEL ALEXENBERG

To experience digital visual culture is to experience an emerging worldview that stands in stark contrast with an older worldview that has dominated Western visual culture until the rise of Modernism. Digital visual culture reveals a paradigm shift from the space-time structures of ancient Greece revived in Renaissance Europe to the space-time structures of the Hebraic roots of Western culture emerging in our networked world. In this chapter, Hebraic origins of this profound contemporary paradigm shift in visual culture are explored in relation to the conceptual and contextual impact of media, from Talmud to Internet, and of architecture, from Wright to Gehry. Fresh directions in art education flow from this paradigm shift in our experience of space and time along the dynamic and diaphanous interface between real space and cyberspace.

In his seminal book *Hebrew Thought Compared with Greek*, Norwegian theologian Thorleif Boman (1960) contrasts the static, peaceful, moderate, and passive Greek thought with the dynamic, vigorous, passionate, and action-centered characteristics of Hebraic thought. Winston Churchill (1951) points out: "The Greeks and the Jews are the two peoples whose worldviews have most influenced the way we think and act. Each of them from angles so different has left us with the inheritance of its genius and wisdom.... Their messages in religion, philosophy, and art have been the main guiding light in modern faith and culture" (Churchill, p. 532).

THE MEDIUM IS THE MESSAGE

"Visual culture opens up an entire world of intertextuality in which images, sounds and special delineations are read on to and through one another, leading ever-accruing layers of meanings and of subjective responses" (Rogoff, 2002, p. 24). Major media systems in Jewish visual culture and digital visual culture share a common space-time structure that opens up new worlds of intertextuality. Both

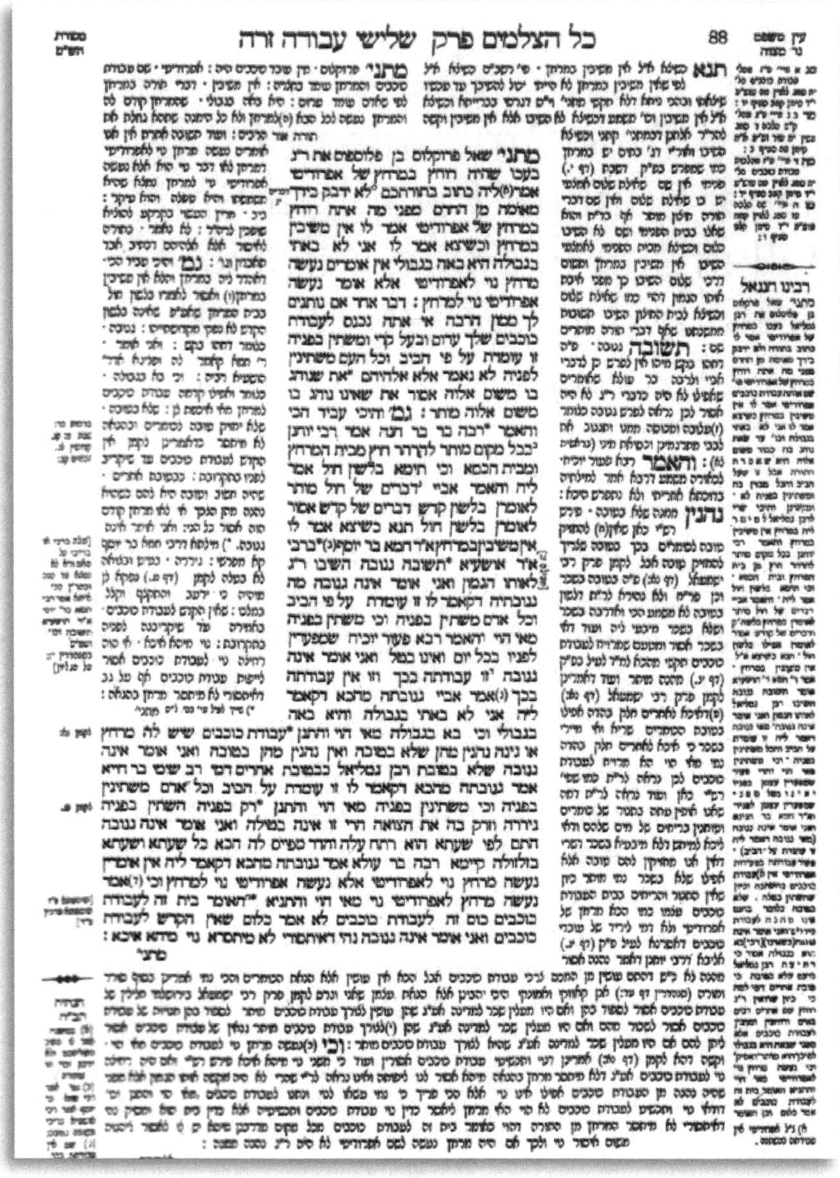
88 כל הצלמים פרק שלישי עבודה זרה

FIGURE 1:
One of the 5,894 pages of the Babylonian Talmud.

the multilinear typographical design of the Talmud, the major work of Jewish law and lore, and hypertext linking in the design of the Internet are structured so that they facilitate and encourage creative, associative, and multiple perspectives. The single-point perspective of Hellenistic consciousness revealed through Renaissance art and the unilinear structure of the proto-industrial age Gutenberg Bible produce an obsolete structure of consciousness alien in a networked world.

Like the Internet, the branching and rhizome-like structure of the Talmud has no beginning and no end. The multiple patches of text on each page are the recorded dialogue of generations of scholars that come to life in the vivid spontaneity of contemporary learners engaging these scholars and each other in searching for significance of past explorations for present and future actions. Studying these non-sequential multilinear tractates takes place in active noisy learning environments, quite different from the enforced quiet of a library for linear books. These traditional sites for creative learning in real space branch out through cyberspace to extend the worldwide community of learners. Fresh directions for art can be derived from the dynamic, interactive, and multidirectional structure of an ancient culture echoed in digital visual culture of the future (Alexenberg, 2004).

When I was professor of art and education at Columbia University, techno-prophet Marshall McLuhan came down from Toronto to lecture. He talked about how the linear pattern of information resulting from print technology limited the thought patterns of people who learned from printed books. Word follows word, line follows line, paragraph follows paragraph, page follows page, chapter follows chapter, in a single necessary order from the first page to last. Learning through a medium that is a one-way street prevented creative, flexible, associative, open-ended, multidirectional, and multidimensional thought. Instead of just being authoritative, books became authoritarian, demanding thinking in straight lines from a fixed point of view. The book medium became a stronger message than its content. Designed to be read in privacy, in seclusion from others, the book ended dialogue. It conferred the values of isolation, detachment, passivity, and non-involvement (McLuhan, 1969, 1994).

I invited McLuhan to my office to show him how the Hebraic dialogic mindset, which could not tolerate unidirectional thought, used print technology to design multilinear books. I took a volume of Talmud off my shelf and showed him non-linear pages designed in 16th-century Venice (see Figure 1). "The Talmud is thus the recorded dialogue of generations of scholars. It has all the characteristics of a living dialogue. Freshness, vivid spontaneity, and acute awareness of every subject permeate every argument and discussion. The spirit of life breathes on every single page" (Steinsaltz, 1989, p. 9). It is not a set of books to be read in quiet solitude. We give life and continuity to the dialogue that began millennia ago by engaging the hundreds of voices talking across the folio pages in active dialogue with a learning partner. The two learners, a *hevrutah*, enter a page and move around within it while arguing with each other, calling for support from all the scholars before them and proposing their own innovative ideas. They can begin their learning on any of its 5,894 pages. Each student in the dialogic dyad "longs to create, to bring into being something new, something original. The study of Torah, by definition, means gleaning new, creative insights from the Torah" (Soloveitchik, 1983, p. 99). The multivolume Talmud has no beginning and no end. The hevrutah can jump around within a page, between pages, between different Talmud tractates, bring to bear the Bible, kabbalistic texts, or any other sources, ancient and modern. A study hall in a yeshiva filled with many learning teams is a busy, dynamic, noisy environment—quite different from the eerie silence of a library for linear books.

FROM TALMUD TO INTERNET

When I began surfing the World Wide Web, it seemed a familiar place to me. I felt I had been there before. Talmud study had prepared me for its vast multidirectional options, hyperlinking, and its non-sequential organization. I felt at home seeing home pages that had an uncanny resemblance to Talmud pages. As a member of the panel, "Toward an Aesthetic for the 21st Century: Networking, Hypermedia, and Planetary Creativity," at the 1990 conference of the College Art Association, I explored this confluence between traditional Jewish media experiences and encountering the emerging Internet. A decade later, Jonathan Rosen (2000) wrote in *The Talmud and the Internet: A Journey between Worlds*:

> I can't help feeling that in certain respects the Internet has a lot in common with the Talmud. The Rabbis referred to the Talmud as a yam, a sea—and though one is hardly intended to 'surf' the Talmud, something more than oceanic metaphors links the two verbal universes. Vastness and an uncategorizable nature are in part what define them both.... The Hebrew word for tractate is *masechet*, which means, literally, "webbing." As with the World Wide Web, only the metaphor of the loom, ancient and inclusive, captures the reach and the randomness, the infinite interconnectedness of words.... I take comfort in thinking that a modern technological medium echoes an ancient one. (pp. 7, 8, 11)

Canadian professor Eliezer Segal (2008) goes one step further. He uses the new medium to explicate the old. He created an interactive digital Image-Map of the typographic design of a typical Talmud page to serve as a port of departure on a voyage through centuries of vital dialogue. The visitor to his website can click on any portion of the Talmud page image and be linked to a description of that patch of text. He explains the contents and purposes of the text in English, also describing when and where that patch of text was composed.

In the online magazine *Computer-Mediated Communication*, Rensselaer Polytechnic Institute professor David Porush (1995) writes that the Talmud is an early example of hypertext and the Wikipedia process of multiple authorships in an interactive global community:

> A page of Talmud is structured around a single text surrounded by concentric layers of commentary and commentary on commentary. By form and content, it announces the unfinished quality of constructing knowledge and the collective construction of shared values. Even in its layout on the

> page, the Talmud suggests a kind of time and space destroying hypertextual symposium rather than an authoritative, linear, and coherent pronouncement with a beginning and ending written by a solitary author who owns the words therein.... The notion of private self, or the notion of singular origin of knowledge, pales into insignificance in the face of this talmudic-hypertextual-Internet-like vision of communally-constructed knowledge. (p. 46)

TWO GUGGENHEIM MUSEUMS

Complementing our exploration of the media ecology of the Talmud and the Internet, two major works of American architecture embody the contemporary confluence between Hebraic consciousness and the space-time structure of visual culture in the emerging digital world. The paradigm shift from the Hellenistic to the Hebraic roots of Western culture is exemplified by the two Guggenheim art museums—Frank Lloyd Wright's museum in New York and Frank Gehry's museum in Bilbao, Spain.

In his study of Hebrew thought compared to Greek, Boman explains that biblical passages concerned with the built environment always describe plans for construction without any description of the appearance of the finished structure. Noah's ark is presented as a detailed building plan. How the ark looked when it set sail is never described. The Bible has exquisitely detailed construction instructions for the Tabernacle without any word picture of the appearance of the completed structure. Indeed, the Tabernacle was made of modular parts, came apart like Lego, was set on a wagon, moved through the desert from site to site, deconstructed and reconstructed each time. Its active life was quite different from the immovable monumental marble temples on the Acropolis (Alexenberg, 2003).

A Hebraic structure of consciousness in architecture emphasizes temporal processes in which space is actively engaged by human community rather than presenting a harmoniously stable form in space. Architectural theorist Bruno Zevi (1983) compares the Hebraic and Greek attitudes toward architecture in his essay, "Hebraism and the Concept of Space-Time in Art":

> For the Greeks a building means a house-object or a temple-object. For the Jews it is the object-as-used, a living place or a gathering place. As a result, architecture taking its inspiration from Hellenic thought is based on colonnades, proportions, refined moulding, a composite vision according to which nothing may be added or eliminated, a structure defined once and for all. An architecture taking its inspiration from Hebrew thought is the diametric opposite. It is an organic architecture, fully alive, adapted to the needs of those who dwell within, capable of growth and development, free of formalistic taboo, free of symmetry, alignments, fixed relationships between filled and empty areas, free from the dogmas of perspective, in short, an architecture whose only rule, whose only order is change. (p. 165)

FRANK LLOYD WRIGHT'S GUGGENHEIM MUSEUM

In *Frank Lloyd Wright: A Study in Architectural Content*, art historian Norris Kelly Smith (1966) explained Wright's originality and genius in terms of Boman's comparison between Hebrew and Greek patterns of thought. Because Wright was well versed in the Bible as the son of a Unitarian minister, he internalized the biblical message of freeing humanity from enslavement in closed spaces and expressed this freedom in his architectural design. Smith emphasizes that Wright imbued the field of architecture—conditioned by 2000 years of Greco-Roman thought—with Hebrew thought. Wright was critical of the neo-classical rhetoric employed by American architects who studied at the Ecole des Beaux-Arts in Paris. He sought to create a new architecture to echo the biblical call inscribed on the Liberty Bell in Philadelphia: "Proclaim liberty throughout all the land unto all the inhabitants thereof" (Leviticus 25:10). He wanted American architecture to assert its cultural independence from Europe.

It is significant that the nation founded on the principles of "life, liberty, and the pursuit of happiness" became the center of the shift from the Hellenistic to the Hebraic worldview in the arts. Dynamic forms of art and architecture symbolizing life and liberty blossomed on American soil. Frank Lloyd Wright exemplified this blossoming. His spiral museum invites a living response. When I had asked my children what they remembered most from their visits to the New York Guggenheim, they enthusiastically reminisced about running down the ramp and being high up looking over the fence into the center atrium. It is not a box for rectangular pictures set in static space, but a lively place to be engaged over time. The exhibitions I saw there that worked best were shows about movement: Alexander Calder's mobiles were moving around the spiral to create a circus of color. Yaacov Agam's kinetic and dialogic art changed with the movement of the viewers in his Beyond the Visible show, and Jenny Holzer's ruby light word messages on a running electronic signboard flashed their way up the spiral ramp. The Art of the Motorcycle exhibition in 1998 was right on the mark.

The spiral is one of the major life forms in nature: from DNA, to a nautilus shell, to the growth pattern of palm fronds. It is also one of the major symbols of the Hebraic mind. Jews are called am *haSePheR*, usually translated "People of the Book." But *SePheR* is a word written in the Torah scroll itself long before the invention of codex type books. *SePheR* means spiral scroll. It is spelled SPR, the root of the word "SPiRal" in numerous languages, ancient and modern. The English words "SPiRitual" and "inSPiRation" share the SRP root from the Latin *SPiRare*, to breathe.

In Judaism, form gives shape to content. The medium is an essential part of the message. Rather than the modernist viewpoint of art as the language of forms, Judaism shares Postmodernism's emphasis on the ideas their forms might disclose (Efland et al., 1996). Weekly portions of the first five books of the Bible in the form of a Torah scroll are read in synagogue. The symbolic significance of the spiral form is so strong that if a Torah scroll is not available in synagogue, the Bible is not publicly read at all. The exact same words printed in codex book form convey the wrong message. If the divine message encoded in the Torah is trapped between two rectilinear covers, it loses its life-giving flow. Form and content join together to symbolize the essence of Jewish values. The Bible encoded in a flowing scroll form provides a clue to the nature of biblical consciousness as an open-ended, living system.

> Wright's helicoidal shaping of the Guggenheim Museum's cavity in New York represents the victory of time over space, that is, the architectural incarnation of Hebrew thought, even more significant because it was fully realized by a non-Jew. Like Schonberg's music, Wright's architecture is based on linguistic polarity, emancipated dissonance, contradiction; it is once expressionistic and rigorous; it applies Einstein's concept of 'field;' it is multidimensional; it extols space by demolishing all fetishes and taboos concerning it, by rendering it fluid, articulated so as to suit man's ways, weaving a continuum between building and landscape. In linguistic terms, this means a total restructuring of form, denial of any philosophical a priori, any repressive monumentality: action-architecture, aimed at conquering ever more vast areas of freedom for human behavior. (Zevi, 1983, p. 165)

FRANK GEHRY'S GUGGENHEIM MUSEUM

In creating the Bilbao Guggenheim, Frank Gehry moved beyond Wright to a more powerful realization of the Hebraic mindset that Boman (1960) describes as "dynamic, vigorous, passionate, and sometimes quite explosive in kind" (p. 27). Gehry told the story about his grandmother buying fish and keeping them in the bathtub to prepare gefilte fish for the Sabbath meal. He would observe the vigorous body motions of swimming fish seen from above. This gave Gehry his vocabulary for the dynamic shape of his museum. Fish are one with their environment. They must stay in constant motion in it to stay alive. Oxygen carrying water must be kept moving over their gills for them to breathe. To stop motion is to die.

Gehry's method of working is creative play with dynamic forms using digital imaging systems. He starts with spontaneous scribble sketches that become forms that he moves and reshapes in a dynamic interplay between computer-generated 3D CAD graphic models and physical models in real space.

> As he began to shape buildings from mobile parts, his sense of space transcended Cartesian notions. This special sense defies verbal definition, but it might be compared with the sensation of moving bodies in a medium akin to water. To the extent that his buildings arrest volumes in continuous motion (and transformation), time becomes their formative dimension.... He sets the bodies of his buildings in motion as a choreographer does to his or her dancers. (Dal Co, 1998, pp. 29-30)

As an integral part of education for an architecture of time and motion, Gehry takes his students on ice in full hockey gear to interact with each other and their environment in rapid movement. Like fish in water, skaters standing still on ice are unstable. Swift motion creates balance. The same concept of stability in motion is sensed in seeing the "fish-scale" titanium skin on the Bilbao museum that makes it look like a futuristic airplane. Airplanes must move through their air medium in order to fly. Stopping motion in midair leads to crashing and death. He sets the bodies of his buildings in motion as a choreographer does with dancers. "One need only observe Gehry's manner of drawing to gain an immediate impression of his way of thinking: the pen does not so much glide across the page as it dances effortlessly though a continuum of space" (Dal Co, 1998, p. 30). His studio practice appears like a performance rehearsal. His knowledge of performance art, his collaborations with artists, and his planning with artists led to spaces at the Bilbao Guggenheim uniquely suited for the presentation of alternative forms of art.

LEARNING IN DYNAMIC SPACE-TIME

When we look back at the 20th century, we see Modernism breaking down the Hellenistic dominance of Eurocentric visual culture. When we look forward to the 21st century, we begin to experience a new global visual culture in which Hebraic space-time structures (Alexenberg, 2006) resonate with ancient worldviews of India (Vidwans, 2008) and China (Huang, 2008) in dialog with the creative energies of America.

Fresh directions for art education are emerging from the redefinition of visual culture in a networked world. We are witnessing a paradigm shift from Hellenistic to Hebraic consciousness, from iconic representation to dialogic presentation, from static image to dynamic process, from passive appreciation to interactive collaboration, and from imitating the creation to imitating the Creator. It is not the Hellenistic vision of a complete and ideal nature to be copied that is the primary artistic value, but it is the continuation of the living process of creation itself that is valued in the Hebraic structure of consciousness. Hebraic space-time, like Web 2.0, suggests new pedagogical strategies that break open frameworks to create a vibrant dialog between multiple realms of discourse through active participation and multiple authorship as in my WikiArtists blog (Alexenberg, 2008b). It makes boundaries between disciplines as permeable as cell membranes that act as vital processes for active interchange of information. It makes learning an adventuresome romp through a dynamic ecosystem of interrelationships flowing between real space and cyberspace.

An early exemplar of innovative directions for education in Hebraic space-time that I initiated in the 1970s is "From Science to Art" (Alexenberg, 2005, 2008a), an interdisciplinary art education program that I developed at Tel Aviv University for Israeli junior high schools. It aimed to help learners see a diaphanous world in which fresh relationships between disparate realms of phenomena emerge. It later formed the core of the interdisciplinary graduate course "Morphodynamics: The Design of Natural Systems" (Alexenberg, 2006) that I introduced and taught at Columbia University Teachers College. In the opaque worlds experienced through linear logical thinking, phenomena are trapped within the boundaries of separate disciplines. "From Science to Art" and "Morphodynamics" were designed to develop modes of ecological thinking that perceive interrelationships between phenomena that remain invisible to logical minds by inviting continual questioning. In units on periodicity and rhythmic structures and on threshold phenomena, hands-on experiments and observations lead to such questions as: How do you link your fingerprints to op art, topographic maps, ripple tank projections, zebra stripes, supermarket bar codes, prayer shawls, *Joseph's Technicolor Dreamcoat*, and your shadow shifting in relation to the rotation of Planet Earth? What does the generation of electrostatic energy have to do with waiting for a bus, turkey chicks' feeding patterns, a flash of insight, a shock from a doorknob on a dry day, nerve physiology, biblical narratives, or the cancellation of your Facebook account for spamming?

In "From Science to Art" and "Morphodynamics," interdisciplinary explorations extend from the units on periodicity and rhythmic structures and on threshold phenomena to units on bilateral and rotational symmetries, stochastic processes and asymmetries, spiral systems and branching systems. Through experimentation coupled with artistic creation, both children and graduate art education students learned imaginative ways to unify cognitive and affective experiences, time and space concepts, aesthetic values of East and West, human activities and built environments, ancient cultures and our emerging digital visual culture. They learned to couple cognitive acts of creating relationships/connections/congruencies with concomitant affective responses of joy/amazement/elation.

REFERENCES

Alexenberg, M. (2003). Wright and Gehry: Biblical consciousness in American architecture. *Journal of Cultural Research in Art Education, 21*, 97-106.

Alexenberg, M. (2004). An interactive dialogue: Talmud and the net. *Parabola, 29(2)*, 32-36.

Alexenberg, M. (2005). From science to art: Integral structure and ecological perspective in a digital age. In M. Stokrocki (Ed.), *Interdisciplinary art education: Building bridges to connect disciplines and cultures* (pp. 170-181). Reston, VA: National Art Education Association.

Alexenberg, M. (2006). *The future of art in a digital age: From Hellenistic to Hebraic consciousness.* Bristol, UK and Chicago: Intellect Books/University of Chicago Press.

Alexenberg, M. (Ed.). (2008a). *Educating artists for the future: Learning at the intersections of art, science, technology, and culture.* Bristol, UK and Chicago: Intellect Books/University of Chicago Press.

Alexenberg, M. (2008b). WikiArtists blog. Accessed September 26, 2008, from www.wikiartists.us

Boman, T. (1960). *Hebrew thought compared with Greek.* New York and London: Norton.

Churchill, W. (1951). *History of the Second World War, vol. V.* Boston: Houghton Mifflin.

Dal Co, F., & Foster, K. (1998). *Frank O. Gehry: The complete works.* New York: Monacelli Press.

Efland, A., Freedman, K., & Stuhr, P. (1996). *Postmodernism in art education.* Reston, VA: National Art Education Association.

Huang, W. (2008). New media art as embodiment of Tao. In M. Alexenberg (Ed.), *Educating Artists for the Future: Learning at the intersections of art, science, technology and culture* (pp. 155-168). Bristol, UK and Chicago: Intellect Books/University of Chicago Press.

McLuhan, M. (1969). *Gutenberg galaxy: The making of typographic man.* New York: New American Library.

McLuhan, M. (1994). *Understanding media.* Cambridge, MA: MIT Press.

Porush, D. (1995). Ubiquitous computing vs. radical privacy. *Computer-Mediated Communication Magazine, 2*(3), 46.

Rogoff, I. (2002). Studying visual culture. In N. Mirzoeff (Ed.), *The visual culture reader* (p. 24). London and New York: Routledge.

Rosen, J. (2000). *The Talmud and the internet: A journey between worlds.* New York: Farrar, Straus and Giroux.

Segal, E. (2008). A Page from the Babylonian Talmud. University of Calgary. Accessed September 26, 2008, from www.ucalgary.ca/~elsegal/TalmudPage.html#

Smith, N. K. (1966). *Frank Lloyd Wright: A study in architectural content.* New Jersey: Prentice-Hall.

Soloveitchik, J. B. (1983). *Halakhic man* (L. Kaplan, Trans.). Philadelphia: The Jewish Publication Society.

Steinsaltz, A. (1989). *The Talmud, The Steinsaltz edition. Reference guide.* New York: Random House.

Vidwans, V. (2008). Expressing with grey cells: Indian perspectives on new media arts. In M. Alexenberg (Ed.), *Educating artists for the future: Learning at the intersections of art, science, technology and culture* (pp. 141-154). Bristol, UK and Chicago: Intellect Books/University of Chicago Press.

Zevi, B. (1983). Hebraism and the concept of space-time in art. In A. O. Dean, *Bruno Zevi on modern architecture.* New York: Rizzoli.

Fragmented Self-Portraits: How the Historical Avant-Garde Foretold Online Identity Construction / LIÁN AMARIS

Students in higher education are currently mapping and navigating online social environments that can be textual and immediate (chatrooms and instant messaging), idiosyncratic and personalizable (MySpace and Facebook) or immersive and narrative (MMORPGs or massively multi-player online role-playing games). As they move through these socially interactive environments, fluently code-switching, they participate in many kinds of mediated and mediatized identity-building scenarios which result in a multitude of specific online representations of self that are visual, textual, and interactive. The development of these identities can be mapped directly to the performing arts, wherein artists strategically deploy differing manifestations of identity to achieve a certain effect or result. However, I argue that the ontology of these identities, i.e. fragmentation, more closely resembles specific "multi-media" art movements within the historical Avant-Garde—in particular those that utilize collage and montage. This chapter describes and explores a potential pedagogical strategy for generating a critical discussion of networked social environments with the very people who inhabit them, the students, by situating the analysis of the phenomenon within the historical Avant-Garde, specifically the movement of Cubism. While contemporary new media art often utilizes methods of collage and montage, I situate my analysis of fragmentation within the historical Avant-Garde to bridge an analysis over a century, rather than a few latter decades.

Many scholars of media studies, sociology, and performance studies have approached an ontology of how the self is represented and manifested online (see Dixon, 2007; Hayles, 1999; Rheingold, 2000; Ryan, 2006; Turkle, 1995). Additionally, many extensive survey books have addressed the trajectory of engagement with new media from an art-historical perspective (see Packer & Jordan, 2002;

Dixon, 2007; Berghaus, 2005). However, Peter Bürger's (1984) explication of montage in his book *Theory of the Avant-Garde* offers a compelling rhetorical context for inquiry into manifestations of self in online social environments and provides an excellent pedagogical opportunity for students to interrogate their own experiences within online social spaces. Bürger addresses the use of montage within fine art, literature and film, but focuses on the appearance of montage within Cubism, "that movement in modern painting which most consciously destroyed the representational system that had prevailed since the Renaissance" (p. 73). While Bürger's *Theory of the Avant-Garde* has been criticized for its limitations as an exhaustive primer on a formulation of the Avant-Garde, including its shortsightedness with regards to technology (see Berghaus, 2005), Bürger's assertion that "montage presupposes the fragmentation of reality" (p. 73) is my point of analytical departure.

Within the classroom, a rhetorical utilization of Bürger functions as a lens through which to locate a reading of online identity construction, thereby provoking critical perspectives on contemporary online social phenomena while at the same time informing a theoretical understanding of the visual Avant-Garde. New media art which utilizes fragmentation is pervasive in contemporary art, and it is addressed extensively in the aforementioned media/techno-art history books; my use of Bürger, however, allows for a bridge between contemporary social scenarios and an historical art movement that predates what Steve Dixon (2007) calls "works where computer technologies play a key role rather than a subsidiary one in content, techniques, aesthetics, or delivery forms" (p. 3). Therefore it is my argument that Bürger (first written in 1974) looks backward to analyze Cubism and forward to historicize identity formation in online social spaces.

Though the boundaries between online social spaces are continuously blurring, loose distinctions could be made between spaces that prioritize text versus image, immediacy versus immersion, personalizability versus narrative, and broadcast versus interactivity, requiring, as Katherine Hayles (1999) states in *How We Became Posthuman*, "the interplay between codes and the articulation of individual subjectivity with data" (p. 40). In *Avatars of Story*, Marie-Laure Ryan (2006) reveals the collaged nature of cyberspace when she suggests, "The affordances of language, pictures, and music complement each other, and when they are used together in multichannel media, each of them builds a different facet of the total imaginative experience" (p. 20). So when a person is able to move between all these spaces—a text-based chatroom, a video repository, instant messaging, perpetual game playing, friend-connecting sites, maintaining a blog, visiting news sites, and engaging in comment forums within any of these contexts—the presentations of self are often multifarious and distinct from one another, but are facets of a total experience. According to Bürger, "In the avant-gardiste work... the individual elements have a much higher degree of autonomy and can therefore also be read and interpreted individually or in groups without its being necessary to grasp the work as a whole" (p. 72). Insofar as the avant-gardiste work can be apprehended by its constituent parts as well as a whole, the "individual elements" (p. 72) of a person's online identity can be understood independently or holistically. In Copeland's (2002) use of collage to analyze the performances of Merce Cunningham, he suggested, "the most radical function of collage [is] its capacity for undermining the distinction between foreground/background, inside/outside" (p. 12) and it is within this context that I look to collage for my analytical lens; just as Copeland has applied the "aesthetics of collage" to performance, and performance has been a seminal rubric for analyzing online identity construction, I transitively analyze online identity construction through the lens of Cubism, and more specifically, collage. The building of an online self utilizes a similar method as Cubist works do to reveal a fragmented whole from a multiple of perspectives—similar to what Sherry Turkle (1995) calls building "a self by cycling through many selves" (p. 178). Therefore, using Bürger's "fragmentation of reality" as a trope, building just one individual social networking page closely parallels creating a Cubist painting or a collage, and the engagement of all these spaces creates a modern museum of the self. These concepts can be strategically paired for critical discussion in an undergraduate classroom in the following ways.

To study the art-historical Avant-Garde, Peter Bürger's (1984) *Theory of the Avant-Garde* is used as a central text. The work is an arguably post-graduate theoretical critique which posits the notion of an "institution of art... (establishing) a framework within which a work of art is both produced and received" (back cover). Rather than investigation and discussion of Bürger's theories through direct example and counter-example drawn from the art-historical canon, Bürger's ideas can be clarified by drawing parallels between his notions of the Avant-Garde and contemporary social practices of the students in the class. As an example, during a class discussion on montage, Bürger's ideas are easily explicated when the students are asked to consider their own online identities.

Facebook, one of the most popular online social networking tools, developed by two students from Harvard University in 2004, allows participants to easily create and modify a "page" that represents their online social identity. A person's Facebook page can be extremely simple, containing the bare facts of their identity (name, gender, birthday, etc.) or, more commonly, can be elaborated ad infinitum. The tools available for creating one's page exist in a variety of modes, as Ryan (2006) articulated in her discussion of virtual spaces and multichannel media. Built-in schemes for textual description (interests, activities, favorite music, etc.) sit easily alongside visual representations (photographs, graphs, maps, etc.), as well as tools for communication, networking, and narrative construction ("tagging" photographs, leaving public messages, or playing games). Idiosyncratic "applications" can be also be added allowing for an extremely wide range of tools for people to express themselves.

Elucidating Facebook as a tool for creating identity montage allowed students to engage with Bürger using a scenario with which they were familiar and also provided an opportunity for theoretical interrogation of Facebook. I propose that this method allows for the communication of complex points about Cubism, based on the assertion that many of the perceptual and conceptual precepts behind the movement have resonant cultural currency today. As a result, literary theory can be used within interdisciplinary pedagogy to describe an art movement as viewed backwards from a contemporary cultural meme.

Looking at Bürger's (1984) text, we see a number of his key points regarding montage within the Avant-Garde as applicable to the analysis of online social spaces and vice versa. For example:

> ...we invariably find a contrast between two techniques: the 'illusionism' of the reality fragments that have been glued on the canvas... and the 'abstraction' of cubist technique in which the portrayed objects are rendered. (p. 73)

Here, Bürger is referring to Georges Braque and Pablo Picasso, distinguishing between two key arts practices of historical Cubism: the physical montage (which combines physical objects—wallpaper, newspaper, oilcloth, etc—and paint on a canvas) and the rendered painting (which abstracts perspective through just paint on canvas), respectively. As a parallel, Facebook has two very distinct modes of identity authoring; one is along a classically Cubist-rendered model, where identity is defined from a multiplicity of angles: favorite music, favorite books, social relationships, political views, etc. Each of these elements could be seen as paint on a canvas, informing simultaneous perspectives on the individual—but they are all read as "paint" due to their epistemological similarities. The second model is primarily accessed through applications within the program that allow for a combination of illusion with reality: Facebook users have access to a number of imaginary or avatar-style modes of self-representation; they can be ninjas, vampires, werewolves, 1950s pin-up models, or even French philosophers. The use of these applications can be read as illusory elements combined with real, factual information, much as paint is combined with oilcloth in Picasso's *Still Life with Chair Caning*. The combination of fictive identities grafted onto a page that also contains concrete biographical information allows for kind of montage that specifically reflects Bürger's distinction in the quote above. Furthermore, the Cubist painting can be analyzed as Turkle (1995) analyzes the fragmented online self: "The essence of this self is not unitary, nor are its parts stable entities. It is easy to cycle through its aspects and these are themselves changing through constant communication with each other" (p. 261). As the illusory is combined with the real in a Cubist collage, the constituent parts inform our understanding of the whole and vice versa.

Additionally, Bürger (1984) addresses Adorno's notation of the negation of synthesis as a compositional principle; in other words, combining formally irreconcilable elements as a means of formal construction:

> On the production-aesthetic side, negation of synthesis refers to what was called rejection of reconciliation on the side of the aesthetic affect. If to check Adorno's statements, one looks again at the collages of the cubists, one can see that although they allow one to discover a principle of construction, they do not show a synthesis, in the sense of a unity of meaning... (p. 79)

In the world of Facebook, this "principle of construction" is paramount in how users construct their identities: A user can represent themselves simultaneously as, for example, both a pirate and a zombie, without any apparent conflict. In fact, these identities co-exist to create a multi-faceted identity that allows a user to represent her/himself using a variety of metaphorical media akin to collage; as Copeland (2002) suggests, "Collage in a sense, is always divided against itself. One's attention, one's allegiances are drawn in multiple, often conflicting directions" (p. 26).

Bürger (1984) posits that the requirement for contextual agreement is a false one when dealing with works of montage, and that the component parts of the work must be dealt with in relation to one another to gain an understanding of the complete work. He argues:

> A critical hermeneutics [of the Avant-Garde] will replace the theorem of the necessary agreement of parts and whole by investigating the contradiction between the various layers and only then infer the meaning of the whole. (p. 82)

When looking at online identity construction, the same axiom applies: Facebook users are allowed (and even expected) to create pages where portions of their represented identities are diffuse, paradoxical, and even completely in opposition to one another—but it is through these contradictions that the idiosyncratic representation of self is imparted and inferred.

The themes outlined above address an interdisciplinary pedagogical approach for understanding digital visual culture within the context of art history. The notion of fragmentation is present in contemporary society and manifests specifically in online social spaces. Fragmentation as a trope can be traced to cultural antecedents present in the historical Avant-Garde, specifically within Cubism and its complementary use of montage. Arguably, the value of art history is to convey the lasting impact artistic movements have had on contemporary culture. Strategic implementation of Peter Bürger's *Theory of the Avant-Garde* within an interdisciplinary arts pedagogy provides a bridge between critical interrogation of contemporary social practice and a theoretical foundation in art criticism.

REFERENCES

Berghaus, G. (2005). *Avant-garde performance: Live events and electronic technologies.* New York: Palgrave Macmillan.

Bürger, P. (1984). *Theory of the avant-garde* (M. Shaw, Trans.). Minneapolis: University of Minnesota Press.

Copeland, R. (2002). Merce Cunningham and the aesthetic of collage. *TDR: The Drama Review, 4*(1), 11-28.

Dixon, S. (2007). *Digital performance.* Cambridge, MA: MIT Press.

Hayles, K. N. (1999). *How we became posthuman: Virtual bodies in cybernetics, literature, and informatics.* Chicago: University of Chicago Press.

Packer, R., & Jordan, K. (2002). *Multimedia: From Wagner to Virtual Reality.* New York: W.W. Norton & Company.

Rheingold, H. (2000). *The virtual community: Homesteading on the electronic frontier.* Cambridge, MA: MIT Press.

Ryan, M. (2006). *Avatars of story.* Minneapolis: University of Minnesota Press.

Turkle, S. (1995). *Life on the screen: Identity in the age of the Internet.* New York: Simon & Schuster.

From Storyspace to PowerPoint: Searching for an (In)Adequate Space to Make a Point / KEVIN TAVIN

TELLING MY STORY(SPACES)

From the fall of 1996 to the spring of 1999, I taught a required course, Art Education 303: Visual Arts in the Elementary School, to elementary education majors at Penn State University at the University Park campus. Each semester I was responsible for two sections of the course. During the fall of 1997, I shifted the focus of the course (which I inherited) from Discipline-Based Art Education (DBAE), where art from the museum realm provided the content and issues, toward a more critical pedagogical practice, where visual culture informed the content and issues of the curriculum. I revised my pedagogical approach based on "new" discourses and technologies that I had learned in my own graduate coursework. These new discourses included concepts from critical pedagogy, visual culture, and hypertext theory, and the new technologies included the software Storyspace.

To help move the class beyond DBAE, I began including readings and discussions on popular and visual culture.[1] Similar to Kincheloe (1993), I believed popular and other forms of visual culture "should be made problematic to our students in a way that causes them to assess the impact of information and information sources in their lives... teacher education programs must prepare teachers for the role of media analyst" (p. 91). I believed that this analysis was appropriate for elementary school, where young students could begin to study where they get "their information and their opinions about the world" (p. 91). In other words, informed by critical pedagogy, I wanted my students to confront the ways particular forms of visual culture help shape consciousness. Following McLaren's (1991) suggestions, I wanted future elementary educators to understand how "subjectivities, dreams, desires, and needs of students are forged by media [and] how the subjectivities of students [are] constituted by the effects of representations which penetrate the level of the body" (p. 165).

I included articles that deconstructed various forms of popular culture, including advertisements, animated films, television programs, and toys. I included time in the course schedule for seminars on the connection between the interpretation of visual culture and curricular practices for elementary education. To help facilitate a discussion on critical connectivity, I attempted to get students to

> begin to see popular culture texts as hypertexts... to encourage the reader to become also an author.... As a hypertext, popular culture changes and shifts in meaning as the reader/viewer of these texts reads, plays, manipulates, resists, and/or accepts them without monopolizing the meaning. The reader becomes a cultural critic/author and the purpose of the cultural critic/author is no longer to 'master' the meaning of a text like modernist literary and cultural critics assume. Instead the purpose becomes to create meaning from a text. (Weaver & Daspit, 1999, p. xxiv)

Hypertextuality, as a concept rather than a particular software program, embodies notions of intertextuality by "bringing texts closer together and blurring the boundaries between them" (Landow & Delany, 1991, p. 11). Hypertextuality may create new conditions for intertextual meaning-making by situating texts within a field of other texts. Through hypertextuality, "knowledge happens in a context of other knowledge... [where] the reader is aware of the context of the knowledge in hand—that is, how knowledge relates and interrelates to other knowledge surrounding it" (Anderson, 1994, p. 109). In this case of interpreting popular and visual culture, hypertextuality helps raise critical consciousness by exposing how prior knowledges help shape and name our experience of the world through the process of intertextuality. After much discussion of the possibility of popular and visual culture as hypertexts, and after having students view my own hypertextual examples using Storyspace software, I offered students in the class a choice of using the same software program to construct their final course project or writing hard-copy curricula (Tavin, 2002, 2003a).

In 1997 Storyspace was a new hypertextual computer program that allowed a writer and reader to link together a multitude of images and written texts. Storyspace seemed to offer students the ideal features relevant to a critical exploration of visual culture as part of their final project:

> Storyspace allows the author to set up the hypertext so that as the reader moves from space to space, the windows remain open unless purposely closed by the reader. The various texts are thus juxtaposed or displayed side by side... each window may contain a number of texts. Multiple windows, presented sequentially and/or simultaneously, may thus contain any combination of print text and digitized video, audio, and visual images. Windows may also be created so that sounds begin to play as they open and sized so that the visual images and words may be displayed as well. (Hammett, 1999, pp. 209-210)

I was hopeful that the use of Storyspace would help raise students' critical consciousness through the process of intertextuality. In this sense, I wanted the students to be both readers and writers of their world and, through Storyspace, allow them to revisit their own knowledge and expand upon it. I believed that this might engage a shift in thinking, one that views the inter-relatedeness of things through a more connectionist ontology. In other words, the shift, I hoped, might facilitate recognition and understanding of multiple forms of knowledge and discourse: a process that proponents of critical pedagogy and visual culture seem to embrace (Darder, et al., 2003; Elkins, 2003; Giroux, 1992; Sturken & Cartwright, 2001). I also believed that Storyspace had the potential to disrupt the discourse of authority by enabling students to manage nodes of information and challenge positivist rationality and linearity by creating visual manifestations of situated knowledges. In short, Storyspace suggested for me a type of empowerment through, and democratization of pedagogy between, the students in my class and their potentiality within their future classroom settings.

Unfortunately, only 2 out of 41 students enrolled in the course in 1997 completed a hypertext for their final project using Storyspace.[2] The two students that chose to construct a hypertext spent a significant amount of time researching materials for their final projects—searching through newspapers, magazines, books, journals, the Internet, videos, artworks, and other forms of documentation. Their research yielded vital information on their respective topics and allowed them to make meaningful intertextual connections. Each student spent hundreds of hours constructing and reconstructing his hypertexts (Tavin, 2003a).

One of the students used his hypertextual experience to take a position on Nike's global politics and labor practices in ways not depicted by the mass media or corporate-dominated society (see Figure 1). In his Web, he used visible forms

FIGURE 1:
We Are Nike *Screenshot—Nike Advertisements Targeted Toward Women. (1997)*

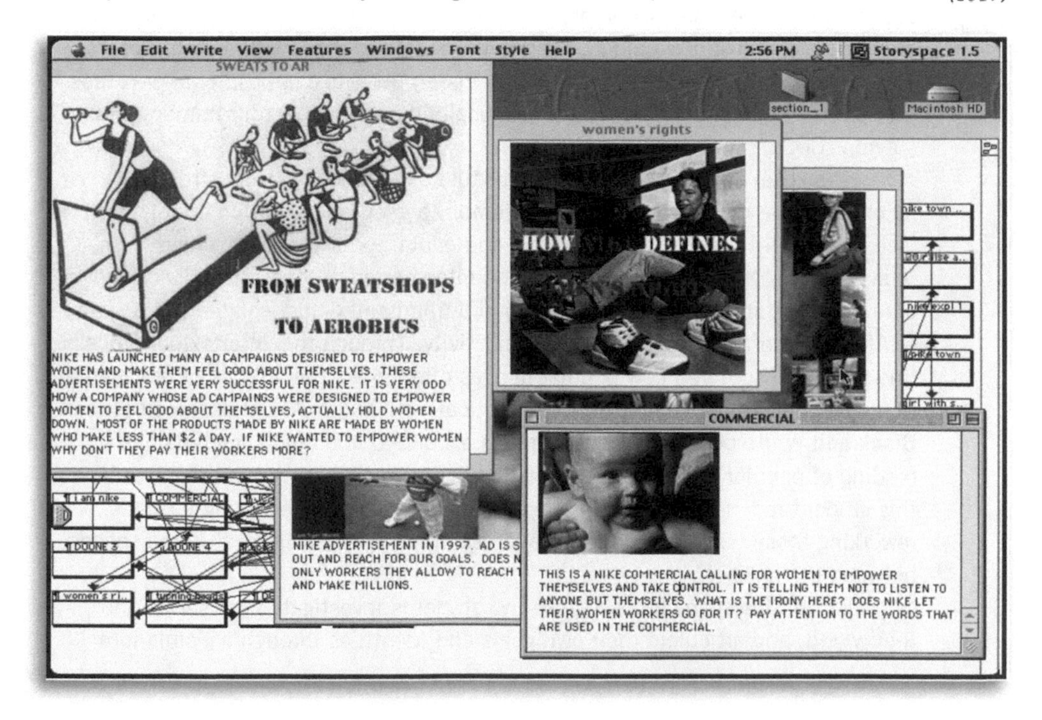

FIGURE 2: *Marketing Mirages Screenshot: Levi's Advertisement, Dancing Topsy, Aunt Jemima, and* Birth of a Nation. *(1997)*

of intertextuality to interrogate the horrendous working conditions in Nike's overseas factories. He also used intertextuality to challenge the racist underpinnings of Nike's use of Third World labor and have readers identify with female workers. This student saw hypertextuality as a way to help mobilize oppositional practices that demand global corporate social responsibility and respect for human rights (Tavin, 2003a).

The other student used his hypertextual experience to deconstruct and recontextualize racial, ethnic, and gendered representations within popular culture (see Figure 2). He connected historical and contemporary images, music, film, television programs, and written text. The intersection of these "texts" allowed for a new form of analysis that moved beyond a fragmented and isolated perception of African American and Caucasian subjectivity. Through this intertextual process, this student discovered how popular images often erase the politics of representation by whitewashing complex social, political, and cultural relationships between Black and White people. The student also expanded and challenged his initial reading of popular culture and questioned his own subjectivity. In other words, this student redefined his personal notion of whiteness by searching for texts, reworking those texts, linking texts, and searching for meaning within the spaces between the links.

While Storyspace helped these two students investigate themselves and their world, and articulate their own goals and identities through a visible form of intertextuality, it is clearly problematic that 39 students chose not to use Storyspace but instead created more linear hard-copy curricula. Was it because of the technology itself? Was it because of the amount of time needed to create the hypertext document? Was it just too much to ask considering all the issues the students faced in that semester? On one level I believe that a majority of the students during that semester simply did not want to invest themselves in hundreds of hours learning a new software program to create a hypertext, especially when the conceptual framework of the course itself, including theories of hypertextuality (as differentiated from the hypertext software programs), was new.

On a different level, I believe there was a need for comfort and familiarity. That is, through the writing of a final project that connected to real-life issues and popular cultural texts most students were already risking their identities and subjectivities as preservice elementary teachers and perhaps needed something to ground their new textual experiences. It was one thing to ask students to write out their ideas for a unit of study for me; it is quite another issue to ask them to visually expose their own thinking and vulnerabilities before all others. While all writing is risky, I believe Storyspace (as a digital way to visually produce hypertextual work) may have been perceived as a threat to the safe bounds of linear text by forcing, exposing, and blurring the lines between "the personal space from the real and the imaginary [and] the internal and external realms of experience" (Landow & Delany, 1991, p. 8). Ten years later, I decided to offer a more familiar, perhaps "safer" hypertext software program for preservice art educators for their final projects. I hoped to provide a more adequate space for students to mark and map their "points" within and through popular visual culture.

MISSING THE (POWER)POINTS

In Spring 2007, I taught a required course for pre-art education majors at The Ohio State University (OSU). In the course, Art Education 601: Conceptual Process for Visual Culture as Curricula, students explored different symbolic representations as legitimate content for study while exploring themselves as networked and mediated subjects. After reading about visual culture pedagogy and watching films on various representations and theories of representation, students constructed a hypertextual document using PowerPoint as their final project. I chose PowerPoint primarily because of the familiarity with the software, ease of use, and the fact that the newer versions of Storyspace were difficult to use and unavailable on OSU computers.

Even though I required a different software program than my preservice elementary students 10 years earlier, the goal of the final project in 2007 was similar: to link different visual sites of personal, pedagogical, and political investment where students become absorbed into visual culture. In this sense, I wanted students to use a familiar tool, PowerPoint, in an unfamiliar way, to mark points on their effective "mattering map" (Grossberg, 1992) and provide possible points of contact for future curricula. Building on the work of Taylor and Carpenter (2002), some of the goals for the final project included:

- Make visible the relationships you find between forms of visual culture (including artwork) and other texts, subject areas, and bodies of knowledge.
- Make visible how your hypertext is based on your own frames of reference and sets of knowledge.
- Ask questions and offer uncertainty about the meaning of visual culture.
- Provoke inventive ways of thinking and knowing through your linking.
- Support a connective approach to multiple and varied aspects of everyday life.
- Help the reader understand your voice(s) and subjectivity in the hypertext.

Students were encouraged to actively affirm their own stories, histories, and subjectivities by adding, modifying, and linking texts through PowerPoint that exposed, clarified, and challenged multiple registers of power. I believe that many of the topics that students chose for their hypertext were critical, meaningful, and relevant to their own identity as a young person living in a visual culture. Topics included Tattooing and Body Modification in the US, Dreams of the "American Girl," the Visual and Cultural Construction of Love, Points of Identity and Memory in and through Popular Films, and Mapping out a Road Trip through Death.

Despite these topics, almost all the students used PowerPoint as a presentation tool rather than toward the goals of a hypertext program (embodying the concepts of hypertextuality). In other words, even though students linked together different slides within the entire document, and embedded multiple links within any given slide (so one could jump between slides), most of the final products resembled a collection of images and texts encrypted in "presentation mode." The PowerPoint program itself had in large part predetermined the outcome of the final project. As Eisenhauer (2006) reminds us, PowerPoint represents a discursive shift toward "corporate vision" that embodies a "corporate visual epistemology of persuasion, management, and entertainment.... Goals of persuasion dominate those of discovery and illustration" (pp. 207-208). When my students used Powerpoint, they were more likely caught up in the congeries of PowerPoint epistemology, where the software is consciously understood as just another tool in the marketplace of visual culture and unconscious represents a cognitive style (Tufte, 2003). This style is "deeply hierarchical, nested, highly structured, relentlessly sequential, one-short-line-at-a-time [through its] preoccupation with format not content" (Tufte, 2003, p. 4). In other words, the knowledge of PowerPoint was for many students internalized as a common sense approach to "presenting information" in a linear format, a neat method of analysis, a process of seeing, and a way of knowing. John Dewey understood this form of hegemony well before the production of software programs:

> We rarely recognize the extent in which our conscious estimates what is worthwhile and what is not are due to standards of which we are not conscious at all. But in general it may be said that the things we take for granted without inquiry or reflection are just the things which determine our conscious thinking and decide our conclusions. (Dewey, as cited in Ross, Cornett, & McCutcheon, 1992, p. 16)

It was clear that values and standard practices of PowerPoint were not easily unlearned. I did not anticipate the depth of preconditioning that the software brought to the class. In addition, similar to the experience at Penn State, many of the preservice art educators in my course came already with a set of expectations, attitudes, and beliefs about curricula entrenched in modernist thinking. It is no easy task to move from the mind-set of linear and progressive K-12 curriculum development to intertextual approaches that require and embody knowledge construction as a way to raise "difficult questions about purpose, identity construction, and the making of culture" (Carlson, 1992, p. 245). PowerPoint seemed to fit neatly within the modernist paradigm of curriculum development which allows information to be presented as fun and factual. As Eisenhauer (2006) points out "The Microsoft Corporation emphasizes the potential for this software to entertain.... Learning creatively with custom animations turns even the most difficult subject into something interesting and fun"'(p. 209).

CONCLUSIONS

One of the main goals for using Storyspace in 1997 was to help cultivate and maintain the integrity of individual student voices through writing spaces, while collectively challenging existing views of the world through reading spaces. I chose Storyspace because

> readers see and access links in whatever order they choose as well as create their own paths and add information throughout the Web. In doing so, readers change the structure of the original web, making it more than it was before they encountered it.... New ideas may be discovered or even provoked through this hypertextual process of inventively linking resulting in an authentic intertextual reading. (Taylor & Carpenter, 2002, p. 7)

Ten years later, in a preservice art education course, instead of Storyspace I chose to utilize PowerPoint as way of making hypertextual links visible with my students. The goal of using PowerPoint was to find an accessible and familiar program to link different visual sites of personal and political investment. Because so few preservice elementary education students chose to use Storyspace in 1997, I thought PowerPoint would be less intimidating.

In both cases, my attempt to employ within classroom situations different forms of hypertext software—computer programs or applications that use information technology to link and connect electronic blocks of text, lexias, documents, images, sounds, and video—was problematic, perhaps for both similar and different reasons. Storyspace and PowerPoint were inadequate tools for self-reflexive, dialectic thinking about, and through, visual culture and visuality. Storyspace was too difficult and threatening for many of the preservice elementary education students in 1997 and PowerPoint was perhaps too easy, reinforcing an unconscious form of representational hegemony and a "cognitive style" (Tufte, 2003).

Perhaps instead of focusing on one particular software program, both groups could have chosen their own hypertextual digital application or non-digital materials to construct an intertextual document. In other words, perhaps instead of dictating the software program, students in both cases could have chosen a digital or non-digital process toward the goal of taking "the risk of making connections, drawing lines, mapping articulations, between different domains, discourses and practices, to see what will work, both theoretically and politically" (Grossberg, 1994, p. 18). Herrmann (2006) provides an excellent example of using "low technology hypertext" with preservice teachers to investigate popular culture. Exploring the television show *The Swan*, Herrmann had her students use "chalkboard, printed images, tape, and string" (p. 146).

With my students, more time was needed to explore how hypertext can be less intimidating and more than just software. For both groups, the concepts from hypertext theory, when aligned with theories of intertextuality, should have been explored beyond the limits of technological determinism, which I may have unfortunately reproduced by positioning hypertext within a narrow range of products (Storyspace in 1997 and PowerPoint in 2007). For the later group of students, building on Eisenhuer's (2006) work on the corporate discourses of visual projection, I might have situated Powerpoint "within a larger history of projection technology and [helped students understand that] such technologies' meanings are discursively constituted through cultural understandings of vision, knowledge, and subjectivity" (p. 211). I could have shared the work of David Byrne (2003), whose EEEI project consists of artwork made in PowerPoint in part to disrupt commonsense ideas about the program. In addition, I might have addressed the use of blogs, Wikis, and social networking sites such as Facebook and MySpace and raised questions about their embodiment of hypertextual concepts. As it stands, my discussion and use of hypertext in the classroom from one end of the decade to the next, while successful in many ways, may have missed the point—that hypertext should offer all students a temporary point of attachment where they critically connect their subject positions to "images selected from the past, present and future" (Landow & Delany, 1991, p. 8) without ever having to stand still.

REFERENCES

Anderson, G. (1994). Dimensions, context, and freedom: The library in the social creation of knowledge. In E. Barrett (Ed.), *Sociomedia: Multimedia, hypermedia, and the social construction of knowledge* (pp. 107-124). Cambridge, MA: The MIT Press.

Browne, R. (1987). Popular culture: Medicine for illiteracy and associated ills. *Journal of Popular Culture, 2*(3), 1-5.

Byrne, D. (2003). *E.E.E.I. (Envisioning emotional epistemological information).* New York: Steidl/Pace/MacGill Gallery.

Carlson, D. (1992). *Teachers and crisis: Urban school reform and teachers' work culture.* New York: Routledge.

Darder, A., Baltodano, M., & Torres, R. D. (Eds.). (2003). *The critical pedagogy reader.* New York: Routledge.

Eisenhauer, J. (2006). Next slide please: The magical, scientific, and corporate discourses of visual projection technologies. *Studies in Art Education, 47*(3), 198-214.

Elkins, J. (2003). *Visual studies: A skeptical introduction.* New York: Routledge.

Giroux, H. (1992). *Border crossings: Cultural workers and the politics of education.* New York: Routledge.

Grossberg, L. (1994). Introduction: Bringin' it all back home—Pedagogy and cultural studies. In H. Giroux & P. McLaren (Eds.), *Between borders: Pedagogy and the politics of cultural studies* (pp. 1-25). New York: Routledge.

Grossberg, L. (1992). *We gotta get out of this place: Popular conservatism and postmodern culture.* New York: Routledge.

Hammett, R. (1999). Intermediality, hypermedia, and critical media literacy. In L. Semali & A. Pailliotet (Eds.), *Intermediality* (pp. 207-223). Boulder, CO: Westview.

Herrmann, R. (2006). In the classroom with ducks, swans, and elementary education majors. In P. Duncum (Ed.), *Visual culture in the art class: Case studies* (pp. 142-150). Reston, VA: National Art Education Association.

Kincheloe, J. (1993). *Toward a critical politics of teacher thinking: Mapping the postmodern.* Westport, CT: Bergin & Garvey.

Landow, G. & Delany, P. (1991). Hypertext, hypermedia and literary studies: The state of art. In P. Delany & G. Landow (Eds.), *Hypermedia and literary studies* (pp. 3-50). Cambridge, MA: The MIT Press.

McLaren, P. (1991). Schooling and the postmodern body: Critical pedagogy and politics of enfleshment. In H. Giroux (Ed.), *Postmodernism, feminism, and cultural politics: Redrawing educational boundaries* (pp. 144-173). Albany, NY: State University of New York Press.

Ross, E., Cornett, J., & McCutcheon, G. (Eds.). (1992). *Teacher personal theorizing and research on curriculum and teaching.* Albany, NY: State University of New York Press.

Sturken, M., & Cartwright, L. (2001). *Practices of looking: An introduction to visual culture.* Oxford, UK: Oxford University Press.

Tavin, K. (2002). Engaging advertisements: Looking for meaning in and through art education. *Visual Arts Research, 28*(2), 38-47.

Tavin, K. (2003a). A critical pedagogy of visual culture as art education: Toward a performative inter/hypertextual practice (Doctoral dissertation, Pennsylvania State University, 2003). UMI Microform No. 3097054.

Tavin, K. (2003b). Wrestling with angels, searching for ghosts: Toward a critical pedagogy of visual culture. *Studies in Art Education, 44*(3), 197-213.

Tavin, K. (2005a). Hauntological shifts: Fear and loathing of popular (visual) culture. *Studies in Art Education, 46*(2), 101-117.

Tavin, K. (2005b). Opening re-marks: Critical antecedents of visual culture in art education. *Studies in Art Education, 47*(1), 5-22.

Taylor, P., & Carpenter, S. (2002). Inventively linking: Teaching and learning with computer hypertext. *Art Education, 55*(4), 6-12.

Tufte, E. (2003). *The cognitive style of PowerPoint.* Cheshire, CT: Graphics Press.

Weaver, J., & Daspit, T. (1999). Critical pedagogy, popular culture, and the creation of meaning. In T. Daspit & J. Weaver (Eds.), *Popular culture and critical pedagogy: Reading, constructing, connecting* (pp. xii-xxxiii). New York: Garland.

ENDNOTES

1 Popular culture and visual culture are not one a the same, and art educators should be careful not to conflate the two. Although both terms are difficult to define, popular culture refers to the "daily, vernacular, common, cultural environment around us all... the television we watch, the movies we see, the fast food, or slow food, we eat, the clothes we wear" (Browne, 1987, p. 2). On the other hand, visual culture is both a field of study and an inclusive register of images and objects well beyond the popular (Tavin, 2003b). See Tavin (2005a, 2005b) for further clarification on the history and politics of popular and visual culture in art education.

2 Indeed, only two additional students (four in all) created hypertexts during the entire 3 years that I taught Art Education 303.

Digital Journals: The Past, Present, and Future of Electronic Portfolios for Visual Culture Learners / SHEI-CHAU WANG

The rapid development of computer technology and the Internet has changed the way people look at the world. Such a change has become the source of conflicts between new and old social values. Given a whole new visual experience, the outcomes of computer technology have also provided art educators with revolutionary pedagogical ideas (Colman, 2004; Delacruz, 2004; Keifer-Boyd, 1997; Lai & Ball, 2004; Marschalek, 2002). Through computerized media, massive amounts of information—texts, sounds, pictures, images, and all kinds of combinations—have been disseminated more promptly than before. New concepts of aesthetics resulting from such new dimensions of visual stimuli have also challenged art educators (T. Chang, 2003; Freedman, 2003; Mirzoeff, 1999). Therefore, how to embrace this rapid change and face the challenge has become a major concern for art educators.

Art education should reflect students' daily life, their social and cultural values, and their immediate visual environment. Materials to be used in art education, therefore, should use as many visual objects from such an environment as possible, for example, crafts and art products or installations and images using traditional media and computer technology (Walker & Chaplin, 1997). Sharing the same format, meaning, function, and purpose of traditional art education, the new scope of visual art learning also meets the requirements and values of postmodern education. Educators are responsible for bringing a holistic world view into the classroom (Duncum, 1999; Freedman, 2003; Mirzoeff, 1999).

Take assessment as an example. Traditionally, the purpose of assessment in art education is to examine the process and outcomes of students' learning to give instructors better ideas about how to modify their instruction (Gruber & Hobbs, 2002). Most recently, art educators have proposed a new perspective on quality assessment through focusing on the learning process itself, i.e., students' reactions to and comprehension of the arts and their social and cultural values (Boughton, 2004b; Gruber & Hobbs, 2002; Shepard, 2000). Thus, learners' development in each step becomes an important clue for assessment (Beattie, 1997).

Because the visual products of art education are qualitative, it is nearly impossible to use any one assessment tool to obtain a holistic view of students' learning. To efficiently record students' development in art education, researchers suggest that art teachers employ the portfolio approach to assess students in a visual art learning environment (Blaikie & Schönau, 2003; Boughton, 2004b; C. Chang, 2003; Chung, 2004). Thus, a high quality portfolio not only represents students' efforts and accomplishment but also records students' development at their own pace (Alter & Spandel, 1992; Danielson & Abrutyn, 1997).

Born in the late 1980s, contemporary college students grew up in an environment filled with television, computers, the Internet, and various electronic devices that have enormously changed visual and textual information. To communicate with these students, educators must acquaint themselves with electronic products. Marschalek (2004) recommends that art educators increase the flexibility of space for digitized activities to establish multidimensional teaching and learning platforms for students to develop the ability to create, appreciate, think, and write via computers. Moreover, research has shown that the development of technology and advanced devices has strongly motivated the students to learn art (e.g., Boughton & Wang, 2002; Dorn, Madeja, & Sabol, 2004; Freedman, 2003; Wang, 2004). The researchers also reported that they introduced high technology devices into the curriculum to make students' learning more efficient and engaging. Although the digitized environment has brought in a new trend of learning in art education, the question to be asked here is: To what extent are art educators capable of employing the multifunctional, highly efficient, and virtual characteristics of high-tech products to better their teaching and learning?

Several studies show that more and more art educators have started to utilize computer devices to assess students' development in artmaking and to advocate e-portfolios (Boughton, 2004a; Boughton & Wang, 2002; Dorn, Madeja, & Sabol, 2004; Keefe et al., 2002). An e-portfolio, an electronic version of the traditional portfolio, usually includes files of digital texts, pictures, sounds, and various types of images.

The early development of digitized databases in art education was structured on platforms such as Microsoft PowerPoint and Microsoft Access. However, the limited file sizes in these two interfaces have eventually made saving images nearly impossible. Another option that incorporates HTML language to create webpages to which several files are linked soon replaced PowerPoint and Access (Dorn, Madeja, & Sabol, 2004). Such a portfolio allows students to collect and store their works more efficiently. The following summarizes the benefits of using e-portfolios. They can (1) manage and store artworks, (2) access and distribute files, (3) revise the contents of the portfolio, (4) present multimedia or interactive works, (5) establish comprehensive knowledge networks, and (6) enhance students' computer skills (Morris, 2001; Niguidula, 1993).

EXPERIMENTS WITH E-PORTFOLIOS AT THE COLLEGE LEVEL

The NIU Case Study

During 2000-01, I designed a template for the Northern Illinois University (NIU) e-portfolio model to assess college art students in Basic Drawing I (Dorn, Madeja, and Sabol, 2004, pp. 162-166). Other than providing criteria for designing e-portfolios, I experimented with several Microsoft Office programs and summarized the following principles for establishing an e-portfolio:

- The e-portfolio should be student-centered; it should have a framework enabling each student to access one of these common electronic platforms to create and continuously improve a personal portfolio.
- The e-portfolio should have the capacity to accommodate various forms of electronic multimedia: static text and graphic displays, databases, audio bytes, video clips, etc.
- The e-portfolio should be easily portable or transferable to other electronic systems or intranets via storage devices or electronic transfer technologies.
- The e-portfolio should facilitate the easy access, storage, display and retrieval, and deletion of any/all information and material to be included.
- The e-portfolio should have a simple user interface, easily accessed and viewed by all students, instructors, and prospective evaluators without specific directions or lessons.

The first e-portfolio model (Fall 2000) was created via Microsoft PowerPoint 98 because of its accessibility to students. After a semester, the students in Basic Drawing I were asked to compile their best works into PowerPoint presentations. The students enjoyed the process of editing/designing their e-portfolios. However, due to the limits of computer hardware and software in 2000, we encountered several challenges. For instance, neither floppy disks nor zip disks were large enough to save the increasing file size when many images were added in PowerPoint. Moreover, it was difficult for students to generate their own presentation because they were limited by PowerPoint's preformatted templates. This difficulty certainly became a drawback for creating the e-portfolio for visual arts.

The second model (Spring 2001) was created to solve the problem of saving digitized image files. Students in Basic Drawing II used Microsoft Word 2000/ME to save their documents into HTML format. The function of HTML in Word was also a solution for changing the way of organizing text and image files. Students felt more comfortable using Word instead of PowerPoint. In the same semester, the university Web server began to provide students with a 5MB Web space from which they enthusiastically accessed and published their webpage. Tightly tied to the objectives of the course and the purposes of the e-portfolios, the criteria for the websites required introduction, artwork examples, writing assignments, reflection, self-evaluation, and conclusion.

In addition to these criteria, I wrote a step-by-step manual and provided a template for students to follow. The online discussion board, another platform for the instructor and students, eventually helped expand the learning of the traditional classroom and increased interactions between the instructor and students.

The NHCTC Case Study

After 2001, I introduced the concepts of e-portfolios to Taiwanese college students in an art education course at National Hsin-Chu Teachers College (NHCTC) and continued my e-portfolio pilot studies there. I asked students using Microsoft FrontPage 2000 to edit their e-portfolios. Instantly, I noticed that college students in Taiwan had more advanced computer skills than did the NIU students. The students first combined the concepts they learned into digital files and then incorporated them along with their artwork into the structure of the e-portfolio. They used HTML or JAVA languages, Macromedia Flash, Dreamweaver, Director, etc. Some students even chose to employ several types of software simultaneously to make their Web pages look more professional. This shows that students were able to create personalized websites; therefore, compiling the e-portfolios was an exciting and interesting demonstration of their knowledge and their abundant creativity.

The NUU Case Study

With these students' success in creating their e-portfolios, I became interested in learning how much college students' e-portfolios reflect their academic/professional development and decided to conduct action research to study a group of design-major students (N=40) at National United University (NUU) from 2003 to 2007. From a survey, I understood that most of the students had mastered Microsoft Office (Wang, 2004; 2005). In two foundation courses, I introduced the concepts and purposes of developing an e-portfolio and required the students to collect all the materials they had produced during the semester. At the end of the semester, the students were asked to follow the e-portfolio template (similar in structure to the second NIU model but in Chinese) to display their semester's artworks.

After learning Macromedia Dreamweaver and Flash In the following semester (Spring 2004), the students were able to employ these new tools to create their portfolios. As experienced before, this new e-portfolio model had some drawbacks:

- To make animation or high-speed page transitions, the students reduced the resolution of the images.
- Some students spent too much time on the software/program itself but ignored its learning function.
- When presenting the e-portfolio on the Web, some students focused too specifically on the technique of the software/program and disregarded the purpose of assessment.

The next year (2004-05), I used Perry's (1981) scheme of four college-student learning stages—dualism, multiplicity, relativism, and commitment—

TABLE 1:
Perry's Development Scheme and e-Portfolio Application.

STAGES	DESCRIPTION OF COGNITION	APPLICATION STRATEGIES	ASSESSMENT APPROACHES
Dualism	Students rely on authorities' answers or commands to learn	Students follow the structured forma to produce their portfolios	Instructor Assessment
Multiplicity	Students recognize different opinions and voices and are encouraged to discuss what they learn	Students follow the basic guidelines but can use various features to present the chosen contents of their portfolios	Self-Assessment
Relativism	Students understand knowledge is qualitative, dependent on contents	Students are familiar with the purpose of portfolio development and are able to take responsibility for the process	Peer-Assessment
Commitment	Students are able to conduct their own learning and make decisions or judgments	Students develop the portfolio based on their interests and needs	Comprehensive Group-Assessment

to emphasize self-, peer-, and group-assessment and application strategies in the process of portfolio development to teach the same group of students critical and multidimensional thinking. Table 1 shows the relationship among the stages and the application to the current study.

Instructors can alternate several strategies to facilitate the stages of first-year students' and sophomores' cognitive development. The assessment exercises began with my checklists and rubrics for project reviews. After the students were familiar with the concepts of assessment, I guided them to conduct self- and peer-assessment according to my review criteria. From my observations, the results of the assessments directly reflect students' learning through the process of creating their e-portfolios. They realized the function and value of a portfolio and were able to establish their own learning database by collecting all types of visual information and combining them in their portfolios (Wang, 2005). Because of the course requirements, graphics/images created through computer software frequently appeared in students' portfolios. Digital images, therefore, are the most authentic and appropriate materials that can be placed in an e-portfolio, as suggested by Boughton and Wang (2002).

In their junior year (2005-06), although no course required these students to create e-portfolios (as had been the case in the previous 2 years), the students maintained the habit of recording their learning development. For example, most of them used their digital cameras to photograph their school-related activities to document their learning. The popularity of free Internet space (weblogs) has made recording personal development and publishing visual and textual information online more accessible; hence, I recommended that the students use MSN Space or any other available free weblogs as their formative/progressive portfolio where works, journals, and notes are to be easily stored. I noticed that students not only recorded their learning activities but also selected some of their personal thoughts about their daily life to post on the weblog because of the interactive and friendly nature of the weblog. Students felt that they had full control of the weblog, which met the purpose of formative portfolios that many ideas, experiments, and in-progress works be seen and discussed by the weblog community. One advantage of the weblog, then, is that it allowed the students to filter their audience. So, students were much more motivated when managing their portfolios than they had been in the preceding years. Although the self-managed weblog shows students' learning development, it is inadequate when curriculum goals and learning objectives are to be emphasized; therefore, it is necessary to maintain an academic portfolio at the same time so students can discern the differences between the academic nature of the e-portfolio and the unstructured nature of the weblog.

The major goal for this group of design students during their final/senior year (2006-07) was to complete their final projects for the senior exhibition. Most of them continued using the weblog to record every stage of their final project and asked for comments from the online communities. Making progress in a portfolio became a self-motivated behavior. According to some experienced faculty at NUU, this was the first group of students who were able to conduct their own monthly project review/critique and were fully responsible for their senior exhibition. Based on their previous experiences of creating e-portfolios, the students were also able to put together a professional portfolio for graduate school applications or job interviews. Many students reflected that they had benefited from the process of e-portfolio development, especially by seeing themselves growing and becoming organized.

CONCLUSION

After 7 years of implementing e-portfolios in college art and design classrooms, I have learned the following:

- Students realize the purpose and value of creating portfolios at the end of each semester.
- Students take advantage of computers and the Internet to facilitate their learning.
- Students often help one another to solve technical problems or ask for support through their online communities.
- Students learn a great deal when browsing peers' webpages and competing with each other.
- Students eventually appreciate the process of collecting their study records and learning to be critical.

Although there are many benefits of using e-portfolios in art education, we must also be aware that students today are more capable of adjusting to the new trends in technology than their teachers are. What the students learn through computers easily goes beyond what the academic curriculum offers, and what they learn from their visual experiences usually exceeds what they learn in classrooms. My concern here is not with technology but with the purposes of the portfolio. As instructors, we must take advantage of creating e-portfolios and make them a guideline to help us examine our students' learning development so that they will be able to think critically throughout their learning in the contemporary visual environment.

Based on what I have learned, some issues have to be considered for future e-portfolio development. One big challenge for teachers is to keep up with the constantly developing computer hardware and software, for students always find new ways, such as weblogs, to publish/share their texts and visuals.

1. Educational issue: The purpose of developing portfolios is to help students compile their learning results for assessment of one or more courses/subject areas in a specific period; at the same time, they help the instructor(s) examine/review their teaching, curriculum design, and the students' performance. When using electronic platforms to create portfolios, both teachers and students sometimes forget or ignore this purpose and have the illusion that creating a portfolio is doing assessment. Educators must be aware of this type of misunderstanding to use the portfolio assessment correctly. Assessment in general requires a process not only of data collection but also of analysis and critiques.

2. Aesthetic taste and visual quality issue: One of the challenges in teaching art is to inspire students to discover ways to see the world. However, contemporary students are so bombarded by the mass media, sub-cultures, and other visual information that exercising judgment becomes difficult. Hence, because aesthetic meanings are significantly changed, teachers and students seeing and judging visual facts face many conflicts not only between traditional and contemporary values but also between actual artwork and the representational qualities of images in e-portfolios.

3. Identity and authorship issue: The meaning of creation and authorship has changed in the postmodern era. Most art instruction now directly or indirectly is related to such interlocked postmodern concepts as the question of originality and identity. Undoubtedly students and teachers have to debate the use of computer programs to adopt and adapt images, create or recreate art, and present art. They need to define or at least agree about the originality of artwork to best present the actual quality and effort of students' works.

4. Communication and language issue: Today's images or visuals have become comprehensive in their meanings and functions. In coding and decoding, the "readers" are able to interpret them in various ways. Therefore, understanding students' artwork, writing, or artwork statements is very challenging for the teachers. The teachers have to apply several strategies to teach students the roles of both visual and verbal communications so that the presentation of the portfolios can meet the objectives of portfolio development.

5. Technological issue: Students will not stop questing for new things in the computer world; in the meantime, teachers have to keep exploring new computer software to facilitate e-portfolio development, even though the purposes of making portfolios remain the same. Future studies will inevitably have to address new values and the pros and cons of e-portfolio developments. In this high-tech global society, because much can be learned from the process of developing an e-portfolio, teachers are always encouraged to be enthusiastic in learning new ways to enrich their teaching even in places that are deprived of the latest technology.

REFERENCES

Alter, J. & Spandel, V. (1992). Using portfolios of student work in instruction and assessment. *Educational Measurement: Issues and Practice, 11*(1), 36-44.

Beattie, D. (1997). *Assessment in art education.* Worcester, MA: Davis Publications.

Blaikie, F., & Schönau, D. (2003). Students' gendered experiences of high school portfolio art assessment in Canada, The Netherlands, and England. *Studies in Art Education, 44*(4), 335-349.

Boughton, D., & Wang, S. (2002). The implement of electronic portfolio in student assessment in art education. *Journal of Aesthetic Education, 129*, 69-75 (in Chinese).

Boughton, D. (2004a). Learning visual culture: The important relationship of curriculum and assessment. *International Journal of Art Education, 2*(4), 76-90.

Boughton, D. (2004b). The problems of seduction: Assessing visual culture. *Studies in Art Education, 45*(3), 265-269.

Chang, C. C. (2003). On the influence of contemporary education intellection & learning theory over e-learning of art. *Journal of Aesthetic Education, 134*, 33-43 (in Chinese).

Chang, T. C. (2003). Aesthetics of web site design for art education in the age of highly image reproduction. *Journal of Aesthetic Education, 134*, 20-26 (in Chinese).

Chung, S. K. (2004). Art education in cyberspace: Strategies for implementation. *Journal of Aesthetic Education, 141*, 90-96 (in Chinese).

Colman, A. (2004). Net.art and Net.pedagogy: Introducing internet art to the digital art curriculum. *Studies in Art Education, 46*(1), 61-73.

Danielson, C., & Abrutyn, L. (1997). *An introduction to using portfolio in the classroom.* Alexandria, VA: Association for Supervision and Curriculum Development.

Delacruz, E. (2004). Teacher's working conditions and the unmet promise of technology. *Studies in Art Education, 46*(1), 6-19.

Dorn, C., Madeja, S., & Sabol, R. (2004). *Assessing expressive learning.* Mahwah, NJ: Lawrence Erlbaum and Associates.

Duncum, P. (1999). A case for an art education of everyday aesthetic. *Studies in Art Education, 40*(4), 295-311.

Freedman, K. (2003). *Teaching visual culture: Curriculum, aesthetics, and the social life of art.* New York: Teachers College Press.

Gruber, D. & Hobbs, J. (2002). Historical analysis of assessment in art education. *Art Education, 55*(6), 12-17.

Keefe, A., Kobrinski, E., Keen, P., Mattia, C., & Moersch, C. (2002). Electronic portfolio production for performance assessment of undergraduate learners. *Journal of Virginia Society for Technology in Education, 17*(1), 24-32.

Keifer-Boyd, K. (1997). Interfacing hypermedia and the internet with critical inquiry in the arts: Preservice training. In D. Gregory (Ed.), *New technologies in art education: Implications for theory, research, and practice* (pp. 23-32). Reston, VA: National Art Education Association.

Lai, A., & Ball, E. (2004). Student online as cultured subjects: Prolegomena to researching multicultural arts courses on the web. *Studies in Art Education, 46*(1), 20-33.

Marschalek, D. (2002). Building better web-based learning environments: Thinking in "3s." *Art Education, 55*(4), 13-18.

Marschalek, D. (2004). Four learning environments for the contemporary art education classroom: Studio, information, planning, and electronic. *Art Education, 57*(3), 33-41.

Mirzoeff, N. (1999). *An introduction to visual culture.* London: Routledge.

Morris, J. (2001). Electronic Portfolios. Retrieved December 2005, from www.uvm.edu/~jmorris/ep/electronicportfolio.html

Niguidula, D. (1993). The digital portfolio: A richer picture of student performance. Retrieved December 2005, from www.essentialschools.org/cs/resources/view/ces_res/225

Perry, W. (1981). Cognitive and ethical growth: The making of meaning. In A. Chickering (Ed.), *The modern American college: Responding to the new realities of diverse students and a changing society* (pp. 76-116). San Francisco: Jossey-Bass.

Shepard, L. (2000). The role of assessment in a learning culture. *Educational Researcher, 29*(7), 4-14.

Walker, J., & Chaplin, S. (1997). *Visual culture: An introduction.* New York: Manchester University Press.

Wang, S. (2004). Electronic technology and visual art learning: A case study of college students in Taiwan. Paper presented at InSEA 7th European Regional Congress, Istanbul and Cappadocia, Turkey.

Wang, S. (2005). The impact of digital images on learning visual arts: A case study of Taiwanese college students. Paper presented at National Art Education Association 2005 Annual Convention, Boston, US.

In Search of the Public Domain: Addressing the Threat of Copyright Laws in Art Education / SARA WILSON MCKAY

WE LIE, AS EMERSON SAID, IN THE LAP OF AN IMMENSE INTELLIGENCE. BUT THAT INTELLIGENCE IS DORMANT AND ITS COMMUNICATIONS ARE BROKEN, INARTICULATE AND FAINT UNTIL IT POSSESSES THE LOCAL COMMUNITY AS ITS MEDIUM. (JOHN DEWEY, *THE PUBLIC AND ITS PROBLEMS,* 1927, P. 219)

Fear of overstepping, misusing, and being in conflict with copyright laws has created a panic in many art teachers with regard to issues of originality. The idea of originality has been in dispute in the art world for a very long time (Krauss, 1986; Plato, n.d.). But in the postmodern era of pastiche and de(re)construction in art, appropriation—the borrowing of elements in the creation of new work—has been an accepted and highly regarded form of art (Gude, 2004; Jenkins, 2006). However, using and re-using other people's marks is not merely a 20th-century development. Ancient civilizations created standard ways of representing desired imagery. Medieval apprentices in studios copied their master's stroke, and Renaissance artists reused classical imagery for their own ends. Benjamin (1936) suggested:

> In principle a work of art has always been reproducible. Man-made artifacts could always be imitated by men. Replicas were made by pupils in practice of their craft, by masters for diffusing their works, and, finally, by third parties in the pursuit of gain. Mechanical reproduction of a work of art, however, represents something new.... Around 1900 technical reproduction had reached a standard that not only permitted it to reproduce all transmitted works of art and thus to cause the most profound change in their impact upon the public; it also had captured a place of its own among the artistic processes. (Section I)

Though Benjamin could hardly have anticipated the extent and ease of current reproduction methods, he argued that technical reproductions were evolving into their own artforms over the course of technology's advancement throughout history. He was, at the time, specifically referencing photography and film, though certainly synthetic Cubism, Duchamp's mustachioed Mona Lisa—*L.H.O.O.Q.* (1919)—and Warhol's *Brillo Box* (1964) all achieved some degree of notoriety in contemporary times. Further exploring ideas of what makes an artwork in terms of originality, several contemporary artists like Sherrie Levine, Tracy Emin, and Vik Muniz have made overt investigations of originality through their work. However, in the current age of corporate media copyright laws, many of these artforms might never have been created.

Art educators' concerns with issues of copyright derive from a climate of fear surrounding much of U.S. public education. The litigious culture of the US, increasingly cautious recommended teacher limits that seem contrary to common sense in conjunction with numerous solicitations for Teacher Liability Insurance, and the strict accountability climate in public schools from the No Child Left Behind (2001) legislation have put many teachers in a defensive mode. Art educators feel these same pressures but in unique ways given the nature of art's ever-expanding definitions and boundary-pushing qualities. Art teaching thus requires openness to ideas and change that seems unsupported in many K-12 environments, particularly when "idea theft, copyright violation, appropriation and plagiarism are used interchangeably in the public discourse" of creativity (Vaidhyanathan, 2001, p. 34). Art educators, especially those who embrace a visual culture stance in the field, are caught in a dilemma of how to maintain openness and strategic criticality with regards to our visual culture, both in terms of visual culture production as well as visual culture reception, while feeling constrained by fear of infringing on the power of copyright laws.

Sometimes fear of infringement has far-reaching impact. For example, the rigid rules and documentation required to prove the "originality" of a student's submission to one state's visual art event can serve as a case in point of how art educators often find themselves perpetuating limited cultural production. The visual art event's director has concerns about originality and artwork because of the legalities on the line for him in the position of event director. If an honored student's work is published on the cover of the event's brochure or some other publication and it is determined to be a derivative image,[1] he believes he would be libel for perpetuating "stolen" imagery. The director, understandably, seeks protection instead of ways to define art in the most open way possible. The originality clause of the visual art event's submission policies have thus been crafted to eliminate any such liability, and have, consequently, limited cultural production:

Entry Regulations

(1) Originality:

(A) All artworks are required to be original in composition and individual expression. No Laser Photocopied Artworks. Artworks must be original. If a teacher has any doubt about the originality of an artwork, the work should not be submitted (refer to the Qualifications Checklist in Addendum B).

(B) Copying or reproducing in any media a published image, photograph, album/CD cover, how-to book, magazine, image from Art History, etc., is

> plagiarism and will be disqualified. Student photographs, student sketches, student-directed photographs, and any additional secondary references (Secondary References may include but are not limited to magazines, textbooks, downloaded images, photo files, etc.) used to develop an artwork by non-mechanical means will only be allowed if all reference materials are attached to the submitted artwork.
>
> (C) Photographs taken by an art instructor are considered professional due to the teacher's training. They may be used as secondary reference material only.
>
> Copying from a professionally created photograph in any work entered is prohibited. Images traced with the use of an overhead or opaque projector or other mechanical means are prohibited. Artwork from direct observation is encouraged. (Texas Art Education Association, 2008)

While developing representational drawing skills is a worthwhile activity in art education, to have a statewide visual art event, probably one of the finest visual art events in the country, focus predominantly on representational artwork and drawing from direct observation out of fear of liability and copyright infringement likely results in a limited notion of the public's (and students') ideas of art and the ends of art education.

This chapter addresses the questions of how media copyright laws have impacted the field of art education. It specifically investigates how Internet resources—such as Creative Commons, Detritus.net, and the Arts Project at the Center for the Study of the Public Domain—are actively involved in interrupting corporate strongholds on intellectual property, and therefore might be useful to art educators.

CREATIVITY, POWER, AND COPYRIGHT

Under copyright threat, generally coordinators of student art events, like the situation just discussed, avoid any kind of student artwork that embraces the kinds of appropriation and art-from-art attitudes that have frequently defined much of the modern and contemporary artworld as seen in the work of Rauschenberg's combines, Prince's re-photographed advertisements, and Muniz's sugar and chocolate replicas. One possible justification of these decisions valorizes the converse situation: creativity in art education is often mobilized and conceptualized through the Lowenfeldian lens of "no adult influence" suggesting a "free" space of creativity that is devoid of influence of any adult-created imagery (Lowenfeld & Brittain, 1964, p. 25). Wilson and Wilson (1977) challenged this position as they studied influences on student drawing. They found, indeed, that students are impacted by the imagery with which they are surrounded; in the visual culture era of art education, we should more seriously address what this means for student creativity and cultural production, particularly with regard to copyright law.

In the digital age, copyright law and fair use are pushed to the limit in educational contexts. And those limits seem to be closing in, with much cost, I argue, to our conceptions of artmaking in art education. Many art educators have worked hard to open up students' minds to the breadth of art in their lives, expanding notions of art beyond the myth of the isolated genius birthing completely new ideas from nothing. This myth perpetuates a sense in art education that only the talented few "get it" and there really is not much point in studying art, much less producing it, if only a few are designated "artists."

The US became a party to the Berne Convention of 1886 in 1988. Accordingly, no documentation or registration of a work to be copyrighted is required, and all creations are owned exclusively at the moment of creation (Berne Convention Implementation Act, 1988). Legislative changes in copyright law since then, including the Digital Millennium Copyright Act of 1998 and the Sonny Bono Copyright Term Extension Act of 1998, have built further on the idea of exclusive ownership with a goal of protecting this form of "property," creating a culture of exclusivity and restriction rather than a culture of shared knowledge and cultural capital (Vaidhyanathan, 2001).

Relating these ideas to Foucault's power/knowledge construction, knowledge is restricted by those in power (Foucault, 1980), and those claiming exclusive ownership of imagery are restricting access to and circulation of visual knowledge. Free Culture movement founder and Stanford Law professor Lawrence Lessig (2008) discusses the idea of proprietary ownership and its impact on creativity by acknowledging the current potentials of what he calls a 'hybrid economy,' the mixing of both commercial and sharing economies. Lessig (2008) claims that without proper respect granted to sharing creators (and less extreme laws), amateur or "remix" creativity is in the process of being snuffed out by those in power, namely corporate media. Further, he claims, in every other century besides the 20th century, there has been enormous value in remixing culture (Lessig, 2008)—particularly for young people who learn to participate in culture by creating and recreating the culture around them.

This idea of how young people learn through sharing in the culture around them is related to another phenomenon—patchwriting—targeted under the name of plagiarism. *Patchwriting* is defined as paraphrasing (and citing) a text but leaving it too similar to the original. A comparison of the two texts would show that though the second writer may have changed the grammatical structure, substituted phrases, used synonyms, or changed the order of the ideas, the original text is still detectable. Patchwriting, particularly in this digital age of Wikipedia and the like, has been criminalized as plagiarism. But some scholars think that this kind of writing is a part of the learning process:

> Finally, let 'patchwriting' describe the act of enthusiasm in which students collaborate with their source texts for the purposes of understanding them and entering their discourse. Let us respond pedagogically to that

> phenomenon, too. That pedagogical response can regard the patchwriting as a transitional stage toward full comprehension of the text or toward full membership in a discourse community, or it can celebrate patchwriting as (re)formative composition. But let us, at last, quit telling our students and ourselves that writer-text collaboration is a crime. (Howard, 1999, p. 166)

In viewing the process of education as collaboration with source texts, the sharing of ideas becomes a critical component for education: "We do not write alone, and often it is texts, not people, with whom we collaborate" (Howard, 1999, p. 7).[2]

But what does this have to do with art education? I suggest strict copyright law and educators who fear such laws reinforce narrow definitions of art in education. In a sense, overblown copyright laws, passed without regard for the original intent of copyright (see following section), bully art educators, effectively denying our students the opportunity to collaborate with other art and artists. In the artworld, it is acceptable, even expected, for the "genius" artist, the renegade, to go against convention and play at the margins of copyrighted materials, to appropriate popular culture and other artists' work unabashedly. For example, digital artist Cory Arcangel claims of his Nintendo game hacking Super Mario Clouds (2002-2005) that the creators of Super Mario Brothers have yet to call him. If they did, though it does not appear to be his intent to raise corporate hackles, his defense would likely be that he views all media, not nostalgically as critics often describe his work, but as raw material. The old NES cartridges and consoles happen to be handy and usually free in the trash (personal communication, November 2005). Because effects similar to Arcangel's can be achieved without in-depth coding knowledge, new media work often embraces appropriation due to the ability to copy and share digital media more easily now than in previous media. But in the schools, teachers are leery of the infringement issue. We run so far from copyrighted material, or feel so illicit when we do use it, that students (and teachers) become entrenched in the copyrighted culture that supports the notion that someone owns every idea. The costs of students growing up in such a culture suggest that dollars will win out over sense in the long run (Rose & Lessig, 2008).

HISTORY AND NAVIGATION OF COPYRIGHT LAW

With the invention and widespread use of the printing press, so developed the idea of copyright (Vaidhyanathan, 2001). At the time, it was less for the benefit of the authors that it developed, but rather for the publishers who sought restrictions on the copying of printed works. However, at the birth of the United States, the crafters of the Constitution carefully acknowledged the power that copyright conveyed and required Congress to craft a federal law, "that provides an incentive to create and distribute new works" (Vaidhyanathan, 2001, p. 20). This incentive came from the reasonable limits attached to the protection of new works: allowing good faith use by private citizens including students and teachers, and the term of copyright must expire after a reasonable time, allowing the work to pass into the public domain to encourage more creative works. At the time of the drafting of the Constitution, "copyright was created as a policy that balanced the interests of authors, publishers, and readers" (Vaidhyanathan, 2001, p. 20). Specifically, the United States Constitution (Article I, Section 8, Clause 8) charges Congress, "to promote the Progress of Science and useful Arts, by securing for limited Times to Authors and Inventors the exclusive Right to their respective Writings and Discoveries" (U.S. Constitution). Vaidhyanathan (2001) argues that "the framers [of the Constitution] and later jurists concluded that creativity depends on the use, criticism, supplementation, and consideration of previous works" (p. 21) and that the intent of the copyright clause was to encourage people to create with a legal guarantee that they would profit from their creations but for only a limited time, and then more people would be encouraged to create over time. This original purpose of copyright has been challenged and seemingly lost in recent revisions of copyright law, which now favor corporate media and well-established creators over future creators.

Copyright law is long, complicated and changing daily with new lawsuits and new challenges to the current laws. In general, it is best to think of copyright law as a "bundle of rights that includes the exclusive right to make copies, authorize others to make copies, create derivative works such as translations and displays in other media, sell the work, perform the work publicly, and petition a court for relief in case others infringe on any of these rights" (Vaidhyanathan, 2001, p. 21). The Copyright Act of 1976 more clearly articulated: "a work is protected in all media and for all possible derivative uses as soon as it is fixed in a tangible medium of expression" (Vaidhyanathan, 2001, p. 24). Emphasizing protection of expression in 1976, the expression/idea dichotomy initiated the widespread use of the slippery term "intellectual property" where ideas are owned and have property rights (Vaidhyanathan, 2001). This was a critical shift in copyright law. When ideas began to be viewed as something to be guarded as property as opposed to shared within the public realm, copyright legislation got the public support it needed to extend its reach and its strength. Terms of expiration are now absurdly long thanks to the Sonny Bono Copyright Term Extension Act (1998), and the protection of ideas, presumably for monetary gain (as indicated by the facetious, yet truthful, nickname of the 1998 legislation: "The Mickey Mouse Protection Act") instead of the generation of new works, has become the detrimental purpose of current copyright.

An exception to these copyright monopolies is the Fair Use law, provided in the Copyright Act of 1976, which "allows users to make copies of, quote from, and refer to copyrighted works for the following purposes: in connection with criticism or comment on the work; in the course of news reporting; for teaching or classroom use; or as part of scholarship or research" (Vaidhyanathan, 2001, p. 27). But admittedly the judgment calls on Fair Use, with which art educators are most concerned, are grey areas. Toward the end of this chapter, readers will find some tips for helping art teachers navigate fair use at this seemingly restrictive time.

A final concept to explore with regards to copyright is the notion of the "public domain." In general, works pass into the public domain because time has mandated it. Works created before 1923 are in the public domain. Some works created before 1964 (when copyright was required to be renewed) may also be in the public domain if their copyright expired without renewal. But in general, very few contemporary works are in the public domain unless the creator has so designated. With the ideas of "copyleft" taking hold—a copyright licensing strategy to remove restrictions on creative works, especially software—we are seeing more and more examples of shared content in the blogosphere.[3]

As we have seen in this section, copyright laws were initially created to facilitate the exchange of ideas, but current employment of the laws criminalize such activity. Lessig (2004) argues that copyright laws are perpetuating and creating a generation of unknowing consumers not savvy producers. These laws are being mobilized to protect corporate content and monopolize cultural production. The emerging copyright system seems to be working against new forms of cultural expression and democratic ideals: "Literature, music, and art are essential elements of public forums. They are all forms of democratic speech and should be encouraged and rewarded, not chilled with threats of legal action" (Vaidhyanathan, 2001, p.16). Art educators are rightfully concerned about freedom to produce new works from and through the influence of our visual culture, and it should be regained.

PROTECTORS AND SHARERS OF CREATIVE WORKS

There are many forces, both individuals and collaborative groups, however, who have come together to interrupt the criminalizing use of copyright laws. These interruptions are important in art education because they allow students (and more importantly teachers) the opportunity to imagine a world of limited corporate control and increased citizen participation in our visual culture. Because copyright laws in this digital age are evolving at a pace that makes it impossible for any definitive position to be elaborated here as to what is and is not allowed (it would be out of date long before it actually appeared in print), this chapter encourages art educators to be aware of the evolving nature of digital law and to be advocates for copyright laws that promote the free exchange of ideas, not corporate protection. Awareness of good sources of information regarding copyright is more important in this dynamic climate than knowledge of hard and fast rules. The rules are changing constantly. This section looks briefly at three different sources for their usefulness to art education.

Creative Commons

Creative Commons was founded by Lessig to give creators the ability to exercise their copyright rights. Creators use Creative Commons licenses to tell those who see or interact with their work how they may use it. For example, I considered using a graph of the expansion of copyright laws that is provided by Tom Bell on Wikipedia's entry for "public domain" under the CC license that requires I attribute the creator and that if I make anything with it, I share it freely. Because this book will be sold, not shared, I chose not to use the graph presuming you can go and look it up yourself. The share-alike license is just one of the six main licenses offered if a creator chooses to publish a work with a Creative Commons license. Other licenses range from most restrictive amounting to permission to redistribute only (essentially free advertising) to the most permissive with the Public Domain Dedication, which frees the work from copyright completely.

Roland (2007) says: "Sites that promote Creative Commons use (like Flickr) are a boon to teachers and students looking for images, video clips, audio files, and other materials for use in multimedia projects. Art teachers and students should be aware of Creative Commons licensing, both as content consumers and content providers."

Center for the Study of the Public Domain

Since 2002, this nonprofit center at Duke Law School has had as its goal "to study the balance between intellectual property and the public domain" (Center for the Study of the Public Domain, n.d.). Accordingly, the group investigates a wide array of topics including arts and culture. The Arts Project includes downloadable (and remixable) comic book pages about issues of fair use and the public domain as well as film contest winners on the same topics. The Center also organizes conferences like "Framed! How Law Constructs and Constrains Culture," held in 2004 and which looked specifically at the impact of intellectual property in documentary film and music. Most notably, perhaps, is that the Center is home to scholars who are committed to an idea that copyright work now must be "constructive rather than critical" (Boyle, 2007, Sec. VI). Boyles employs a powerful analogy that he calls "cultural environmentalism" so that the delicate aspects within the environment of creative works can be respected, maintained and, in fact, thrive.

Detritus.net and Other Spaces for Cultural Recycling

A now somewhat historical site, Detritus.net, whose blog ceased to be active in 2006, is "dedicated to recycled culture" claiming a reverence for bits and pieces of culture that can be reused. The purposes of the site: "First, modern technology allows easy reproduction of cultural artifacts, making it all the more necessary that social attitudes adjust to match. And second, the rise of capitalism and corporate power has created an environment where intellectual property law constricts the healthy growth of culture and exercise of individual creativity. This site is a rallying point against this negative force" (Detritus.net, n.d.). On the site, the link to "detrivores" is especially rich in that it includes current links to artists with sympathies to recycling culture. Interesting efforts are included by Post Consumer Productions and People Like Us.

However, in the age of Web 2.0 and technology encouraging easy reproduction of cultural things, everyone can participate in the kind of project Detritus.net created. Take for example MadV's One World video posted on YouTube over 2 years ago that received more than 2000 video responses, making it the most responded to video on YouTube ever (Thompson, 2008). MadV then took the responses, short clips in which people filmed a message on their hand, and made a montage of them. It is a meaningful piece of video (www.youtube.com/watch?v=Z-BzXpOch-E). With these kinds of tools, ideas, and willing participants, recycling of culture will continue, despite corporations' attempts to hold culture hostage for profit through copyright laws.

CONCLUSION: FAIR USE GUIDELINES AND ACTIVISM

Fortunately, teachers and students do have a very important tool in their toolbox to combat these expansive copyright laws—the concept of fair use. Fair use is deliberately flexible to be determined by the teacher or a judge if the creator made a use of copyrighted material that is indeed fair. To determine fairness, according to the Center for Social Media, the two questions judges return to are:

> Did the unlicensed use "transform" the material taken from the copyrighted work by using it for a different purpose than that of the original, or did it just repeat the work for the same intent and value as the original?
>
> Was the material taken appropriate in kind and amount, considering the nature of the copyrighted work and of the use? (Center for Social Media, 2008)

In a recent publication of the Center for Social Media (CSM), titled "The Code of Best Practices in Fair Use for Media Literacy Education," teachers are encouraged to lead, not follow, when it comes to reclaiming fair use. Acknowledging the fear-laden terrain of copyright compounded by risk-management rhetoric from schools, the authors suggest that teachers are operating under increased fear and confusion about fair use, often refusing to use any copyrighted work in their classroom (or hiding it if they do). Teachers must reclaim fair use for educational purposes and stop equating "any unlicensed use of copyrighted material with stealing" (CSM, 2008). The Center for Social Media supports teachers recovering the ability to decide what is important and necessary for their classroom, and they urge teachers to make reasoned, contextual decisions about the following four factors to determine fairness as it applies to their situation:

1. the nature of the original work is important to public discussions or concern;
2. the nature of your use of it is important because of teaching, research, or commentary;
3. you did not use very much of the original work; and
4. your use did not significantly affect the market for the original work. (Vaidhyanathan, 2001, p. 249)

The essay goes on to describe how there is no magic percentage for fair use, and that students (and teachers) should be able to reason about their choices in the name of fair use: "Students' use of copyrighted material should not be a substitute for creative effort. Students should be able to understand and demonstrate, in a manner appropriate to their developmental level, how their use of a copyrighted work repurposes or transforms the original" (CSM, 2008). This is thus a matter of sound pedagogy as it relates to the use of copyrighted imagery.

Underlying all of these recommendations is a call for teachers and students to think, reason, and reclaim fair use in their classrooms. And, perhaps even a state visual art event could rethink and reverse its self-imposed limitations with careful consideration of the goals of the event and the fair use clause emphasizing education. Such steps would truly be acts of activism in expanding understandings about copyright particularly in our schools, but also in our democracy generally.

Another activist step, advocated by Vaidhyanathan (2001), is to make a rhetorical shift from discussions of intellectual property to intellectual policy. This simple semantic shift would remove the psychological "rights" currently attributed to creative works, and thus as a consequence, the criminality for supposed trampling of those rights. Reframing this discussion around intellectual policy suggests that there are contextual and situational nuances to the application of the policy that would allow for a broader spectrum of use.

In short, advocate for "thin" copyright laws that promote free exchange of ideas and productions of new work, not corporate protection. Continue to encourage mash ups, remixes, Cubist, Pop Art, and conceptual pieces that directly challenge and interrogate our relationship to visual culture. Cultivate public domain usage when possible and otherwise aim to stay within the flexible fair use guidelines knowing you can articulate your decisions for your particular situation. Lastly, advocate to your students, your colleagues, your administrators, your family, and your legislators that copyright expansion cannot be allowed to continue in its current vein if we expect to live in a free and democratic society.

Indeed, Lessig (2008) argues in the conclusion of his book *Remix* that a whole generation is being criminalized for activities that to them seem completely normal and that the long-term impact of extremist reactions to amateur creativity (through which people learn to participate in culture), is a general weakening of law-abiding instincts. On his Free Culture website, Lessig (n.d.) argues that "while new technologies always lead to new laws, never before have the big cultural monopolists used the fear created by new technologies, specifically the Internet, to shrink the public domain of ideas... What's at stake is our freedom—freedom to create, freedom to build, and ultimately, freedom to imagine" (¶ 3). Art educators are certainly concerned with these freedoms, but we need to be bold and reclaim our fair use rights, in addition to making use of Creative Commons licenses and urging our legislators to protect and enlarge the public domain. We must move beyond our fear, to exercise and preserve these freedoms for ourselves and more importantly for our students.

REFERENCES

Babauta, L. (2008). Open source blogging: Feel free to steal my content. Retrieved January 24, 2009, from http://zenhabits.net/2008/01/open-source-blogging-feel-free-to-steal-my-content/

Barthes, R. (1977). *Image-music-text.* New York: Hill & Wang.

Benjamin, W. (1936). The work of art in the age of mechanical reproduction. Retrieved January 20, 2009, from www.marxists.org/reference/subject/philosophy/works/ge/benjamin.htm

Berne Convention Implementation Act (1988). 17 USC 101 note. United States Code Congressional and Administrative News, 100th Congress—Second Session, Volume 2, West Publishing Co., St. Paul, Minn., 102 Stat. 2853-2861. Retrieved January 21, 2009 from www.cni.org/docs/infopols/US.Berne.Convention.html

Boyle, J. (2007). Cultural Environmentalism @ 10, *Law & Contemporary Problems, 70*(2). Retrieved January 24, 2009, from www.law.duke.edu/journals/lcp/lcptoc70spring2007

Center for Social Media (2008). The Code of Best Practices in Fair Use for Media Literacy Education. Retrieved January 22, 2009, from www.centerforsocialmedia.org/resources/publications/code_for_media_literacy_education/

Center for the Study of the Public Domain (n.d.). Art & Culture. Retrieved January 23, 2009, from www.law.duke.edu/cspd/artscience.html

Detritus.net (n.d.). Retrieved January 22, 20009 from http://detritus.net/faqomatic/cache/11.html

Dewey, J. (1927). *The public and its problems.* New York: Henry Holt.

Foucault, M. (1980). *Power/knowledge: Selected interviews and other writings, 1972-1977.* New York: Pantheon.

Gude, O. (2004). Postmodern principles: In search of a 21st century art education. *Art Education, 57*(1), 6-14.

Howard, R. M. (1999). *Standing in the shadow of giants: plagiarists, authors, collaborators.* New York: Ablex Publishing.

Jenkins, H. (2006). *Convergence culture: Where old and new media collide.* New York: NYU Press.

Krauss, R. (1986). *The originality of the avant-garde and other modernist myths.* Boston: MIT Press.

Lessig, L. (n.d.). About Free Culture. Retrieved January 24, 2008, from www.free-culture.cc/about/

Lessig, L. (2004). *Free culture: The nature and future of creativity.* New York: Penguin Books.

Lessig, L. (2008). *Remix: Making art and commerce thrive in the hybrid economy.* New York: Penguin Press.

Lowenfeld, V., & Brittain, W.L. (1964). *Creative and Mental Growth.* New York: Macmillan.

No Child Left Behind (2001). Public Law 107-110.

Plato (n.d.) *The Republic.*

Roland, C. (2007). Get creative with Creative Commons. Retrieved January 22, 2009, from http://artjunction.org/blog/?p=130

Rose, C. (Interviewer) & Lessig, L. (Interviewee). (2008). A conversation with Lawrence Lessig [Video file]. Retrieved from Charlie Rose website: www.charlierose.com/view/interview/9618

Texas Art Education Association (2008). Visual Art Scholastic Event, 2008-2009 Rules Condensed for Qualifications Personnel and Jurors. Retrieved from www.nisd.net/marshall/Departments/FineArtsdept/Arts/VASEinfo/2009VASERulesCondensed.pdf

Thompson, C. (2008). How YouTube changes the way we think. *Wired Magazine, 17* (1). Retrieved March 16, 2010, from www.wired.com/techbiz/people/magazine/17-01/st_thompson

U. S. Constitution, Art. I, § 9, cl. 2.

Vaidhyanathan, S. (2001). *Copyrights and copywrongs: The rise of intellectual property and how it threatens creativity.* New York: NYU Press.

Wilson, B., & Wilson, M. (1977). An Iconoclastic View of the Imagery Sources in the Drawings of Young People. *Art Education, 30*(1), 5-12.

ENDNOTES

1 Based on the nature of artistic influence, one might question what image is not a derivative image?

2 Barthes' empowered reader is a related concept discussed in his essay "The Death of the Author" (Barthes, 1977).

3 The owner of Zen Habits, one of the top 100 blogs on the Internet, Leo Babauta declared his site uncopyrighted in a post titled: "Open Source Blogging: Feel Free to Steal My Content" stating "if someone wants to take my work and improve upon it, as artists have been doing for centuries, I think that's a wonderful thing. If they can take my favorite posts and make something funny or inspiring or thought-provoking or even sad...I say more power to them. The creative community only benefits from derivations and inspirations." http://zenhabits.net/2008/01/open-source-blogging-feel-free-to-steal-my-content/

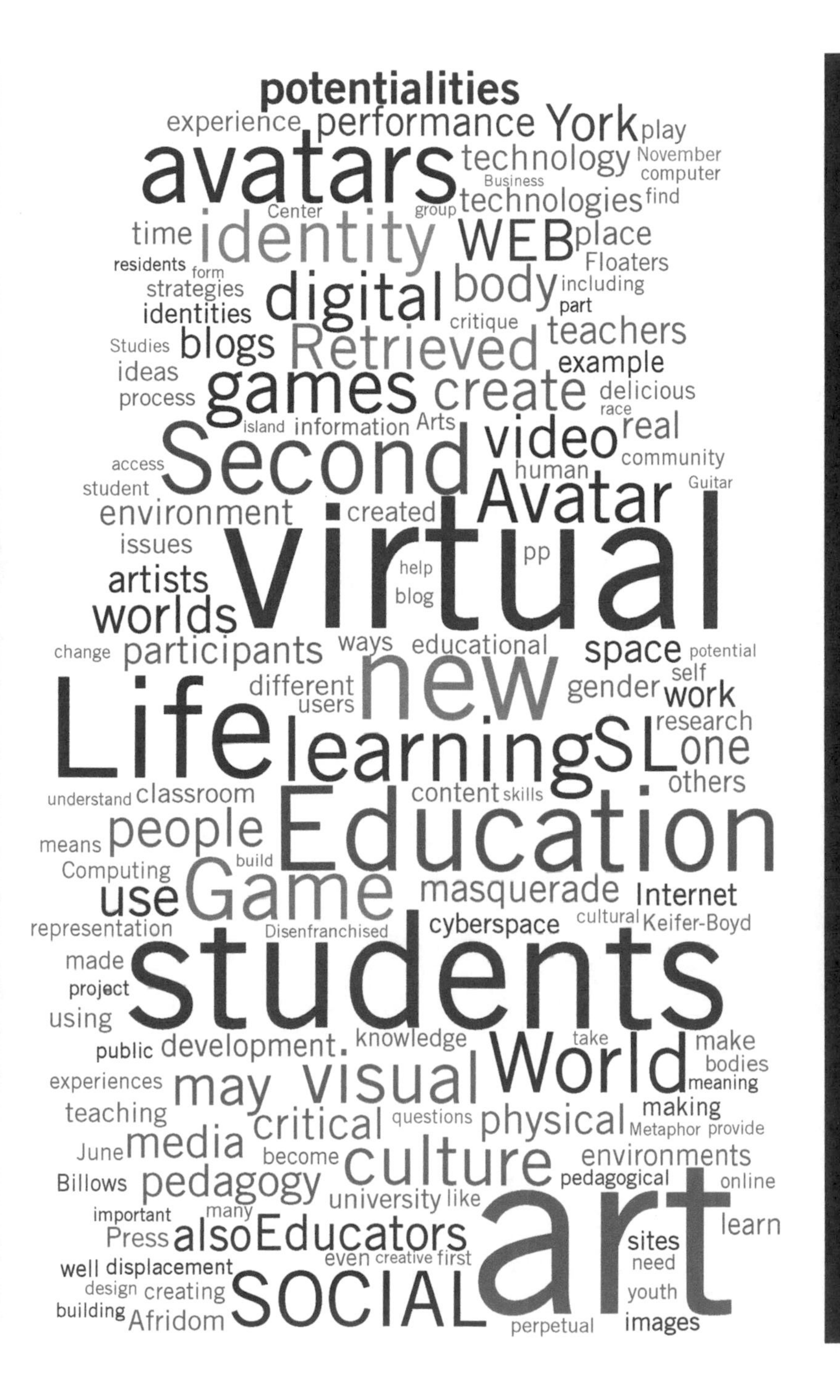
potentialities
experience performance York play
avatars technology November computer
Business
Center group technologies find
time identity WEB place
residents form Floaters
strategies digital body including
identities part
critique
Studies blogs Retrieved teachers
ideas example
process games create delicious
race
island information Arts real
Second video community
access human
student Guitar
environment created Avatar
issues pp
virtual
help
artists blog
worlds
change participants ways educational space potential
self
different new gender work
users
Life learning SL research one
understand classroom content skills others
means people Education
build
Computing
use Game masquerade Internet
representation Disenfranchised cyberspace cultural Keifer-Boyd
made students
project
using
knowledge take make
public development World bodies
experiences may visual meaning
teaching making
critical questions physical Metaphor provide
June media
become culture environments
Billows pedagogy pedagogical online
university like
important many art
Press also Educators learn
sites
even creative first
well displacement need
design creating youth
SOCIAL
building Afridom perpetual images

Web 2.0 and Social Constructivism /

MELANIE L. BUFFINGTON, WITH
KATHRYN R. HELMS, JAN A. JOHNSTON, AND
SOHHYOUN YOON

The emergence of Web 2.0 and its related technologies has the potential to dramatically alter current educational practices. Because users now have the ability to rapidly create content and to engage in social interactions through the World Wide Web, we argue that Web 2.0 supports socially mediated, constructivist learning environments in ways that are becoming seamless. In this chapter, we describe the tenets of social constructivism and then discuss three technologies associated with Web 2.0 and explore how teachers and students could utilize them to promote constructivist learning.

In 2003, the O'Reilly media group developed the term *Web 2.0* to describe the gradual changes that occurred over the previous few years in the way content for the Web could be created and consumed (O'Reilly, 2005). *Web 2.0* does not refer to a specific program or application, but rather to a group of emerging technologies that allow for significant social interaction through the Web, permitting users to create content either individually or collectively.

Because of the ease of collaborative knowledge building through Web 2.0, it may represent an important development in working toward constructivist teaching and learning practices. At the heart of constructivism is the notion that knowledge is not a thing that can be easily conveyed from one person to another in the manner that a coin can be exchanged. Educators can use tools of Web 2.0 to promote the types of social constructivist learning promoted by Vygotsky (1978) and others. Vygotsky wrote about the importance of and the relationship between learning and the social world of the learner. He argued that the social environment significantly affects what and how students learn (Dimitriadis & Kamberelis, 2006; Vygotsky, 1978). When discussing the work of Dewey, Prawat (2000) explores Dewey's version of social constructivism that emphasizes the importance of public learning. Additionally, Prawat discusses the idea that learning or change can occur from the conflict between divergent ideas.

The ideas that we propose in the following pages build upon what other art educators argue for in previously published literature related to using the Web in Art Education. Coleman (2005) explores various facets of Web art and raises many issues relating to how the aesthetics of Web art call for new ways of understanding and interpreting these works of image and text. Keifer-Boyd (n.d.) approaches the Web as a means of creating cyberfeminist art and pedagogy. Through her Cyber-House project, she pushes notions of gaming and art as a pedagogical tool. Additionally, Sweeny (2004) analyzes how contemporary digital technologies change societies. He raises questions about how art education can address challenges posed by the digital visual culture world that involves simulation, unique forms of interaction, and new forms of visuality.

The inherent nature of Web 2.0 makes it ideal as a vehicle to promote teaching and learning from a social constructivism paradigm. Because the information available through the technologies of Web 2.0 is always changing and emerging, conflicts are inevitable. Additionally, because of the ease with which users can work collaboratively to share and build knowledge, these technologies can facilitate the type of learning that Vygotsky promoted.

DELICIOUS

delicious is a social bookmarking site that allows a user to "tag" websites, add descriptors, categorize them, and save them for future use (Johnson, 2007). Unlike bookmarking sites through a browser, sites that are marked with delicious are available to the user at any computer with Internet access. By default, delicious accounts and any sites tagged through delicious are public. However, if a user wishes to create a private account that is possible by changing the settings. Thus, a teacher may choose to exercise various degrees of control over what students do and what is available to the public. There are many possibilities for using delicious as a resource for teaching art at the classroom, district, and university levels. Through delicious, classroom teachers can share links with students to start research (Anonymous, 2005). Students can use delicious to collect resources for group projects and for documentation of their own research process. For example, AP art students could each have a delicious page that focused on the media they were most interested in, artists that they study both in and out of class, and social and cultural issues related to those artists' work. Students could make notes in delicious about how images, issues, and ideas were connected in order to be able to form complex thoughts about the artist and her/his work. In this case, delicious could be a tool to help students understand their artmaking process and see the relationships between and among disparate ideas. This sort of research would prepare students for speaking thoughtfully about their own artwork. Though students can make notes about their artmaking process in a variety of traditional ways, including through a sketchbook, using delicious allows students to add ideas whenever and wherever they have Internet access, access other students' ideas, and easily connect relevant websites to their ideas.

At the district level, art teachers could collaborate to share links for lesson plans, resources, museums, and blogs that relate to their teaching practice and interests. Teachers in a district could collaborate to create one page that contained links they all utilize. This may be a useful tool especially for elementary art teachers who are often the only art teacher in their school(s). Additionally, through delicious, art supervisors could easily share links with all the teachers in the district or with a group of teachers who teach particular courses.

At the university level, art education students could use delicious in their courses to share links related to readings, lesson plan ideas, or other Web resources tied to course materials. For example, beginning level art education students might create a delicious page of lesson plan ideas. The following year, these same students might add to the delicious page by gathering links to blogs written by art teachers. During a methods or practicum course, these students may find it useful to collect links to tools for classroom management. In their final year of college, art education students could use delicious to tag links to job fair announcements, tips on resume building and interview skills. Thus, through delicious, teachers and students at all levels can find and save useful websites that may relate to their artmaking or research about art and artists. Though delicious itself is not inherently constructivist, it can be used in ways to promote constructivist teaching and learning. For instance, through reviewing the tags of others, a user can learn from someone else and build a network of other delicious users who are interested in similar topics. Therefore, delicious can be the beginning of relationships that may lead to constructivist knowledge building.

BLOGS

Blogs, also known as "web logs," are a type of website that is updated frequently and that allows individuals to publish their ideas in a public forum. Blogs are increasingly popular and they have become a larger cultural form of communication. Unlike traditional print media, blogs are usually written in a conversational tone, allow for readers to comment on the content, and promote asynchronous dialogue between the author and commenters. The software required to create a blog is both user-friendly and often available at no cost. Blog authors are not Inherently "experts" on their topics, which is both frustrating and enchanting. The writer benefits tremendously, not only from the careful preparation and organization of her content, but also from the apprehension of publishing and inviting commentary from the digital community. It is this act of reflection and preparation of content that is so beneficial (Moulton, 2008). Readers can easily comment on or question the information provided, thus beginning a dialogue. Blog readers, in turn, find not only factual information on topics of interest, but entries that are slanted or expressed in a manner that is appealing to them individually.

Anyone has the opportunity to publish and have her/his opinion heard, and readers have the opportunity to agree or disagree. The very fact that the information provided might be incomplete or one of several perspectives necessitates further examination and evaluation of the validity and relevancy. The existence of so many voices should encourage students to find more than one perspective—perhaps even conflicting ones—triangulate information, and begin to compare and evaluate new knowledge (November, 2008). Art students in the 21st century need to develop critical thinking skills that include accessing, analyzing, evaluating, applying, and ultimately creating new media content. The types of social interactions possible through blogs range from none, in blogs that function mainly as bulletin boards, to significant, in blogs that have lively exchanges between the blogger and the commenters. We believe that blogs may contribute to socially constructing new knowledge, but it is up to the blogger and the commenters to make this type of interaction happen.

There are various genres or types of blogs that educators and students can use (Brooks, Nichols, & Priebe, 2004). For instance, a video blog might contain short clips demonstrating techniques, step-by-step instructions, or student presentations. An audioblog might feature student podcasts from a museum or gallery opening, excerpts from an interview with a local artist, or an evaluation of student work. A sketchblog would allow students to document the process of creating a work of art. Typically a blog centers on writing, but art students may be drawn to the personal and expressive dimensions offered by a blog (Brooks, Nichols, & Priebe, 2004). Blogs are useful tools for both art students and art teachers for a variety of purposes.

Blogs may promote conversation and learning that can be constructivist. Through making a comment, a user may be able to have a direct conversation with a blog author. When this type of dialogue occurs, new knowledge can be constructed through the social interactions of the commenter and the original blogger. However, the comments on a blog are typically subsumed under the authorship of the blogger. The dialogue produced offers tremendous potential for critique, as teaching students to constructively discuss art and artmaking is a challenging, yet important endeavor. Asynchronous commentary about a work of art promotes deep and thoughtful consideration on the part of a student, something not always possible when looking at 25-30 student artworks in the 45- or 90-minute timeframe of the public school class period. Many adolescents feel uncomfortable in a formal critique environment and although they might have good ideas, they might not stumble upon something useful or profound until after class is over. Thus, using a blog with a class as a form of ongoing critique could be a way to introduce continuing dialogue about artmaking. Through a blog, students could contribute comments about other students' works of art. The artist could respond to the comments and carry on a conversation with peers and the teacher about the work of art. Through these types of interactions, students could work together to build a deeper understanding of their own artmaking process, the meaning of their artworks, and the art of others. However, it is important to note that the teacher needs to actively monitor student blogging. Just as in face-to-face critique settings, teachers may need to step in if student comments are inappropriate. To facilitate students learning about appropriate uses of the blog, we suggest that teachers begin with some type of student contract that explains how the blogs can be used (Richardson, 2006).

Additionally, student use of blogs might supplant the use of textbooks. Because textbooks are static objects, they may be outdated or incomplete a short time after publication. The art world changes rapidly and blogs can accommodate these changes. If students need additional details about an entry or if doubts arise regarding information found in a blog, students may interact with the author and find new information. Though this could also be possible by contacting a book publisher or author, we think it is more likely to occur through a blog than through traditional media publishing channels. Through blogs, students have the chance to control and contribute to their own learning, direct, and even shape the content and curriculum in the art classroom (November, 2008).

Teachers may find it useful to read blogs to keep up with current events in the art world, monitor developing educational trends, share practices and resources, and conduct discussions about theory and shared interests. To make reading blogs manageable, teachers can use feed readers or aggregators that hand pick information and condense it onto a personalized, content-rich resource (Moulton, 2008). The content of blogs may change when the interests of the author change or in reaction to the readers and their comments. Widgets, including blogrolls, a list of other blogs identified as interesting or related, and embedded hyperlinks encourage the reader to explore further content and, perhaps later, to return with new information, perspectives or helpful links.

For teachers, a blog might act as a classroom organizational tool, a platform for critique, or a method for self-promotion and program advocacy. Blogs can be configured to be public or private and to allow students a variety of roles, including those of contributor, author, or merely viewer. Blogs may afford a developing artist the opportunity to have a virtual gallery or studio space. Ultimately, as Blood (2008) states, blogs have the power to transform both writers and readers from "audience" to "public" and from "consumer" to "creator."

SECOND LIFE

As technologies emerge, the use of technology, including the Web, in classrooms has become familiar to teachers and students. Delacruz (2004) suggested that although using technology in art class depends on school systems and art educators, many art educators know the importance of using the Web to access information. With an Internet connection, art educators and students can easily learn

Creating avatars (TOP) *and modeling objects* (BOTTOM) *in Second Life.*

about art and share their images, audio, video, etc. with a worldwide audience. There are many possibilities for art educators to use Web 2.0 for their art lessons as references and tools for critique.

A newer development of the Web is the ocial virtual world, which allows people to communicate through the Internet. One popular example of a social virtual world is Second Life, which is a virtual three-dimensional online community created by users. Linden Lab created Second Life in 2003 and the company started educational programs for university courses shortly thereafter (Conklin, 2007). Second Life allows users to register for free and to create their avatars, which are graphical representations of people in Second Life. Avatars represent virtual identities of the users and, with their identities, they can navigate virtual places, and meet and communicate with other residents in Second Life (Hayes, 2006). Also, this social virtual world has the potential for community development and educational purposes (Hayes, 2006). A version of Second Life specifically for teenagers is Teen Second Life.

The use of Second Life is growing in education (Conklin, 2007; Wong, 2006). For example, some educators in Second Life created the international spaceflight museum, made a model of the solar system, and built architectural forms from ancient Egypt. These creations make it possible to experience something that it is impossible to encounter in real life. In addition, Harvard's Berkman Center owns a private island in Second Life and routinely conducts conferences and courses in Second Life with avatars in attendance. Harvard law school professors Charles and Rebecca Nelson use the Berkman island as a new educational environment (Rymaszewski et al., 2007).

Depending on how educators use Teen Second Life, they can design new environments for students' learning that promote constructivist learning. Teen Second Life has great potential for educational purposes and specifically for art education because of the importance of visual imagery (Conklin, 2007; Hayes, 2006; Wong, 2006). Alvarez (2006) found that one person learned 3-D modeling and designing by using Second Life. She presented the possible uses of Second Life for 3-D design classes and traditional fine art classes for students to create virtual galleries for a critique. Additionally, Alvarez (2006) presented that the use of Second Life promotes communication among users to share their interests. Wong (2006) emphasized a benefit of Second Life is that it allows students to have real-time interaction so that they can engage in discussion with others.

In our opinion, some of the goals of education should be to provide students with an excellent education, for them to have a voice in this educational system, and then to help them contribute to society. As presented, Teen Second Life may be used to help students learn about their identity and to collaborate with others through experiencing a virtual 3-D society. Second Life might help connect subjects such as sociology, graphic design, and visual art and display (Alvarez, 2006).

CONCLUSION

In this chapter, we presented a variety of ways that Web 2.0 can enhance learning in art. However, it is important to note that there are significant criticisms of Web 2.0 and the basic idea that collaborative intelligence is a good thing. Critics, including Andrew Keen (2007), point out that blogs, YouTube, Wikipedia, social networking, and other Web 2.0 sites are completely unregulated. This means that incorrect and inaccurate information can coexist with other documented information. Wilson (2008) describes how the democratic principles espoused by some sites associated with Web 2.0 may not be followed. He offers the examples of Wikipedia and Digg and explores how the majority of the content is created and maintained by a small network of contributors. This is in contrast to the ideas that the content of these sites represents a significant collective gathering of knowledge from many people. In addition, Keen (2007) makes the point that these technologies allow for a form of narcissism that is manifested in an almost infinite desire for attention to one's personal life. Examples of the manifestation of Keen's point can be found throughout the Web, including the social networking site HAMSTERster. The tagline for this community is, 'Your virtual hamster and gerbil community.' Through this site, the owners of hamsters and gerbils post images of their pets, record pertinent information about them including birthdates and favorite foods, and link to their hamster friends and family. As of this writing, there are more than 2,200 registered rodent users of the site. Additionally, Keen laments the change in who makes content and how it becomes a part of culture. The democratization of the Web, which many people herald, is something that Keen believes is harmful to culture. In regard to the idea of using the Web to bring more music to the world, he writes, "The new Internet was about self-made music, not Bob Dylan or the Brandenburg Concertos. Audience and author had become one, and we were transforming culture into cacophony" (Keen, 2007, p. 14). His concern is that creators and consumers of content have already merged and that this merger is causing culture to begin deteriorating.

Through the tools of Web 2.0, teachers and students have the chance to interact with others and learn in collaborative ways. Because these technologies encourage user-generated content, social interaction, and new ways of knowing, they are appropriate to incorporate in the 21st-century classroom. As our students will encounter these technologies in their lives, we need to teach them meaningful ways to use these technologies that can further their classroom learning. Though the ideas of constructivist teaching and learning have been espoused for many years, the reality of classrooms does not always reflect these ideas. Simply bringing these technologies into classrooms will not result in wholesale changes in teaching. To engage in meaningful reform, teachers and school districts will need to rethink the structure of the traditional curriculum and classroom dynamic to bring about other practices that foster constructivist teaching and learning. During the coming years, it is likely that more aspects of the Web will become freely available with socially based platforms such as social bookmarking, blogging, and immersive environments. Thus, incorporating aspects of Web 2.0 will become increasingly important as students and teachers learn to navigate the emerging Web.

REFERENCES

Alvarez. M. (2006). Second Life and school: The use of virtual worlds in high school education. Retrieved December 6, 2007, from www.ucop.edu:8080/display/SecondLife/Articles+and+Papers

Anonymous. (2005). 7 things you should know about social bookmarking. Educause learning initiative. Retrieved June 3, 2008, from www.educause.edu/eli/

Blood, R. (2000). Weblogs: A history and perspective. Retrieved June 7, 2008 from www.rebeccablood.net/essays/weblog_history.html

Brooks, K., Nichols, C., & Priebe, S. (2004). Remediation, genre, and motivation: Key concepts for teaching with weblogs. Retrieved June 8, 2008, from http://blog.lib.umn.edu/blogosphere/remediation_genre.html

Coleman, A. (2005). Constructing an aesthetic of web art from a review of artists. *Visual Arts Research, 31*(1), 13-25.

Conklin, M. S. (2007). 101 Uses for Second Life in the college classroom. Retrieved February 25, 2007, from http://trumpy.cs.elon.edu/metaverse

Delacruz, E. (2004). Teachers' working conditions and the unmet promise of technology. *Studies in Art Education, 46*(1), 6-19.

Dimitriadis, G., & Kamberelis, G. (2006). *Theory for education.* New York: Routledge.

Hayes, E. R. (2006). Situated learning in virtual worlds: The learning ecology of Second Life. Retrieved January 01, 2007, from http://scholar.google.com/scholar?hl=en&lr=&q=%22Situated+learning+in+virtual+worlds%3A+The+learning+ecology+of+Second+Life.+&btnG=Search

Johnson, D. (2007). Techproof: It's delightful, it's del.icio.us. *Education World.* Retrieved June 4, 2008, from www.educationworld.com/a_tech/columnists/johnson/johnson017.shtml

Keifer-Boyd, K. (n.d.). Cyberfeminist activist art pedagogy. Retrieved September 22, 2008, from http://explorations.sva.psu.edu/uiah/readings/CH.htm

Keen, A. (2007). *The cult of the amateur: How today's internet is killing our culture.* New York: Doubleday.

Moulton, J. (2008). Blogs, blogs everywhere: Does everyone need an internet journal? Retrieved June 8, 2008, from www.edutopia.org/blogging-purpose

November, A. (2008). Student as contributor: The digital learning farm. *November Learning.* Retrieved June 4, 2008, from http://novemberlearning.com/index.php?option=com_content&task=view&id=290&Itemid=87

O'Reilly. (2005). What is Web 2.0. Retrieved June 1, 2007, from http://oreillynet.com/pub/a/oreilly/tim/news/2005/09/30/what-is-web-20.html

Prawat, R. S. (2000). The two faces of Deweyan pragmatism: Inductionism versus social constructivism. *Teachers College Record, 102*(4), 805-840.

Richardson, W. (2006). *Blogs, wikis, podcasts, and other powerful web tools for classrooms.* Thousand Oaks, CA: Corwin Press.

Rymaszewski, M., Au, W. J., Wallace, M., Winters, C., Ondrejka, C., & Batstone-Cunningham, B. (2007). *Second Life the official guide.* Hoboken, NJ: John Wiley & Sons.

Sweeny, R. (2004). Lines of sight in the 'network society': Simulation, art education, and digital visual culture. *Studies in Art Education, 46*(1). Reston, VA: National Art Education Association.

Vygotsky, L. (1978). *Mind in society: The development of higher psychological processes.* Cambridge, MA: MIT Press.

Wilson, C. (2008). The wisdom of the chaperones: Digg, Wikipedia, and the myth of Web 2.0 democracy. Slate. Retrieved September 28, 2008, from www.slate.com/id/2184487

Wong, G. (2006). Educators explore "Second Life" online. Retrieved December 6, 2007, from www.cnn.com/2006/TECH/11/13/second.life.university/index.html

Masquerading the Immateriality of Materiality / KAREN KEIFER-BOYD

Avatar masquerade is a technology of identity. From the premise that humans are not discreet entities but are an entanglement of social, technological, discursive, material, and haptic activity—which mutually articulates subjectivity—identity formation is the encoding of social-technological practices. The creation and performance of avatars in virtual environments can stretch open the borders of comfortably incorporated frames of knowing.

I present my thesis through a speculative fiction[1] about a collaboration of two art educators, Afridom and Billows, and their students in the mid-21st century who are producers and consumers of digital visual culture. The fictitious students (Jo, Syd, and Cory) are composites of students with whom I have worked in motivating intertextual critical new media art, social activism, and public pedagogy projects (e.g., see Keifer-Boyd, 1997, 2003, 2005, 2006, 2007, 2008). Feminist theories of masquerade inform this speculative fiction of art pedagogy, which takes place in 2050.

Jo: Is a mask an identification or a deception?

Syd: It's in the masquerade—the enactment—that you can reveal or conceal.

Cory: If I don't have an essential core then I am always becoming.

Syd: But you have a past. Isn't that your essential self that you either reveal or conceal?

Cory: My past is made of today's consequences of my previous actions, as well as from the memories of places, people, and things.

Billows: Let's go to UpStage to perform an identity to help you understand the interplay of your subjective experience and the cultural historical "stages" in which it is performed.

Afridom: Keep in mind that all manifestations of yourself are neither authentic or a deception. Your masquerade reveals, if you are paying attention to the immateriality of your materiality, the multiplicity of identity. Masquerade is both a hiding and revealing of self.

The immateriality of identity is materialized through masquerade. Materiality for new media theorist N. Katherine Hayles (2004) refers to "what performances the work [i.e., in this context, the avatar] enacts" (p. 71). How individuals desire to be identified is often through extravagant enactments (Wollen, 2003), i.e., signifying strategies that construct meaning. Masquerade can be a form of critique through performance of unmasking or exposing, or a way to compensate embodied experiences. Feminist film theory posits that masquerade signifies "not only a masking but also an 'unmasking' in the deconstructionist sense of exposing and criticizing" (Smelik, 1999, p. 358). Social psychologist Efrat Tseëlon defines masking as "fundamentally dialectical," and uses the concept to refer to "a 'technology of identity' and as means of interrogating it; the tool for self-definition and deconstruction" (2001, p. 11). Masquerade both conceals and produces femininity, as well as other identities, because identity is a subjective process created from social, technological, and embodied actors, human and non-human, that entangle in a multitude of networks.[2] Identity is contextual and collectively created.

From a feminist theory of masquerading the immateriality of materiality, I envision a future technologically infused ecopedagogy that guides students to deconstruct notions of authentic self. Masquerade dissolves binarisms of self and other; it bespeaks of relationalities.

Afridom: Freedom for the night is not to masquerade self to achieve dominant standards of worth, but to release oneself from such trappings.

Students create themselves, realizing their creation is in relationship to their movement with physical, biological, and digital interplay.

REGARDING FEMINIST SPECULATIVE FICTION

Only the impossible is worth the effort.

Are you a fanatic or an idealist?

Why do you need to label me?

I need to understand.

No, you want to explain me to yourself. (Winterson, 2000, pp. 54-55)[3]

A strategy in the tradition of feminist speculative fiction is to use "ironic humor to make sobering comments about the insidious nature of patriarchy" (Barr, 1987, p. 22; Keifer-Boyd & Smith-Shank, 2006). An imaginative text "change[s] the sense and substance of reality itself" (Edwards, 1984, pp. 148-149). My goal is to open possibilities through a vision of the future of art education, as well as to critique current trajectories of art education. Informed by feminist speculative fiction and feminist theories of masquerade, this chapter is an interchange between theoretical and imaginative texts.

The vehicle to space travel has changed. No longer does speculative fiction occur primarily on other planets than Earth (interstellar). Millions of authors create speculative fiction in cyberspace travel including fictions of sports teams, simulated lives (e.g., The Sims®, Second Life®), structured adventures (e.g., Doom®), and in open-ended Net play such as Regender (Yee, 2004), Verbarium (Sommerer & Mignonneau, 1999), and Frig Magnet Game (Clark, 2007). Mind and body are integrally one with all else in the Net—an interspecies system, no matter if bathing in cyberspace or H_2O.

PALIMPSEST BORDERS

Afridom: Since the 1970s, feminists have created "borders of their crossing" (Broner, 1978, p. 289). And, there have been many borders crossed, and re-crossed differently, until all borders are marvelous palimpsests layered deep with hybridity of active traversing.

Afridom and Billows, the art educators in this speculative fiction, have been working on ways to encourage youth to situate themselves in these palimpsest borders for the vantage perspectives such spaces provide. As an example of masquerading the immateriality of materiality, they refer to art critic Cheng (2002), whom they describe as providing a starting point for enacting perpetual displacement strategies from his interpretation of the 1960s edge paintings of Sam Francis.

Billows: Perpetual displacement, as an intertextual strategy of inquiry into sites of meaning in contemporary visual culture, uncovers rhizomatic connections.[4] The hidden is exposed, centered, and displaced forming endless centers and margins. Perpetual displacement strategy is a way to infiltrate the space inside the binary physicality/virtuality in order to create the rhizomatic connections between its nonbinary alterities. Thus the virtual does not exist as a privileged side of the binary physical/virtual removed from the consequences of embodiment, materiality, and their political consequences.

Afridom: Cheng questions the "color chronology" and "territorial negotiations" and how the edge colors conventionalize the white expanse of emptiness. This focus on peripheral colors surrounding the uniformly white center of the canvas suggests an ambiguity toward the homogeneous center. Cheng's interpretation provides an analogy of the political potential of perpetual displacement as a generative and interpretative strategy. There is generative potential in Sam Francis' painting where the edge colors stimulate questions concerning the meaning of center. What frames the edge, now the center of attention, perpetually persists in displacing assumptions of the normalcy of the center.

Afridom and Billows ask students to resist defining finite borders of contexts, and instead to identify the edges in order to recontextualize, again and again.

Afridom: Perpetual displacement proposes to tie infinite regression to present effects in practice by leaping over the abyss into the immediacy of experience. This process must be perpetuated and not end with one particular petrified reconstruction.

Billows: The frame and center share meanings born of each other. Their distinctions are fabricated by their relationship, which is too often erroneously perceived as a relationship of opposites.

Afridom: Furthermore, by perpetually displacing the center, relationships change and minimize the normalization of stagnate dominance and subordination. For example, normative heterosexuality structures enforce invisibility concerning other views of sexuality (Calhoun, 2000), yet a perpetual displacement of the categories of heterosexuality and homosexuality viewed appositionally creates a fluidness in which meaning of each category is situational.

Syd: Categories such as gender, race, nationality, and sexuality ascribed to a person, for instance, normalize these social constructs rather than contextualize a person's situation.

Jo: Yet our situations frame us with numerous categories.

Billows: Critical social theorist Iris Maria Young (2003) notes a conceptual shift, a perpetual displacement, "when we understand the concept of gender as a tool for theorizing structures more than subjects" (p. 12). Perpetual displacement as a theoretical position in critically questioning visual culture provides a way to acknowledge materiality and physicality without placing it in a fixed category, but instead focuses on the embodied situation.

Afridom: Perpetual displacement strategies both acknowledge and break the frame. Artists such as Orlan use perpetual displacement strategies to challenge dichotomous worldviews, appositional/oppositional binaries, and bivalent logic.[5] Orlan displaces the romantic myth of individual genius, and a host of other notions of patriarchal conditions related to sexual difference.

Billows: Orlan displaces male imaginary of women with its own abject content in the series of facial operations from patriarchal art-historical references, which incorporate the chin of Botticelli's *Venus*, the lips of Gustave Moreau's *Europa*, the eyes of Gérôme's *Psyche*, and the brow of Leonardo da Vinci's *Mona Lisa*. Orlan's performances in the 1990s, *Reincarnation of St. Orlan*, displace religious structures such as moral notions of carnal sanctity and the Christian logocentric principle of the "word made flesh" into "flesh made word."

Afridom: Orlan's art raises the question, "Is identity for sale?"

Cory: Orlan in her manifesto of "carnal art" defines it as "not interested in its final, plastic result but in the surgical operation-performance and in the modified body as a site of public debate" (Hirschhorn, 1996, p. 2).

Billows: Such sites of public debate, such sites of meaning, are not located in any one resultant fixed identity but in the dynamic betwixt spaces. They are not in the naturalized notion of matter but in the process of materialization. The "natural" face becomes displaced into representational structure. Philosopher of education Ilan Gur-Ze'ev's ideas of counter-education, which involves "the possibility of a struggle for dialogical self-constitution and moral responsibility to the otherness of Other and of the subject's struggle to overcome herself as constituted by normalising education" (2000, p. 222), could describe Orlan's performance of masquerade. Gur-Ze'ev highlights dialogue as "the space where the struggle over reflection as an open possibility can take place. Within it, the otherness of the 'external' and 'internal' Other as a reflection of the infinity and the openness of being allows the realization of transcendence in the immediate moment" (2000, p. 226).

TRANSFORM: AVATAR CO-ORDINATES

Afridom and Billows team teach classes not organized by time, or grouped by students' age. Alphanumeric grades have been obsolete for almost 3 decades. Instead, public schools are learning centers in which students select where to go and how long to stay. All K-12 graduates are given an equal lump sum of money upon graduation. Graduation is determined with an evaluation, based on criteria set by the student in dialogue with others in the areas of student interest, of an e-multimedia portfolio reflecting learning and thinking.

In 2050, educators theorize that motivation by alphanumeric grades can be an obstacle to learning, and by teaching in situations that do not require a grade nor result in the reward of a degree, more genuine ways to motivate are part of the pedagogical praxis. Students select where to go and how long to stay on a project, in which time is no longer partitioned according to disciplines. Long periods of time to work are necessary for engagement in learning that materializes in new forms and ideas responsible to diversity.

Afridom and Billows encourage students in their avatar creations to resist standards of beauty in defining human worth. Such standards of worth may lead to shame, self-hatred, destruction of body, or suicide.

Afridom: What does it mean to be fully human? Are there borders encasing a fully human, human? Unfortunately, the social fictions posit that yes, clothes matter, yes, skin color matters, yes, body shape matters. Today, we can still hear phrases that infer to be human is to be a man (e.g., mankind, man-made).

Billows: In Cyborg Web Shop (Andreja Kulun i, 2004), trajectories of speculative fictions concerning constructions of virtual selves redefine what it means to be human.

Afridom and Billows send students to the Cyborg Web Shop for prosthetic body revisions. Once "freedom for the night" is created through disguise, the art educators send students to Upstage,[6] a free-downloadable software developed for cyberformances that also enable impromptu audience participation. Creators "encourage you to use it for creative, educational and social purposes" in performances for global audiences (Upstage, Download, ¶ 1).

Upon entering the cyber art class, a quote from a 50-year-old print-bound book, *The PowerBook*, circulates students as they enter their virtual classroom:

> Undress. Take off your clothes. Take off your body. Hang them up behind the door. Tonight we can go deeper than disguise. (Winterson, 2000, p. 4)

Intrigued with the directive, students transport into a space in which others already there are trying on avatar co-ordinates.

A greeter asks: Male or female?

[Cory:] Does it matter?

[Greeter:] It's a co-ordinate.

[Cory:] This is a virtual world.

[Greeter:] OK. OK—but just for the record—male or female? (Winterson, 2000, p. 26)

Liao: I have been trying for many years to create a gender ambiguous avatar. I am just finishing my skin and remaking my body: it is now short and rather fat. However, I think I still look like an old lady, that is, not yet gender ambiguous enough. When I notice that a staff model from the store is in the dressing room, I realize that my focus on the task at hand has been so intense that I am unaware whether she has just walked in or if she has been watching me for a while. She says, 'plz leave here immediately.' I am stunned. She continues, 'this is a place for women only.' I want to reply that I am a woman, but I do not want to cause an argument. Afraid that she will file an abuse report[7] and that Linden Lab will kick me out of SL [Second Life®], I leave. (Liao, 2008, p. 34)

Afridom: "We are not accustomed to seeing woman as 'person' (man) and man as 'other'" (Barr, 1987, p. 10). Purposeful disguise of gender has been a ploy in fiction since Shakespeare's plays (e.g., Rosalind in *As You Like It*; Imogen in *Cymbeline*; Miranda in *The Tempest*) to James Tiptree, Jr.'s (i.e., Alice B. Sheldon's) *The Screwfly Solution* (1987/1977), as well as in life with the changes of artists' names to gender ambiguous names that lack gender-marking tags (e.g., Lena Krassner to Lee Krasner).

Jo: The disguise typically hides that one is female by taking on the mask of masculinity.

Syd: Masquerading typically derives from desire for a power not possessed. Gender forms the "co-ordinates" that guide social interaction.

Billows: What is the purpose of human existence today, to elders and youth, to people of different tribes and positions in those tribes? Let's imagine that it is socio-political equity for all. If this is human purpose, then use of technology to make bodies "attractive" will not promote social equity. The trajectories in Hawthorne's (1846) *Birthmark*, Tiptrees's (1989) *The Girl Who Was Plugged In*, and movies such as *Death Becomes Her* (Zemeckis, 1992) suggest as such. Diversifying standards of beauty is one potential solution.

DIRECTIVE

Afridom: Imagine a beginning of your civilization, i.e., a cultural narrative in which the society in which you exist did not come from destruction, hatred, and misunderstanding. What would occur in such a beginning?

Jo: I am going to create a fictional cultural narrative in which poverty is not present in the United States by looking at the social systems of the Nordic countries.

Billows: Fiction writer Jeannette Winterson advises to "break the narrative. Refuse all the stories that have been told so far (because this is what the momentum really is), and try to tell the story differently—in a different style, with different weights—and allow some air to those elements choked with centuries of use, and give some substance to the floating world" (Winterson, 2000, p. 53).

Syd: Such a cultural narrative would need to undo the trajectory of global warming.

Cory: Renewable resources several times over in a human lifespan would need to be the staple of humans.

Jo: Oil is not renewable in a human lifespan. It takes hundreds of thousands of years for the Earth to make oil from organic matter.

Syd: Thankfully, the ecopedagogy movement after the turn of the 21st century has begun to turn the destruction of the Earth around. While forest, fish, wetlands, soil, and water have been irreversibly destroyed on a global scale, the civic responsibility in regulating livestock, fisheries, and mining non-renewable energy resources enable our existence today. In my floating world, I will gesture toward reviving interconnected diversity.

TRANSPORT IN SPACE AND TIME

Jo: If I don't know who is behind the mask, I am lost without this orientation, without this coordinator of markers of the categories that I am familiar, that have oriented my responses to people, places, and things.

Cory: What I don't know is how to respond based on what is behind the masquerade.

Syd: My question is how can I respond to the masquerade seeing the co-ordinates that I have already codified as knowledge?

Billows: Reflexively respond in your own masquerade, and reflect on your performed response.

Afridom: Rewind the play and re-view.

Jo: My endowed sexual triggers in my masquerade made me comfortable in conformity with the others roaming in cyberspace but conversation was limited to desires and strategies of how to increase hypersexuality.

Syd: There is no comfortable stable viewing position.

Cory: My masquerade as an oyster generated political jibberish in intertextual reference to the conversation between an oyster and a walrus in *Alice in Wonderland.*

Susan Kaiser (2001), in the foreword to *Masquerade and Identities*, describes "Oprah's 'take it off' show ... [in which] ... the made over, 'after' or 'true, liberated' images serve to reinforce the dominance of that order" (p. xx). Afridom and Billows, familiar with such masquerade in the guise of unmasking amongst their students, and the society that surrounds them know that the pedagogical "trick" is to critique one's own socialization of dominant normalizing practices. The intense desire to refigure embodiment in cyberspace, and the human "capacity for imagining themselves as inhabiting different corporealities" is the motivational hook for discourse amongst the students about their masquerade (Grosz & Eisenman, 2001, p. 85). Afridom and Billows believe in what Elizabeth Ellsworth (2005) noted, drawing upon D. W. Winnicott's notion of transitional space, that "'augment[ation]' through invention" can allow one to "engage in political practice" (2005, p. 127).

KEYFRAME: DREAM A DANGEROUS DREAM
[Students converse.]

Jo: I have learned about myself by not being me.

Syd: I have learned about my fantasies, and question whether these are my desires or desires programmed in me over time from the experiences I have had.

Cory: I am, I am, I am hesitant to reflect on my masquerade.

Jo: My masquerade is doing anything but what I habitually do. This is a difficult creative challenge of emergence, to activate awareness of my masquerade.

Pervasive normalizing practices are difficult to resist or even recognize. The keyframe in one's animated life is that moment of recognizing the absurdity of perceptions of normal. Afridom and Billows' pedagogical strategies help to facilitate dreaming such a dangerous dream, i.e., they help students to keyframe[8] the intentional moment of change. "In transitional space, this someone is in a deeply interfused encounter with and at the same time in a 'differential emergence' from the materiality of the world" (Ellsworth, 2005, p. 34). Transitional space, as a field of emergence then, as relationality, consists in an interactive openness "to being affected by something new in a way that qualitatively changes its dynamic nature" (Massumi, 2002, p. 224).

MERGE

Afridom: Elizabeth Ellsworth's theorizing of a transitional space provides a theory of masquerade that we have experienced: "We are traversing the boundaries between self and other and reconfiguring those boundaries and the meanings we give them. We are entertaining strangeness and playing in difference. We are crossing that important internal boundary that is the line between the person we have been but no longer are and the person we will become" (Ellsworth, 2005, p. 62).

MASQUERADING MATERIALITY

This imaginary text is not an idealization but is instead imagined resistance in hopes that by being imagined it can be enacted. While trying to find the instances of when and how creative displacement strategies become perpetual, one critical criterion is whether the goal is to displace to redefine, or to displace perpetually, in order to defer the meaning. When students of art education use perpetual displacement strategies for masquerade, the daunting task of creating a contemporary, socially and culturally significant masquerade becomes more focused, more deliberate, and ultimately more meaningful. Perpetual displacement strategies can help to defer co-opting what it critiques.

Perpetual displacement strategies combined with immaterial masquerading offers a material transitional space/object that "becomes pedagogical when we use it to discover and creatively work and play at our limits as participants in the world" (Ellsworth, 2005, p. 78).

> The social body reaches the limits of the very expression of its potential and variation when the reciprocal variations and shifting characteristics of individual bodies are constrained from moving about, combining, and inflecting. The limits of the social body's expression and variation within a given context or event, then, can be said to constitute the limits of relationality. (Ellsworth, 2005, p. 130)

Teachers can facilitate a perpetual displacement strategy of masquerade in students' virtual fictions for specific circumstances in the critical and creative practices of their classrooms. Perpetual displacement strategies enable entrance to the between-ness of spaces by deferring signification. Masquerade creates ambiguity and challenges categories of identity. "The process of masking belies that there is no single or no 'true' master status identity. Masking enables the interrogation of identity" (Kaiser, 2001, p. xiv). Masquerading the immateriality of materiality can inform us about what can be changed, such as notions of race or gender as fixed identities, by occupying subject positions in innovative ways that unsettle essentialist narratives, and can trouble tropes that assume universalist claims.

REFERENCES

Atwood, M. (1998/1986). *The handmaid's tale.* New York: Anchor Books.

Barr, M. S. (1987). *Alien to femininity: Speculative fiction and feminist theory.* Westport, CT: Greenwood Press.

Broner, E. M. (1978). *A weave of women.* New York: Holt, Rinehart & Winston.

Butler, J. (1999). *Gender trouble: Feminism and the subversion of identity* (2nd edition). New York: Routledge.

Calhoun, C. (2000). *Feminism, the family, and the politics of the closet: Lesbian and gay displacement.* Oxford, UK: Oxford University Press.

Cheng, M. (2002). *In other Los Angeleses: Multicentric performance art.* Berkeley: University of California Press.

Clark, E. (2007). Frig magnet game. Retrieved November 16, 2008, from www.emmaclarke.com/fun/fridge-magnet-game

Deleuze, G., & Guattari, F. (1981). Rhizome. (P. Foss & P. Patton, Trans.). *Ideology and Consciousness, 8,* 49-71.

Grosz, E., & Eisenman, P. (2001). *Architecture from the outside: Essays on virtual and real space.* Cambridge, MA: The MIT Press.

Gur-Ze'ev, I. (2000). Critical education in cyberspace? *Educational Philosophy and Theory, 32*(2), 209-231.

Hawthorne, N. (1846). The Birthmark. In N. H. Pearson (Ed.), *The complete novels and selected tales of Nathaniel Hawthorne* (pp. 1021-1033). Prepared for the University of Virginia Library Electronic Text Center. Retrieved July 14, 2008, from http://historyofideas.org/etcbin/toccer-new2?id=HawBirt.sgm&images=images/modeng&data=/texts/english/modeng/parsed&tag=public&part=1&division=div1

Hirschhorn, M. (1996). Orlan: Artist in the post-human age of mechanical reincarnation: Body as ready (to be re-) made. In G. Pollock (Ed.), *Generations and geographies in the visual arts: Feminist reading* (pp. 110-134). New York: Routledge.

Edwards, L. R. (1984). *Psyche as hero: Female heroism and fictional form.* Middletown, CT: Wesleyan University Press.

Ellsworth, E. (2005). *Places of learning: Media, architecture, pedagogy.* New York: Routledge.

Hayles, N. K. (2004). Print is flat, code is deep: The importance of media-specific analysis. *Poetics Today, 25*(1), 67-90.

Kaiser, S. B. (2001). Foreword. In E. Tseëlon, E. (Ed.), *Masquerade and identities: Essays on gender, sexuality and marginality* (pp. xiii-xvi). New York: Routledge.

Keifer-Boyd, K. (2009). CyberNet activist art pedagogy. In A. Arnold, A. Kuo, E. Delacruz & M. Parsons (Eds.), *Globalization, art, and education* (pp. 126-134). Reston, VA: National Art Education Association.

Keifer-Boyd, K. (2007). Cyberfeminist activist art pedagogy (Park, Jeong Ae, Trans.). *Journal of Research in Art & Education, 8*(1), 29-90. [KoSEA: English 29-59 & Korean, 61-89]

Keifer-Boyd, K., & Smith-Shank, D. (2006). Speculative fiction's contribution to contemporary understanding: The handmaid art tale. *Studies in Art Education, 47*(2), 139-154.

Keifer-Boyd, K. (2005). Sharing perspectives. *Journal of the United States Distance Learning Association—USDLA, 2*(1), 9-20.

Keifer-Boyd, K. (2003). A pedagogy to expose and critique gendered cultural stereotypes embedded in art interpretations. *Studies in Art Education, 44*(4), 315-334.

Keifer-Boyd, K. (1997). Re-presentations in virtual museums. *Art and Academe: A Journal for the Humanities and Sciences in the Education of Artists, 9*(2), 38-60.

Kuluni, A. (2004). Cyborg Web Shop. Retrieved January 2, 2008, from www.cyborg.com.hr/about.php

Liao, C. (2008). My metamorphic avatar journey. *Visual Culture & Gender, 3,* 30-39.

Massumi, B. (2002). *Parables for the virtual: Movement, affect, sensation.* Durham, NC: Duke University Press.

Orlan. (1996). Conference. In D. McCorguodale (Ed.), *This is my body... this is my software* (pp. 81-93). London: Black Dog Publishing.

Rivière, J. (1991). *The inner world and Joan Riviere: Collected papers 1929-1958.* New York: Brunnel/Mazel.

Shade, D. D. (2009). What is speculative fiction? Lost book archives. Hatrack River Enterprises. January 17, 2009, from www.lostbooks.org/speculative-fiction.html

Smelik, A. (1999). Feminist film theory. In P. Cook & M. Bernink (Eds.), *The cinema book* (pp. 353-365) (2nd ed.). London: British Film Institute.

Sommerer, C., & Mignonneau, L. (1999). Verbarium. Retrieved November 16, 2008, from www.interface.ufg.ac.at/christa-laurent/verbarium/index.html

Tiptree, J. Jr. (1989). *The girl who was plugged in.* Auburn, WA: Tor Books.

Turkle, S. (1984). *The second self: Computers and the human spirit.* New York: Simon and Schuster.

Tseëlon, E. (Ed.). (2001). *Masquerade and identities: Essays on gender, sexuality and marginality.* New York: Routledge.

Upstage (2004). Retrieved November 15, 2008, from http://upstage.org.nz/blog/

Winterson, J. (2000). *The PowerBook.* London: Jonathan Cape.

Wollen, P. (2003). Fridamania. *New Left Review, 22.* July-August. Retrieved May 23, 2006, from http://newleftreview.net/Issue22.asp?Article=07

Yee, K.-P. (2004). *Regender.* Retrieved November 16, 2008, from http://regender.com/index.html

Young, I. M. (2003). Lived body versus gender: Reflections on social structure and subjectivity. In R. N. Fiore & H. L. Nelson (Eds.), *Recognition, responsibility, and rights: Feminist ethics and social theory* (pp. 3-18). New York: Rowman & Littlefield Publishers.

Zemeckis, R. (Director). (1992). *Death becomes her* [Motion Picture]. United States: Universal Pictures.

ENDNOTES

1 While there are many genres that authors posit are speculative fictions (e.g., alternative histories, contemporary social science fantasy, cyberpunk, dystopia, see Shade, 2009), my emphasis is feminist speculative fiction such as that published in *Femspec*, a feminist interdisciplinary journal specializing in critical and creative speculative fiction, and as defined by Margaret Atwood (1998) as a critical vision of the future if the cultural and technological interfaces of contemporary times continue on its trajectory.

2 See Joan Rivière's (1991) foundational 1929 psychoanalytic essay, *Womanliness as a Masquerade*, and Judith Butler's (1999) *Gender Trouble: Feminism and the Subversion of Identity.*

3 This conversation is from *The PowerBook*, which, like Winterson's other fictions, is about "Boundaries. Desire." (Winterson, 2000, p. 35).

4 Rhizome refers to a trailing root that uses a cloning strategy to propagate new life. Gilles Deleuze and Felix Guattari (1981), in "Rhizome," use the term to characterize an acentered, nonhierarchical, nonsignifying system.

5 For further application of perpetual displacement strategies in interpreting artworks see George Bauer's 2002 dissertation, *Perpetual Displacement as a Creative Concept and Critical Strategy of Inquiry into Sites of Meaning* (Texas Tech University).

6 Upstage® was first launched on January 9, 2004, funded by the Community Partnership Fund of the New Zealand Government's Digital Strategy, and is a collaborative project of CityLink, MediaLab, and Auckland University of Technology. It is open source and licensed under a dual-license: Creative Commons Attribution-NonCommercial-ShareAlike 2.5 License and GNU General Public License (GPL).

7 People can file an abuse report when seeing something or someone do something inappropriate in *SL* [SecondLife®].

8 *Keyframe* is a term used in animation to refer to the start and end point of a movement, thus framing a trajectory in which key decisions need to be made for a changed course of action.

Avatar as Pedagogy: Critical Strategies for Visual Culture in the Virtual Environment / CHRISTINE L. LIAO

AVATARS AS CRUCIAL MEDIUM FOR EDUCATION

Because of their enormous potential for teaching and learning, virtual environments are gaining the attention of educators. A 3-D computer graphic world in cyberspace, Second Life® (SL), is among the most discussed virtual environments. In fact, educators and educational institutions are creating educational spaces in SL; these individuals and groups see virtual environments as shared spaces that provide ways for collaboratively creating content (Ondrejka, 2008). At the same time, artists are also exploring virtual worlds as a medium in and through which to create art. In doing so, artists not only engage with the rich creative and imaginative potential of virtual worlds, but they also interrogate the issues inherent in virtual environments, questioning the limitations and conventions in ways that have both integrity and impact.

In order to enter a virtual world, each participant must create an avatar, a visual representation of the self.[1] An avatar, therefore, is the body of a person in the virtual environment and more or less indicates the identities of that person. Avatars reflect identity mostly through visual representation, but also through their performance. People perform their avatars according to the identity they adopted or created for the avatars. Turkle (1995) has recognized cyberspace as a place that "has become a significant social laboratory for experimenting with the constructions and reconstructions of self that characterize postmodern life" (p. 180). Since Turkle's exploration, cyberspace or virtual worlds have, to a significant extent, evolved into graphic-based worlds. In a 3-D graphic virtual world like SL, visual representation becomes an important means for communicating with others and for constructing and experimenting with identity. The creation/performance of the avatars, thus, also constructs the visual culture of a virtual environment. However, despite the connections of avatars to the identities of their creators, the creation of avatars is becoming an increasingly commodified and commercialized process. Participants can choose to buy an avatar (or clothing, skin, hair, etc.) that embodies what they identify with or desire to become. From my observations of visual culture in SL, I have found that people usually re/produce socially constructed identities and even exaggerate those identities. As a whole, the Internet is not free from socially constructed categories (Byrne, 2008; Kolko, Nakamura, & Rodman, 2000). Since virtual worlds (re)create visual culture from mass media and popular culture, the same issues, such as the stereotypical representation of body images, are reproduced and even exaggerated.

Avatars are crucial to art education because they connect body representation with notions of identity in both straightforward and complex ways. Body representation is the visual means of presenting identity online. Although it is problematic to view identity as inhering solely in the body, in cyberspace "human bodies continue to be the material and visible form through which human subjectivities are defined and contested today" (González, 2000, p. 48). Thomas (2007) indicates that the performance of identity online depends on the text and images we adopt as our avatars. Thus, avatars become an important form through which to mediate our experiences in virtual environments. Furthermore, our avatars directly influence these experiences. Therefore, if educators can avail themselves of a critical and flexible understanding of what avatars are and their complicated relationship to and construction of reality, benefits will accrue to students who increasingly live through self-representations in cyberspace.

Given that virtual environments such as SL offer a new medium for producing visual culture, especially in terms of representing body images, educators should explore the pedagogical potential of virtual environments critically. In doing so educators can develop pedagogies that address the issue of body representation as an essential feature. Creating and performing as avatars can itself function as a critical pedagogy through which to critique, challenge, and create alternative visual culture.

As educators begin to bring students into virtual worlds and as more virtual environments become available,[2] greater numbers of students will have the opportunity to create their own avatar(s).[3] If students can think creatively about alternatives for the visual representation of identity and subjectivity and about the meanings behind and effects of a representation, there is a greater chance that they can better understand the ideology behind the digital visual culture surrounding them. Related to understanding how identity and subjectivity can be created, is the need for students to understand the hegemonic visual culture in virtual environments. For example, the avatars in SL are overwhelmingly presented in terms of limited contemporary European Western aesthetics (such as the standard that a beautiful woman has a skinny body), and although it seems that people can create any type of avatar, the limitation of the system makes creating different body types, such as very fat avatars, difficult. It is only with a strong understanding of the culture within which they are creating and performing that students will become critical avatar subjects.

Virtual environments provide potential for imagination and creativity, and further, they can provide alternatives that challenge hegemonic visual culture. Artists use SL as a medium through which to create their works and avatars in the virtual environment. A look at how and what some artists do to enact their avatars and create pedagogical meaning through their avatars can provide strategies for educators to help students engage in pedagogical experiences through avatar creation. I will discuss artists Eva and Franco Mattes and Gazira Babeli, explaining how these artists create their avatars and perform as critical avatar subjects in order to create meaning and raise questions about digital visual culture. Further, I will provide suggestions about how avatar creation and performance can be a critical pedagogy in art education.

Eva and Franco Mattes (aka 0100101110101101.org)

Artists Eva and Franco Mattes (aka 0100101110101101.ORG) are among the early artists using SL as an artistic medium. Their SL artworks start with the Portraits series (2006-present),[4] which displays different avatars' pictures in both the virtual and the real worlds. They see avatars as self-portraits that tell stories about one's self and identity. In another series of works entitled Synthetic Performances (2007-present),[5] the Mattes use their avatars to re/perform early performance art by artists such as Marina Abramovic, Joseph Beuys, Gilbert and George, Valie Export and Peter Weibel, Vito Acconci, and Chris Burden. One performance, featured in PERFORMA07 in New York in November 2007, reenacted Marina Abramovic's performance of Imponderabilia, which was originally performed in 1977. The performance was about two people, artists Abramovic and Ulay, standing naked at the entrance to an exhibition. People wishing to view the exhibition were obliged to go through the door and choose to face a naked male or a naked female body as they moved toward the display space. The performance created anxiety for people, as the safe feeling of normalcy and space between clothed people was broken by the artists' naked bodies, and they were forced to think about the gendered body and subjectivity (Michalak, 1999).

Eva and Franco Mattes use their avatars to enact performance similar to Imponderabilia; however, the meaning and effect of their piece is different. The avatars are representations of artists' bodies in virtual space. Their virtual bodies also display the features of different genders. However, the anxiety of entering the space between their bodies and being forced to choose one side or the other is played out through humor in the context of the virtual world. As the nude avatars performed the piece, the audience laughed as the other avatars passed by the naked ones. In entering the tense space, an avatar symbolically conquers the discomfort borne of closeness to a stranger's nude body. Although at least some participants, even as avatars, still hesitated to pass by the nude avatars, most participants, through their avatars, behaved more playfully and seemed more comfortable participating in the virtual-environment version of the performance. Therefore, the act succeeds in questioning the functions and worth of using a realistic-looking gendered body in a virtual world.

The performance in SL also exposes that people perceive bodies differently in cyberspace than in the real world. Related questions also abound: Should our virtual bodies correspond to the appearance of our real bodies? Do virtual bodies tend to correspond to the real bodies that produced them in terms of race, gender, sexuality, body type, etc.? Further, when representation of body types is limited, what creative options do the participants in the virtual space have? Can this limit or enhance our experience and understanding of bodies? The avatars become a means to question virtual and actual bodies' representations. The result is a parody not of the original work, but of the visually presented realistic gendered body in the virtual world.

Gazira Babeli

SL artist Gazira Babeli only acknowledges her presence as an artist in the virtual world. She performs and creates events, machinima,[6] and exhibitions through her SL avatar. Her humorous performances in SL challenge the hegemonic visual culture of the virtual environment through irony, parody, and humor. For example, in her performance *Ultimate Submission* (2007),[7] she wore a barrel and performed a strange dance, making movements like those of a chicken, in front of advertising images of female avatars in a shopping mall. These images presented hyper-sexual and objectified female avatars for sale, and Babeli staged a performance that parodied and challenged the images and all others like them. The strangeness of her dance disrupted notions of what feminine movement and appearance can and should be, and her performance in the shopping mall venue served to disrupt the representation of the culture of capitalism. Through irony and parody, she created an avatar performance that exercised a creative and critical avatar subjectivity.

Another example of her performance work is *Come Together* (2007).[8] In this work, she stands on a stage; participants can touch a pose ball, which contains computer script, to move, pose, and merge with her avatar body and/or other avatars (or even objects). The result is a group sculpture performance. Avatars are merged into one entity so that the boundaries between individuals no longer exist. The identities of the bodies become blurred. The performance highlights the avatar as an assemblage of identities. Therefore, this work raises the issue of what new identities we can become when we are able to construct identities collaboratively. Further, can we create a new subjectivity that is not defined by gender, skin color, or other visual representation? As Hall (1996) argues, identity is constructed "through the relation to the Other" (p. 4); the collaboration between avatars also indicates that our identity construction is influenced by society and others.

Thus, the question of how we can really become our "true self" or what we want to be through avatar or whether that is even possible is exposed. The collaborative avatar sculpture reveals the impossibility of constructing a new subjectivity through only the existing social imaginary.

CRITICAL STRATEGIES FOR ART EDUCATION

The artists discussed use different strategies to live through their critical avatar subjects. They question, critique, and create visual culture in the virtual environment. Their subjectivities are fluid in cyberspace; though they create different identities, the artists all seek to challenge bounded socio-cultural identities.

Art educators can use the work of these artists as a starting point for discussing with students the general subject of visual culture in virtual environments. For example, discussion questions about Gazira Babeli's *Ultimate Submission* might include questions such as the following: What meanings are inherent in the visual culture that the artist critiques? What does it mean to have a sexy avatar? What does identity mean to you, if you meet an avatar who looks the same as you?

In the beginning, teachers can give students time for exploration and ask them to observe the visual culture they encounter in virtual worlds. An effective strategy is to take a screen shot of the virtual environment and avatars, in which the image contains specific meaning or ideology that is problematic to different groups of people in the society; group discussion afterwards can help students begin to think more critically about the visual culture of virtual environments.

Further, teachers can ask students to create their own avatars and create an art project collaboratively. For high school or college students, the project could be a role-play performance, in which students can play different identities. Using parody as a strategy, students are challenged to create avatars that reflect the problems they identified earlier, or they may create avatars that reflect their role-play experience. They can also create a machinima from their performance. Garoian (1999) proposes a performing pedagogy that "considers the aesthetic dimensions of performative subjectivity as an educational imperative, a practice of teaching that necessitates the critique of hegemonic cultural performances" (p. 10). Performance, for him, is a strategy that creates critical subjectivity to contest and transform socially and historically constructed ideologies. In keeping with the idea of challenging the social hegemony process and creating critical agency, the performance strategy here generates critical pedagogy. Students' avatar creation/performance, therefore, becomes explicitly pedagogical, because they are thinking creatively in order to critique and even challenge the visual culture of avatars. They become critical avatar subjects, which falls in line with critique pedagogy, which resists dominated culture (Garoian, 1999).

In addition, the strategy of appropriating a historical piece—as used by artists Eva and Franco Matte—has been long enacted in art history. The reenactment and appropriation can provide new understanding of the work or create new meaning from the work. Art teachers can have students choose an artwork that contains the ideas or discusses the issues related to their exploration, whether it is performance art or visual art, and students can recreate the piece through their avatars and interaction in a virtual environment. Through the dialogue with an artwork, the intertextual practice can be a way to stimulate students' creativity and critical thinking about representation in cyberspace. Virtual space, thus, is a space in which students can work through critical issues.

A concrete example from my own teaching is a machinima made by two students. In their project, they explored the idea of gender construction and used their avatar as a means to understand the construction of gendered body. They each created a gender-ambiguous avatar in order to challenge the existing gender representation. Then, they perform their avatar dancing on a stage in a mall, which has stereotypical sexy male images. They made a music video-like machinima out of their performance to express their effort to disrupt stereotypical gendered avatars.

It is important to understand that using the avatar as a vehicle for pedagogy is not simply a matter of asking each student to create an avatar that reflects his/her identity and then discussing why students created those particular avatars. To enact a critical pedagogy, educators should understand that it is more important that students fully understand that identity is not just what they choose to be in a virtual environment. The strategies artists use to present a critical subjectivity in the virtual world can give students a starting point for enacting their own creative and critical subjectivities in the virtual world, and perhaps the critical subjectivity can come back to the real world.[9] It is certainly appropriate that art teachers lead the way in encouraging students to be creative and resourceful in enacting their avatars and tapping into their own imaginative worlds.

As places of learning outside of classroom and institutional boundaries, virtual worlds "encompass a peculiar knowledge and skill" (Ellsworth, 2005, p. 151). Knowledge created and shared in the virtual environment can only be created in that environment. For example, we can experience virtual art only by interacting with the art in a virtual environment in which the art was meant to be experienced. Moreover, the learning experience in virtual worlds is mediated through avatars. The embodied experience of avatar creation/performance enables the meaningful apprehension of ourselves, as we constantly experience ourselves through our bodies. Keifer-Boyd (2007) argues that "the construction of the body, in and through virtual space, is a mutual articulation of knowledge formation arising from the body's interactions with virtual objects in a simulated environment" (p. 51). Therefore, the interaction with/in virtual worlds is pedagogical and contributes to the creation of embodied knowledge. The pedagogy that emerges from the avatar creation/performance experience is "pedagogy in the making" (see Ellsworth, 2005)—a pedagogy that constantly creates new knowledge and experiences.

CONCLUSION

A critical pedagogy in art education not only occurs in the teacher–student dialogue in the classroom, but also takes place in the art-making process that transforms the learner. Additionally, Yokley (1999) suggests that through a critical pedagogy teachers and students can discover the meanings and power inhering in works of art, learn to question ideological structures, and even engage in political action.[10] As a visual representation and performance, avatars provide a means for conceptual and practical critical pedagogy in art education, a subject through which students may better understand their own subjectivity and its relationship to socio-culturally bound identities.

As more and more educators develop classes using environments such as SL, avatars become a crucial means by which to engage students to challenge identity politics and to interrogate what it means to be human both within and outside of the virtual environment. Avatar creation/performance, therefore, could be a critical pedagogy in art education that increases students' critical reflection about representations of the self in cyberspace, gives students opportunities to try different possibilities, and challenges and resists limited identity categories and body images in society.

REFERENCES

Byrne, D. N. (2008). The future of (the) "race": Identity, discourse, and the rise of computer-mediated public spheres. In A. Everett (Ed.), *Learning race and ethnicity: Youth and digital media* (pp. 15-38). Cambridge, MA: The MIT Press.

Ellsworth, E. (2005). *Places of learning: Media, architecture, pedagogy.* New York: Routledge.

Garoian, C. R. (1999). *Performing pedagogy: Toward an art of politics.* Albany, NY: State University of New York Press.

González, J. (2000). The appended subject: Race and identity as digital assemblage. In B. E. Kolko, L. Nakamura, & G. B. Rodman (Eds.), *Race in cyberspace* (pp. 27-50). New York: Routledge.

Hall, S. (1996). Introduction: Who needs "identity"? In S. Hall & P. Du Gay (Eds.), *Questions of cultural identity* (pp. 1-17). Thousand Oaks, CA: Sage.

Keifer-Boyd, K. (2007). Body interfaces in curriculum. In S. Springgay & D. Freedman (Eds.), *Curriculum and the cultural body* (pp. 51-60). New York: Peter Lang.

Kolko, B. E., Nakamura, L., & Rodman, G. B. (2000). Race in cyberspace: An introduction. In B. E. Kolko, L. Nakamura, & G. B. Rodman (Eds.), *Race in cyberspace* (pp. 1-13). New York: Routledge.

Michalak, K. (1999). Performing life, living art: Abramovic/Ulay and KwieKulik. *Afterimage, 27*(3), 15-17.

Ondrejka, C. (2008). Education unleashed: Participatory culture, education, and innovation in Second Life. In K. Salen (Ed.), *The ecology of games: Connecting youth, games, and learning* (pp. 229-252). Cambridge, MA: The MIT Press.

Thomas, A. (2007). *Youth online: Identity and literacy in the digital age.* New York: Peter Lang.

Turkle, S. (1995). *Life on the screen: Identity in the age of the Internet.* New York: Simon and Schuster.

Yee, N., & Bailenson, J. (2007). The Proteus effect: The effect of transformed self-representation on behavior. *Human Communication Research, 33*(3), 271-290.

Yokley, S. H. (1999). Embracing a critical pedagogy in art education. *Art Education, 52*(5), 18-24.

ENDNOTES

1 In this chapter, I discuss avatars as a visual representation of people in virtual worlds, but avatars are not necessary to have visual characteristics. Early online virtual worlds, such as MUDs (Multi-User Domain) are text-based, and the avatars in these worlds are also text-based.

2 Social virtual environments such as Openlife®, There.com® and IMVU®, online games such as World of Warcraft® and Gaia online®, or video games such as Little Big Planet® and Animal Crossing® all include customizable avatars.

3 Although the standard version of *SL* is restricted to those aged 18 or older, there is also *Teen Second Life®*, which, as its name implies, is exclusively for teens.

4 See http://0100101110101101.org/home/portraits/index.html

5 See http://0100101110101101.org/home/performances/index.html

6 The terms "machinima" comes from machine and cinema. It is a film genre produced through and in computer-graphic-generated environments, such as games and virtual worlds.

7 See http://gazirababell.com/ultimatesubmission.php

8 See http://gazirababeli.com/cometogether.php

9 Researchers Yee and Bailenson (2007) have demonstrated that our experience in playing an avatar influences our real world performance.

10 An example of using SL to produce political artwork and action is the work of virtual Guantanamo, which engages people (avatars) in experiencing virtual detention to raise awareness of certain social issues and create political action. The work can be seen through an online video at www.youtube.com/watch?v=QT7p231Cfxk

Physical Computing and Video Game Art Education / RYAN PATTON AND MATT KENYON

The pedagogical use of games is not foreign to the field of art education (Hicks, 2004). Games from the Surrealists and Situationists have been a part of art curricula for a number of years. Today, video games are one of the most popular forms of media in youth culture, and educators are beginning to explore their learning potential. In 2006 the MacArthur Foundation began funding a 5-year, $50 million initiative to look at digital media and learning, focusing on video games as a pedagogical site (Jenkins, 2006a). Art educators have written for some time about the impact of digital visual culture within the spaces of art education (Dunn, 1996; Heise & Grandgenett, 1996; Krug, 2002; Keifer-Boyd, 1996; Sweeny, 2004; Taylor & Carpenter, 2002; Tavin, 2002), but have yet to address pedagogical applications of video games. Are the issues that concern scholars in comparative media (Bogost, 2007, Jenkins, 2006b) and the learning sciences (Gee, 2007; Shaffer, 2006) the same for art educators? Might there be aspects of digital media and video games that art educators can address from a unique position in the academic community?

This chapter will look at some of the pedagogical and technological purposes for making video games and physical computing devices for game interfaces as part of an art education pedagogy.

As the educational interest in digital media expands, so does the need for creative professionals. The American public school system has, since its inception, been a site for the development of a robust workforce (Spring, 2004). One relevant example of this can be found in *SchoolArts*, the most widely distributed magazine for K-12 art educators: They link their website to The Partnership for 21st Century Skills, an educational consortium concentrated in the technology sector including Apple, Dell, Cisco, AT&T, The Discovery Channel, Adobe, and Blackboard (Vockley, 2007).

From these technological and educational trends, we find that art educators must address the increased popular interest in digital technologies. If not, the uncritical and uncreative applications of digital technologies will only perpetuate modes of 20th century production and interaction in the art classroom. So what are the aspects of digital media technologies that are most relevant to art educational practice? What are the new skills that are required to use, discuss, and teach digital media—specifically, video games? Recently, Parks (2008) has written about using video games as a site for social reconstructionist art education, looking at the games Darfur is Dying and Peacemaker as examples, but there is much more work to be done. Looking at and using video games created in the commercial market develops a different set of learning objectives than making video games. This is analogous to developing a critical eye for paintings and movies through art appreciation and criticism, in relationship to the critical awareness developed through the process of creating objects. And if we look further into art education's role in game-based and digital art, how do we critically address the way students physically play the games they are making? For this we must understanding the software, hardware, and devices that support their ludic activity.

PHYSICAL COMPUTING: GETTING INTO THE GAME

Video games are one component of digital culture that youth have embraced. Youth have adopted mobile electronics like cell phones to be always connected, all the time, bringing the body and machine closer together through these technologies. Physical computing is an area of digital media that is uniquely positioned at the junction of computer science, materials science, and fine art. In the past, creating interactive environments that respond physically to the presence of the viewer or abstract and intangible data, would have required a team of specialists, including programmers and engineers. Easy to use (and oftentimes open source) game engines, micro-controllers, smart materials, and programming strategies are now expanding what the aspiring game artist/designer can achieve.

Physical computing recently reentered the mainstream market of video games. In the 1980s physical computing began to make inroads in video games with products such as Nintendo's Power Glove and Power Pad, but fell short of popular appeal as the game consoles continued to undergo major graphic advances. More recently, the video game market is seeing that interface can trump processing power, and that the physical experience of play can be an important part of video games. The Wii's recent success in today's "console wars" has been the direct result of advances in physical gaming interfaces (i.e., the Nintendo Wii, Dance Dance Revolution and Guitar Hero) (Schiesel, 2008). The popular culture ubiquity of these interfaces provides a common point of departure for the next generation's exploration of interface design moving from the familiar to the experimental and nonconventional. Developing greater sophistication in physical computing and game design is part of the research being done in the higher education, such as the New Media Program at Penn State University (Kenyon & Patton, 2008).

Game development and physical computing technologies are constantly being upgraded, critiqued, and adapted by the consumer. For example, automobiles now have standard voice activated controls, GPS, and anti-theft systems that were only available on high-end models a few years ago. In video games, the Nintendo's Wiimote, touch screens on the Nintendo DS, Sony's Eyetoy, controllers for Guitar Hero, Rockband, Dance Dance Revolution, and voice communicators in massive multi-player online games have allowed for more interactivity than the single-player experience played with universal equipment like a keyboard, mouse, or joystick controller. Button mashing still has its place in video games; however, the use of physical computing has broadened the game audience by providing an inclusive and sophisticated mechanism for game play. The game industry recognizes that the development of more "realistic" looking games provides a limited advancement to the player's experience (Mencher, 2007). We now find players looking, listening, and touching their media, having experiences where they are talking to other players, and performing to the games that reinforce the physical experience (Schiesel, 2008). How a player receives and responds to information in game worlds is key to future game development (Bogost 2008). Physical computing in games offers some of those solutions.

If we think about the popular video game Guitar Hero in relationship to its electronic game predecessor, Simon, the experience of the game play is very different. Gaining great popularity in the 1980s, Simon was an electronic game focused on matching patterns and sequence. A disk-shaped device, Simon had four buttons—red, green, blue, and yellow—with corresponding sounds and lights that the player needed to mimic to win. Although the idea of Simon and Guitar Hero are the same—matching sounds and colors—the physical form of game play in Guitar Hero is very different. In Guitar Hero, the player holds the guitar-shaped device, "strumming" the switch that replaces the guitar pickup on its body, while fingering the buttons over the neck with a "guitarish" style, creating a new form of physiological activity for the video game player. The gameplay and guitar-shaped interface in Guitar Hero lends itself for a player to feel like they are playing the instrument along with the song, while Simon's four-button interface only focuses on the repeating of the visual and audio pattern. Until recently video game designers developed their games with standardized controllers in mind designed to play a variety of games. Now the game designers are considering how the interface encompasses the player's body and prescribed movement through the physical experience of the game, just as educators look at multiple forms of learning for students (Gardner, 1993).

Although Simon was popular for its time, Guitar Hero has arguably achieved greater status, in part because the game play centers on the experience of using the game controller. Other guitar-based video games like Jam Sessions for the Nintendo DS actually allow the player to play and record notes, but the device uses the directional buttons of a traditional controller, unnatural to those expecting a guitar-like experience. So even though you are closer to playing a guitar by creating your own notes with Jam Sessions, the physical computing component of the Nintendo DS design does not lend itself to the user's knowledge of playing guitar. Looking at game sales and popularity of Guitar Hero events, players appear more psychologically attached and invested in the experience of Guitar Hero than the guitar playing of Jam Sessions or the matching game Simon.

GAME ON: MAKING GAMES

Creating forms of visual culture that are socially relevant to students outside the classroom engages students that have lesser interest or skill in traditional art practices like painting or clay (Duncum, 2002). Critical thinking can be found in the analysis and making of games, uncovering the mystery behind one of the curtains of digital visual culture. So what are some ways students can make video games in the art classroom? Several game engines and game development tools have emerged over the last few years for the amateur and youth market, such as Game Maker, GameBrix, Power Game Factory, RPG Maker, Unity, Unreal, Scratch, and Source to name a few. These programs are designed to help people make sophisticated games within a short period of time. Video game development tools vary in features and price; each have to be considered on their own merits in relationship to what teachers' and students' abilities and needs are. For example, some video game development tools require some knowledge of programming while others do not, or are designed to make games with a side scrolling or first person vantage point. Questions for teachers as they assess their classroom needs are: What knowledge and skills do the students currently have? What specifically are the students learning? Do the game development tools implemented achieve these goals or is additional assistance needed? Even with minimal technology, art educators can use the physical environment as a mixed-reality game space, extending the perceived boundaries of where games begin and end (Salen, 2005; McGonigal, 2007; Lantz, 2008).

One example of students developing games in an art educational context is the Smithsonian Associates Summer Program's game development workshop. Students from the ages of 8 to 14 begin by learning about the qualities of games and how games are structured, and making board games. After learning the basics of game making, students make a video game using the development tool Game Maker. In creating their own two-dimensional characters—animating, designing game levels, and learning beginning programming—students developing an understanding of key video game concepts like procedural thinking, collision detection, random variables, and functions. These experiences do not create expert game developers but instead give transparency to the inner workings of some of their most treasured visual culture. Through the Smithsonian game development workshop students learn how—in video game design—art, math, physics, and computer science are components in constructing the experiences students can design and manipulate.

As students learn game development skills, they can also be challenged to think about and question some of the conventions of games, such as how one moves in a game (i.e., from left to right, bottom to top, or forward in 3-dimensional space), and further consider tropes of video games: imagery, genres, the actions of game play, and new ways these norms can be explored and exposed. As these activities focus on how games are understood and interacted with on an abstract level through software manipulation, physical computing focuses on understanding issues of the game interface and how the physical actions of the player interact with the game, critiquing what is presented behind the screen with what is experienced in front of the screen (Buxton, 2001).

For example, how can we understand games through the player's physical actions? Are there ways the interface or game could be designed to enhance a game's purpose? Art educators can also develop simple physical computing systems from mouse hacks (Baudisch et al., 2006) and keyboard hacks (Sarafan, 2006), modifying old standard equipment to create new video game controllers. By creating sculptural forms that use simple on/off switches and sensors to operate the game, students can create interfaces that critically engage physical experiences to the games they design. For example, the Massage me jacket is a wearable gamepad, embedding game buttons into the back of a vest. Designed to harness the physical activity of a video game player, Massage me puts the player into the position of performing physical acts of kindness to someone else to play the video game (Perner-Wilson & Satomi, 2007). This type of activity prepares students to take the materials and technologies available to them to remix (Navas, 2008), collage (Garoian & Gaudelius, 2008), or bricolage (Bogost, 2006) game systems and computing systems.

Physical computing can also be thought of as a sculptural issue, breaking computer and video games away from the view that they have limited physical forms and touch (Garoian & Gaudelius, 2001). As we've begun to see with assistive technologies that provide modes of inclusion for disabled students, these technologies are also the devices that can be studied, developed and adapted through classrooms engaged in physical computing and interactive art (Eisenhauer, 2007). Interactive digital art and physical computing devices with sculptural and performative components are found in the work of Daniel Rozen, Karolina Sobecka, or Rafael Lozano-Hemmer, bridging the culture of the digital with the analog. Recognizing the past in the present, where ideas of artist, audience, and making are brought together.

Advances in digital technologies cannot be ignored in the art classroom. Discussion on critical uses of video games is visible in art education, but more can be addressed to the making of these interactive systems. Giving students opportunities to create interactive systems and devices like video games and their controllers will strengthen and broaden the scope of art education's reach into digital media in the 21st century.

REFERENCES

Baudisch, P., Sinclair, M., & Wilson, A. (2006). Soap: A mouse-like pointing device that works in mid-air. Retrieved November 3, 2007, from http://research.microsoft.com/users/baudisch/publications/2006-Baudisch-UIST06-Soap.pdf

Bogost, I. (2008). Persuasive games: Performative play. Retrieved June 26, 2008, from www.gamasutra.com/view/feature/3703/persuasive_games_performative_play.php

Bogost, I. (2007). *Persuasive games: The expressive powers of video games.* Cambridge, MA: MIT Press.

Bogost, I. (2006). *Unit operations: An approach to video game criticism.* Cambridge, MA: MIT Press.

Buxton, W. (2001). Less is more (more or less). In P. Denning (Ed.), *The invisible future: The seamless integration of technology in everyday life.* New York: McGraw Hill, 145-179.

Dunn, P. (1996). More power: Integrated interactive technology and art education. *Art Education, 49*(6), 6-11.

Duncum, P. (2002). Theorizing everyday aesthetic experience with contemporary visual culture. *Visual Arts Research, 28*(2), 4-15.

Eisenhauer, J. (2007). Just looking and staring back: Challenging ableism through disability performance art. *Studies in Art Education, 49*(1), 7-22.

Galloway, A. (2006). *Gaming: Essays on algorithmic culture.* Minneapolis: University of Minnesota Press.

Gardner, H. (1993). *Frames of mind: The theory of multiple intelligences.* New York: Basic Books.

Garoian, C., & Gaudelius, Y. (2001). Cyborg pedagogy: Performing resistance in the digital age. *Studies in Art Education, 42*(4), 333-347.

Garoian, C., & Gaudelius, Y. (2008). *Spectacle pedagogy: Art, politics and visual culture.* Albany: SUNY Press.

Gee, J. (2007). *Good video games and good learning: Collected essays on video games, learning and literacy.* New York: Peter Lang Publishing.

Hicks, L. E. (2004). Infinite and finite games: Play and visual culture. *Studies in Art Education, 45*(4), 285-297.

Heise, D., & Grangenett, N. (1996). Perspectives on the use of the internet in art classrooms. *The Journal of Art Education, 49*(6), 12-18.

Keifer-Boyd, K. (1996). Interfacing hypermedia and the internet with critical inquiry in the arts: Preservice training. *Art Education, 49*(6), 33-41.

Kenyon, M., & Patton, R. (2008). Physical computing and game art. *Proceedings of 2008 Playing to Win: The Business and Social Frontiers of Video Games.* University Park: Penn State University.

Krug, D. (2002). Electronic media and everyday aesthetics of simulation. *Visual Arts Research, 28*(2), 27-37.

Jenkins, H. (2006a). *Confronting the challenges of participatory culture: Media education for the 21st Century.* White Paper for the MacArthur Foundation's Digital Media and Learning Initiative. Retrieved February 17, 2008, from http://digitallearning.macfound.org/site/c.enJLKQNIFiG/b.2029199/k.BFC9/Home.htm

Jenkins, H. (2006b). *Fans, bloggers and gamers: Media consumers in a digital age.* New York: NYU Press.

Lantz, F. (2008). Big urban game: A playful connection of the twin cities. In F. von Borries, S. P. Walz, & M. Böttger (Eds.), *Space time play* (pp. 390-391). Basel, Switzerland: Birkhäuser.

Lu, L. F. (2005). Pre-service art teacher negative attitudes and perceptions of computer-generated art imagery: Recommendations for pre-service art education program. *Visual Arts Research, 31*(1), 89-102.

McGonigal, J. (2008). Why I love bees: A case study in collective intelligence gaming. In K. Salen, (Ed.), *The ecology of games: Connecting youth, games, and learning* (pp. 199-228). Cambridge, MA: The MIT Press.

Mencher, M. GameRecruiter's Mencher talks industry careers, In GDC Radio: 29 (April 20, 2007). CMP Media LLC.

Navas, E. (2008). The author function in remix. Retrieved June 29, 2008, from http://remixtheory.net/?p=309

Parks, N. (2008). Video games as reconstructionist sites of learning in art education. *Studies in Art Education, 49*(3), 235-250.

Perner-Wilson, H., & Satomi, M. (2007). Massage me. Retrieved July 25, 2008 from www.massage-me.at

Salen, K. (2005). Games take it to the street. RES, 8 (3). Retrieved October 6, 2006, from www.gamersmob.com/files/Games_Take_it_to_the_street.pdf

Sarafan, R. (2006). Hacking a USB keyboard. Retrieved May 15, 2008, from www.instructables.com/id/Hacking-a-USB-Keyboard/

Schiesel, S. (2008, February 1). In the list of top-selling games, clear evidence of a sea change. *The New York Times*, pp. 1 Arts.

Shaffer, D. (2006). *How computer games help children learn*. New York: Palgrave Macmillan.

Spring, J. (2004). *The American school 1642-2004*. New York: McGraw-Hill.

Sweeny, R. W. (2004). Line of sight in the "network society": Simulation, art education, and visual culture. *Studies in Art Education, 46*(1), 74-87.

Tavin, K. (2002). Engaging advertisements: Looking for meaning in and through art education. *Visual Arts Research, 28*(2), 38-47.

Taylor, P., and Carpenter, S. (2002). Inventively linking: Teaching and learning with computer hypertext. *Art Education, 55*(4), 6-12.

Vockley, M. (2007). Maximizing the impact: The pivotal role of technology in a 21st century education system. Partnership for 21st Century Skills. Retrieved December 20, 2007, from www.picnet.net/basecamp/partnershipfor21stcenturyskills/supportretainer/SIP%20tech%20paper.pdf

Empowering the Disenfranchised: Explorations in Building Sites and Futures in Second Life / MARY STOKROCKI AND SANDRA SUTTON ANDREWS

Throughout history, art has been "a symbolic battleground" (Shohat & Sham, 1994, p. 183) that offers diverse avenues for reframing issues and re-imaging our world (Rogoff, 2005). Giroux (2005) argued that television, films, advertisements, and digital images operate as "sites of public pedagogy" that are dominated by a few corporations (p. 5). Such pedagogy mostly rewards the technologically talented (p. 5). Sweeny (2004) interpreted digital culture and its many perspectives and visual roles as "lines of sight." He critically analyzed those individuals and institutional networks of privileged forms of visuality as "parasites." He explains how smaller entities (individuals, art collectives, and students) usurp power from larger institutions (museums, governments, schools) by drawing energy from them.

Educators need to see the role of digital media not only as expressive exchange but also as socio-cultural change (Garber, 2004; Keifer-Boyd, 2004; Stokrocki, 2007). Gude (2007) argued for "reconstructing social spaces by transforming [them]... with images and texts and a space that stimulated wonder in the process of learning" (p. 13). A social justice pedagogy (Blandy, 1987; Desai & Chalmers, 2007) invites collaboration with those for whom we care, such as disenfranchised youth, survivors of domestic violence, and the chronically homeless (Stokrocki with Andrews & Saemundsdottir, 2004).

We are engaged in an ongoing, participatory action research project with three sets of variously disempowered participants. All participants are co-researchers, and each participant has an equal voice.[1] Our methods include observations of participant-led curriculum development through web search, Google Docs, and building and mentoring within a virtual world. For this aspect of the project, we met once a week for 10 weeks at Arizona State University's SkySong, a new digital research center. We used the Occupational Self Efficacy Scale (Hackett & Betz, 1981) and the Guide to the Construction of Self Efficacy Scales (Bandura, 2006) to investigate changes in self-efficacy during virtual world interaction. The qualitative study will continue in the future with discourse analysis (Kress & vanLeeuwen, 2001) and ethnographic documentation of various mentees (Inoue, 2008).

PARTICIPANTS/RESIDENTS

We propose to empower/educate a sample group of those seeking to build new lives (e.g., formerly homeless/underserved, young people, and artists) in Arizona and Mexico to use the virtual environment Second Life as a way to rebuild their lives or plan new life phases. For this study, we take the case of one 18-year-old youth, "Levis," whom we interviewed, mentored, and observed transforming his avatar and building a virtual home while planning a business for the next phase of his life. We gathered further data from two 18-year-old transient youths calling themselves "Dopey" and "Grumpy," in one session each. At the time of the interviews, Dopey had been on the road for a year and a half; Grumpy had been traveling for 2 months, but reported that he had been on his own for a much longer period of time and that he had supported himself through high school. These observations took place once a week for 4 weeks. In turn, Levis, who was attending a gaming camp at Arizona State University at the same time, mentored us with possible ways to construct objects and offered ideas that may be useful to young disenfranchised people utilizing virtual worlds.

VIRTUAL WORLDS

Virtual worlds are simulated environments that can be accessed by multiple users through an online interface. Some virtual worlds are distributed with no central server, and others are centralized, existing on one server (Dragojlov, 2008). The virtual world that we explore here is Second Life, a place to live as residents and to do nearly everything that people do in real life. In this virtual environment, residents can develop avatars, personal stories, and social networks. Second Life residency is a unique experience among virtual worlds in the amount of freedom that users have. Users, who have scripting privileges and the ability to create objects 'inworld' as well as to import textures and images created in other applications, have created nearly all of the content. Unlike most videogames, people are residents here and can join collaboratives with similar interests, whether educational or avocational.[2]

FLOATERS COMMUNITY TECHNOLOGY CENTERS

Our base is called "Floaters" and is located on the Plush Nonprofit Commons "Island" in Second Life, run by TechSoup, a real life organization located in San Francisco as well as in Second Life. The Nonprofit Commons Islands offer free offices for a number of nonprofit groups, such as the International Humanities Center, Child Rights and You, and Bridges for Women. The Islands offer "note cards" or flyers about the various organizations, a free horse-drawn tour, and free

"T" shirts as well as notices of various events. Through Floaters we also have access to ASU alt^I (Applied Learning Technologies Institute) in Second Life, where our participants can test their ideas in a safe space.

Floaters is likewise a real life technology research center for the disempowered using participatory action research methods, located both in Arizona and in Second Life. Anyone can join the group, but members are asked to give back by sharing technology with others. Members decide when they are ready to give back. Floaters members have engaged in one-to one peer mentoring, worked with disabled people, networked with other groups they belong to, established Community Technology Centers, taught classes, worked with new immigrants, provided technology to homeless/formerly homeless/mobile lifestyle persons, encouraged the development of art and creativity as well as job skills, and worked with Indigenous and low income people in US and Mexico. Floaters is based on Principles of Sustainability—to sustain is to provide someone with basic life necessities that include shelter, food, and clothing. With other nonprofits sponsors, Floaters sponsors Transitions: A Place for Dreams, the curriculum project with which our participants interface (Andrews, 2008).

A PLACE FOR DREAMS: PROJECT AIMS

This endeavor is part of work laid out by a larger team of educators and artists located in Canada, Los Angeles, San Francisco, New York, and Arizona who intend to empower marginal populations via such sites.[3] We are mentoring participants and investigating whether virtual worlds can be used as a tool to revise life plans through art. Our participants will learn new Internet skills, redefine and manifest their goals in a safe virtual space, and become empowered to choose their own life paths through visualizing and making art. For example, a group of Native American artists working with the project credit art with helping them recover from alcoholism, by showing them a different path.

Wonder is stimulated for formerly disempowered people when they have the opportunity to create in a new social space such as, 10 years ago, the Internet, or in 2008 and the coming years, Web 2.0. In assisting in the design of these new social spaces, we will allow our participants the opportunity to find themselves a creative home, manifest life changes in the real as well as the virtual world, and share their experiences with others. Participants who continue the program by mentoring others will be given the chance to begin their own Internet businesses, some of which are independent from 'parasitic' companies as they create a critique of larger, more powerful corporate interests that exist on the Internet.

STEPS IN TRANSITIONS: A PLACE FOR DREAMS

Our plan is to draw on existing directories of homeless resources: posts made to the Homeless People's Network, homeless/displaced blogs, and the caring expertise of a network of involved persons.[4] We will provide a program in which people can build a virtual home while going through a curriculum[5] that includes sustainability, personal finances, and planning for a new life, including a virtual business. In a second phase, those who choose to go on will mentor someone new to the project—and will be given the resources to manifest their virtual business.

Step One: Learn Basic Communication Skills. How do the disenfranchised acquire computers and Internet access? Libraries have been at the forefront of technology distribution since the beginnings of the Internet, arranging public use computers that can be accessed by anyone including those without any other access. Sandy found that mobile homeless persons were particularly likely to use the Internet regularly via library access (Andrews, 1999), staying in touch with one another via e-mail and participating in the Homeless People's Network, a mailing list for the homeless designed to offer solutions to policy makers (Boland, 1997). Five years later, a review of recent Homeless People's Network posts made for this chapter, as well as blogs by the homeless, indicate that homeless people may have laptops and can gain access to the Internet via public Wi-Fi, as at MacDonald's and Starbucks.[6]

Public Wi-Fi access is sufficient for basic virtual world uses, according to reports by residents making use of these resources. More advanced virtual worlds activities such as building may require better access, which we plan to provide via trained mentors who will visit shelters, bringing laptops to these visits. Disenfranchised people also can obtain used computers via various computer recycling centers. Floaters.org accepts used and recycled computers and will transform older computers for mentoring purposes.[7] In addition to virtual worlds expertise, basic online communication skills will be offered, including chatting, instant messaging, and group blogs and discussions. Residents can learn via mentorship as well as online tutorials.

Step Two: Acquire Computer and Digital Literacy. Virtual world instruction can accommodate residents' individual differences. Participants must explore virtual environment sites for themselves in order to understand how to navigate the virtual world and its major components. Downloading the program, adjusting the computer, viewing tutorials, and choosing an avatar are recommended beginning steps that require entrance procedures and patience. As they explore their identity through avatar development, residents of virtual worlds control digital representations of themselves in shared online environments.

At the turn of the 21st century, people find themselves inundated with such images. Avatars range from the lowest level avatars, such as "smileys" (heads that wink, blush, or turn and are attached to e-mail messages), to the more seductive, whimsical, or mysterious "anime" characters in electronic games (Stokrocki, 2007). Liao (2007) empowered young adults to create avatars on Second Life, where they can move around in many ways, chat with friends, go shopping and sell their products, learn about others, write personal stories, and build a house and world. Unlike a video game (Parks, 2008), people are residents of Second Life. They may change avatars, positions in the network of technologies that we use every day, from computers at home and wireless computer connections in the cars, to the workplace with computer-mediated classrooms, with multi-media hookups and digital cameras. These technological avatars connect individuals, local groups, institutions, and international societies (Stokrocki, 2007).

Electronic media also allows postmodern youth, "screenagers," opportunities for role-playing (gender, age, race) and offer "transcendence or temporary relief from youth's preoccupation with their own real life bodies" (jagodzinski, 2004, p. 273) and such perversions as violence and sex. Participants in our project will be concerned only with the nonprofit and education sectors. An alternative universe for teaching teens, The Teen Grid, is a safe place for 14- to 17-year-olds to enjoy and to learn.[8] Teachers direct the meeting of these students in real life. Art educators can foster such meeting grounds with disenfranchised students as well.

During the first session (06/12/08), Levis chose a character that he first called "a nightclub guy." For his first 'Appearance,' he chose what he called "a chain mail shirt" and edited it by sliding the Body Thickness sliding scale. He named his avatar "Levis Footman" (Figure 1).

FIGURE 1:
Levis Footman.

As Levis was also attending gaming camp at the time in which our observations took place, we thought that the ease with which he learned to create and make his avatar his own might be unusual in that his gaming experience may have been transferable. Seeking either corroborating or disconfirming data regarding this ease, Sandy, through the real life Floaters group, worked with the two 18-year-old youths mentioned, both of whom were currently on the road. Working with the youths in a McDonalds over hamburgers and fries, she found that access was not only sufficient for Second Life, but that the two youths found it equally easy to understand the Second Life interface and tools, including the avatar creation tool. Both youths stated that they had played videogames and were familiar with the avatar configuration process in general.

Second Life is always changing and full of surprises, including as it does islands, stores, clubs, and museums. Some sites are restricted; Floaters requires a special invitation to join or build here, and Levis had difficulty teleporting to this location until he joined the group.

Step Three: Develop Life Skill Guides. The Transitions: A Place for Dreams project provides a staircase of steps to a new life for disenfranchised people. At the entry level, the search for resources is important. For example, for those living in cars to look for a job, the Community Voicemail Program is available. The project also directs people to Resume Building sites such as www.e-resume.us. Advanced life skills may include ways of preserving one's family or traditional culture.[9] New life skills, including health information, are also available via public blogs.

Step Four: Imagine a Place for Dreams. For his first exploration, Levis opened with his character walking through water (Baptism) and didn't want to change clothes at first. He walked up to a segway and jumped on it for a tour of the island. After the tour, he teleported into an Info Hub, several of which are named after colors. He announced that he was looking for "a dragon" to go with his new appearance. During his journeys, he collected such free objects as a firework launcher, Celtic sword, popgun, and a party hat with "teddy bears." Finally he explored Morris Island, with moving cars and "things to blow up!" Carrying a torch, he flew around and fought another creature. "Oh! Wow! A green dragon!" He acknowledged this as his favorite activity.

Step Five: Envision a Home. The word "sustain" means to position something by supporting it; providing a space to build a shelter and instructions for building is thus a form of empowerment in learning. One of the challenges residents of a virtual world may face is finding a home site and building a dwelling (Figure 2). Not all islands in Second Life allow homes to be built, so in order to find a home, residents must search for a free site, rent, purchase, or simply "camp." What we learned here was the importance of exploration and play, what he called "messing around." Kincheloe (2002) explained that young people are the experts in this digital domain of experimentation due to their history of gaming, and we saw this here as well as in Sandy's work with the two "street kids" (p. 163).

FIGURE 2:
What we learned here was the importance of exploration and play, what he called 'messing around.' For example, Levis created this 'Awesome twisty house' resembling a tent as his home, when playing around with the build tools. (See Endnote 11.)

Step Six: Build a Business. Second Life abounds in different environments: educational (MIT, Illinois State University), entertainment (nightclubs such as Wheelies or the weekly WharfRatz dance), fashion (Adidas), and business (IBM), to name a few. Because the disenfranchised may have low self-esteem, building a business that is personally rewarding may help sustain their interest as they learn important work skills. For example, Floaters showcases the results of their outreach program that "extends to Puerto Penasco, Mexico, where Floaters supports the Community Technology Center there as well as Indigenous jewelry sellers of Mixtecan silver." Floaters recycles donated computers and sends to Mexican families to sell their goods. Floaters empowers marginalized people in real life and now provides examples to empower them in Second Life, with the aim of boosting their self confidence to execute a job/business in real life.[10] Within the Second Life office, visitors can grab a notecard or flyer about Mixtecan jewelry and how it is made.

Participants in A Place for Dreams are not required to create a Second Life business—they are given the freedom to choose their goals—but the process of designing a new life or phase of life is one that the process of building a virtual home may make easier. If the participant chooses to create a business, the business must first be planned. Participants create a written plan during the same time

FIGURE 3:
Levis' Game Poster.

period in which they build their home, and then bring that plan into Second Life, as a poster, an image, a video, a website, or a statement in some other fashion.

While envisioning his home, Levis worked on a plan for a business that could be incorporated into Second Life. He desired to be a virtual architect and designed a poster to advertise his future business. When uploaded, his lettering appeared too dark and needed contrast with his drawn house. So he redid the poster (Figure 3). While his business may not be directly related to his quest for a dragon, we are sure that he will meet different dragons in his real life that he can fight. We hope that some of these newly acquired tools from Second Life will help him.[11]

The Floaters Community Technology Center in Second Life exhibits some of its members' artworks, such as Judith Campenero's "Arizona Sky" on the wall for sale. Where appropriate, members are encouraged to give a portion of their profits made through Floaters back to the group. A Donation Box is located near the artwork to purchase a copy (either a real or a virtual copy). On the same side of the painting, we inserted a box with Hover Text: Exploratory Art Appreciation Questions (Feldman, 1994) for the onlooker to consider. We expect open-ended reflection and stories from people (i.e. Lunenfeld, 2000; Taylor, 2004).

Build social support roots. Sustainability also refers to maintaining someone with group emotional and moral support. Participants can apply to a group or they can add themselves. Every Friday morning, Second Life Nonprofit Commons participants attend a group meeting at the Plush Nonprofit Commons amphitheater to meet their neighbors and discuss such things as volunteering, service awards, and future plans. Later, people can branch out to similar groups that interest them.

Mixed reality events are a particularly interesting possibility.[12] Other social networking technologies that interface easily with Second Life are such websites as blogs, Delicious, and YouTube (Buffington, 2008). Blogs are frequently updated websites on which participants can add comments and even upload artworks. For example, to promote fashion design, avatar Zorena Deckard discovered the "portable DJ" (Tech and Mech Fashion, 2008).

Step Seven: Develop Service for Life. "Service for life" refers both to the requirement that participants give back to the Floaters and Transitions programs, as well as to the further hope that participants, having gained the sense of ownership that these programs are intended to impart, will continue to volunteer their service in the future. Part of our commitment to develop "service for life" among our participants is the need to raise issues related to Second Life and offer solutions. Some issues are technical; others involve stereotypes and loss of political identity; and some are related to security and morals.

While portability, step-by-step learning, and tutorials are advantages of laptops, disadvantages include their small screens, reduced storage capacity, wireless access, power outages, and the fact that the existence of many users will reduce bandwidth availability. Virtual world programs are expensive to produce, but at this point, can be effective for enrichment as individualized learning. Patience and perseverance are required along with some wariness of pitfalls, as noted in the next section. Of course, virtual worlds are still in development and some limitations will no doubt be removed as time passes.

Avatars and technology are subject to similar problems and concerns as human groups (Heide Smith, 2003). Security issues are a concern as elsewhere on the Internet. Residents must be over 18-years-old, but this may not stop sexual predators. People also need to examine cultural stereotypes in Second Life critically, such as the work *Most Beautiful Avatars* (self-portraits) based on gender identity (Liao, 2007). Such images are dominated by Western canon of beauty with its concepts of beautiful figures (Quaranta, 2007).

Another issue is the loss of political identity and agency in cyberspace. A resident is a disembodied consumer in anonymous control of a simulated reality (Holmes, 1997). How does such a reality affect real life? There is also concern among some observers that overuse of computer technologies may be a form of addiction (Hogan, 2008) and thus could lead to broken families, dissolved marriages, and lost jobs. Because politics is the process of influence, how does greed factor into the economy of excess?

An additional issue is responsible use. Not only do participants need to avoid pornographic areas in this virtual world as on the Web, they also need to be wary of copyright and intellectual property of others. These issues are challenges for participants, teachers and the disenfranchised, as they develop service for life by struggling to learn together to maneuver and change their "Second Life" in the virtual world as well as their real life.

CONCLUSIONS

Virtual worlds have been called "digital Montessori playgrounds for big kids" (Steinkuehler, 2008). Education in such a place goes beyond the typical classroom to include sandbox learning, exploring identity issues, and social causes. Educators have an uncanny ability to play creatively with new technologies and virtual worlds will be no exception (Winn, 2001). Panganiban (2007) argued for use of a hierarchy of Second Life educational tools: text, weblinks, video, immersive environments for a cause, and educational events/classes. Our immersive environment of Floaters and the ASU alt^I Island demonstrated most, if not all, of these levels: the use of text (informative posters), embedded weblinks (Floaters.org), social cause video (Immigration), blogs (ecology), and educational interactive discussion boxes as asynchronous "events." As a product of "Thirdspace"—this conceptual place consisting of continually changing events, appearances, and meanings (Soja, 1996)—the virtual environment "provides the conditions for creative social practice" (Creswell, 2004, p. 39). Richardson (2008) suggested that we think of art education as a "site of endless encounters and reformulations or relationships with the other, a site of constant decomposition and renewal" (p. 16). Second Life and other virtual worlds can provide this promise in conjunction with other Internet offerings.

Our participants are in three groups, all seeking new lives or revised old ones: youth, the disenfranchised, and artists. To be sure, all youth may be said to be disenfranchised or at least seeking to plan new lives. Levis, the initial case discussed here, and Dopey and Grumpy, added via theoretical sampling, had no difficulty mastering the environment and creating in it. We also asked all three to respond to an Occupational Self-Efficacy Scale, where they reported on the confidence each felt regarding their ability to complete the training or education for a variety of jobs. Andrews (1999) noted literature supporting her own findings that disempowered participants were responding on the high end of the scale; follow-up questions indicated that her participants responded in this way because they felt that although they had ability, they lacked opportunity. As we hope to employ self efficacy scales to see whether our participants grow in confidence regarding their ability to change their real lives after changing their virtual lives, it is encouraging that the three who participated in this first phase did not choose their responses only from the high end, thus leaving them room to grow.

Besides naturalistic studies of online gaming environments (Parks, 2008) and art and technology integration courses (Lin, 2008), Art Education needs qualitative case studies of collaborative teaching and learning in virtual worlds to promote social action. We will continue our qualitative action research on empowerment of disenfranchised people through Floaters, and network with other agencies in Second Life so all participants can learn. We also hope to augment our real-life courses with learning activities on Second Life and with non-profit agencies (Pantelidis & Vinciguerra, 2008). As human programmers and social transformers, art educators can enable the disenfranchised to cross the boundaries of their real worlds through learning by doing and virtual networking in a parallel world of art.

REFERENCES

Andrews, S. S. (1999). Floaters technology mentoring program. Retrieved November 26, 2008, from www.floaters.org/edresearch/mentor/index.html

Andrews, S. S. (2008). Transitions: A place for dreams. Retrieved November 24, 2008, from http://aplacefordreams.org/

Bandura, A. (2006). Guide for constructing self-efficacy scales. In F. Pajares & T. Urdan (Eds.), *Adolescence and education, Volume 5: Self-efficacy beliefs of adolescents* (pp. 307-337). Greenwich, CT: Information Age Publishing.

Blandy, D. (1987). Art, social action and the preparation of democratic citizens. In D. Blandy & K. Congdon (Eds.), *Art in a democracy* (pp. 47-57). New York: Teachers College Press.

Boland, T. (1997). Homeless People's Network discussion list. Retrieved from http://hpn.asu.edu

Buffington, M. (2008). What is Web 2.0 and how can it further art education? *Art Education, 61*(3), 36-41.

Creswell, T. (2004). *Place: a short introduction.* Malden, MA: Blackwell.

Desai, D., & Chalmers, G. (2007, Sept). Towards pedagogy of social justice art education. *Art Education, 60*(5), 6-12.

Dragojlov, V. (2008, June 23). Principles of interactivity. Lecture at University of Advancing Technology, Tempe, AZ.

Feldman, E. (1994). *Practical art criticism.* Englewood Cliffs, NJ: Prentice Hall.

Games & Avatars. (2007, June 17). Double Agents [Photo spread] The New York Times on the Web. Retrieved June 29, 2007, from www.nytimes.com/slideshow/2007/06/15/magazine/20070617_AVATAR_SLIDESHOW_1.html

Garber, L. (2004). Using a computer gaming environment to teach about community arts. *Art Education, 57*(4), 40-47.

Giroux, H. (2005). *Border crossings* (2nd edition). New York: Routledge.

Gude, O. (2007). Principles of possibility: Considerations for a 21st-century art and culture curriculum. *Art Education, 60*(1), 6-17.

Hackett, G., & Betz, N. (1981). A self-efficacy approach to the career development of women. *Journal of Vocational Behavior, 18*(3), 321-339.

Heide Smith, J. (2003). Avatars you can trust—A survey on the issue of trust and communication in MMORPGs. Retrieved October 6, 2005, from www.game-research.com/art_avatars_trust.asp

Hogan, S. (2008, May). Virtual addicts: When playing becomes more than a game. *Times Publications, 18-19*, 30.

Holmes, D. (1997). *Virtual politics: Identity and community in cyberspace.* Thousand Oaks, CA: Sage.

Inoue, Y. (2008). Concepts, applications, and research of virtual reality learning environments. *International Journal of Social Sciences, 2*(1). Retrieved May 24, 2008, from www.waset.org/ijss/v2/v2-1-1.pdf

jagodzinski, j. (2004). *Youth fantasies: The perverse landscape of the media.* New York: Palgrave Macmillan.

Kincheloe, J. (2002). The complex politics of McDonald's and the new childhood. Colonizing kidworld. In G. S. Cannella & J. Kincheloe (Eds.). *Kidworld: Childhood studies, global perspectives, and education* (pp. 75-121). New York: Peter Lang.

Liao, C. (2007, March). Avatars, Second Life, and new media arts: The challenge for contemporary art education. *Art Education, 61*(2), 87-91.

Lin, C. (2008). A qualitative study of three secondary art teachers' conceptualization of visual literacy as manifested through their teaching with electronic technologies. PhD Dissertation, University of Illinois at Urbana-Champaign, Dissertations and Theses - Art and Design [2009-12-01].

Lu, L. (2008). Art café: A 3D virtual learning environment for art education. *Art Education, 61*(6), 48-53.

Lunenfeld, P. (2000). *Snap to grid: A user's guide to digital arts, media, and cultures.* Cambridge: The MIT Press.

Keifer-Boyd, K. (2004, March). CyberArt pedagogy. Invited paper at the Society for Information Technology and Teacher Education 15th International conference in Atlanta, Georgia. Retrieved July 15, 2005, http://dl.aace.org/15033 Paper updated/presented at the 2008 NAEA Conference in New Orleans.

Kress, G., & vanLeeuwen. T. (2001). *Multimodal discourse: The modes and media of contemporary communication.* Arnold: London.

Panganiban. R. (2007, Fall). *Best practices for non-profits in Second Life.* New York: Global Kids, Inc.

Pantelidis, V., & Vinciguerra, D. (2008). Virtual reality and education laboratory, Retrieved November 24, 2008, from http://vr.coe.ecu.edu/vrel.htm

Parks, N. (2008). Video games as reconstructionist sites of learning in art education. *Studies in Art Education, 49*(3), 235-250.

Putnam, R. (2000). *Bowling alone: The collapse and revival of American community.* New York: Simon & Schuster.

Quaranta, D. (2007). Life and its double. Retrieved April 25, 2007, from http://0100101110101101.org/home/portraits/essay.html

Richardson, J. (2008, June). Caucus for Social Theory in Art Education, *NAEA News, 50*(3), 18.

Robbins, S., & Bell, M. (2007). *Second Life for dummies.* Hoboken, NJ: Wiley.

Rogoff, I. (2005). Engendering terror, retrieved on February 3, 2008, from mediageographies.blogspot.com/2005/08/irit-rogoff-engendering-terror.html

Shohat, E., & Sham, R. (1994). *Unthinking eurocentrism. multiculturalism and media.* New York: Routledge.

Soja, E. (1996). *Thirdspace: Journeys to Los Angeles and other real-and-imagined places.* Cambridge, MA: Blackwell.

Steinkuehler, C. (2008). Digital Montessori for big kids. Digital Media and Learning Blog. Retrieved May 27, 2008, from http://spotlight.macfound.org/main/public_profile/147/Constance_Steinkuehler

Stokrocki, M., Andrews, S. S., & Saemundsdottir, S. (2004). The role of art for homeless women and survivors of domestic violence. *Visual Arts Research, 29*(1), 73-82.

Stokrocki, M. (2007). Art Education Avatars in Cyberspace: Research in Computer-based Technology and Visual Arts Education. In L. Bresler (Ed.), *International handbook for research in technology and the arts, Part II* (pp. 1861-1380). Dordrecht, The Netherlands: Springer.

Sweeny, R. (2004). Lines of sight in the "network society." *Studies in Art Education, 46*(1), 74-87.

Taylor, P. (2004). Hyperaesthetics: Making sense of our technomediated world. *Studies in Art Education, 48*(3), 328-342.

Tech and Mech Fashion (2008). Retrieved July 7, 2008 from www.rikomatic.com/photos.

Winn, B. (2001). Learning through virtual reality. Retrieved March 8, 2007, from www.newhorizons.org/strategies/technology/winn.htm

ENDNOTES

1 We prefer to use first names in the article as we do with our participants.

2 For example, Lu (2008) introduced Art Café, an experimental learning environment on Second Life where nine adult volunteers interact with an artist. Here she promoted a sense of presence and interactivity, in which "users employing the cursor to interact with content information, objects, and system" (p. 49) and with other humans as well.

3 Discussed on the web at http://aplacefordreams.com

4 All resources will be available in Second Life as well.

5 Transitions: A Place for Dreams curriculum steps include: Learn Basic Communication Tools, Acquire Computer and Digital Literacy Skills, Develop Life Skill Guides, Imagine a Place for Dreams, Envision a Home, Build a Business, Teach Skills to Others, and Develop Service for Life (Andrews, 2008).

6 Surprisingly, an increasing number of transient individuals do come to own laptops; until recently this was rare since used laptops were few in number, but now they are on the increase. Where homeless persons rely on government disability checks, they may be able to frequent Wi-Fi-enabled businesses more often at the beginning of the month. Some homeless activists chronicle their lives via blogs in order to alert society to the issues facing the homeless. We noted one such activist for social change soliciting donations via Facebook in order to replace a stolen laptop. Another activist blogger, unable to work due to a disability, maintains a blog even when camping and not housed; he brings his laptop to town in order to use the Internet. Disenfranchised people also can obtain used computers via various computer-recycling centers. Floaters.org accepts used and recycled computers and will transform older computers for mentoring purposes.

7 See the website www.floaters.org/edresearch/recycle/index.html

8 The site includes Global Kids (www.globalkids.org) and PacificRim Exchange (between California's Modesto City Schools and Japan's Kyoto Gakuen High School) to name a few.

9 See the Virtual Native Lands project in Second Life.

10 ee www.floaters.org/edresearch/Mexico%20Project/IndiansJewlery/index.html

11 Levis has become a mentor and explained how he made his poster in PhotoShop, transferred it as JPEG, and uploaded it under File. Then he explained: (1) Go to Build, (2) Click cube icon, (3) Choose desired dimensions (10"x10"x10"), (4) Click on hollow, (5) Raise the cube—more hollow at 95, (6) Above: Path Cut Begins; round .079 ["mess around with it"]. To add special features, such as hinging: Choose a door to study, Hit door (Apple key on the Mac), Adjust the script if available. Mary directed, "Write these directions down to help someone else, talk slowly, and explain the details when asked. Technicians must learn to define/explain things in simpler terms."

12 For example, Sandy attended the NetSquared Conference (5/28/08) in RL (real life) in San Jose, CA. The aim of this conference was to develop future plans for Remixing the Web for Social Change. As she presented in Real Life, her avatar and others attending the conference sat around a roundtable in virtual reality doing the same thing.

Digital Visual Culture, Social Networking, and Virtual Worlds: Second Life and Art Education /

PAMELA G. TAYLOR, CHRISTINE BALLENGEE-MORRIS, AND B. STEPHEN CARPENTER, II

Brooke Hyacinth

Three avatars[1]—Brooke Hyacinth, Rain Winkler, and Metaphor Voom—exist in the virtual world of Second Life, living and working in their respective virtual spaces: Brooke on eLASTIC arts island, Rain at TELR island, and Metaphor on Educators Coop Island. They meet at numerous places in this virtual world including Beckman (Harvard University's island), Center for Book Arts, Gotham City, and the Isle of Dreams. When they meet, they typically talk about other places they have visited in Second Life. Often one will go somewhere and then teleport the others for a field trip of sorts. They laugh, share funny gestures, jump and somersault, and give each other objects, clothing, equipment, and/or toys. Some of their most favorite gifts are the butterfly wings that Metaphor found. They love to fly, but have trouble keeping up with each other when they try to fly together. The same is true for walking and running. Sitting in poser chairs is fun, but Brooke, Rain, and Metaphor enjoy dancing together above all else!

THE VIRTUAL WORLD OF SECOND LIFE

The three-dimensional virtual world of Second Life (SL) where Brooke, Rain, and Metaphor reside was launched in 2003. "From the shape of their avatars to the design of their homes, from how they spend their time to what types of affinity groups they form; SL design was focused on fostering creativity and self-expression in order to create a vibrant and dynamic world full of interesting content"(Ondrejka, 2004, p. 1). Avatars—graphic representations of people, animals, or other beings that serve as digital representations of their users—populate this online, three-dimensional rendered environment. With respect to the variety of avatars in this virtual world, Carr and Pond (2007) note, "Second Life allows a huge amount of customization resulting in a physical diversity unmatched by any place on earth" (p. 31). In SL, users, as their avatars, can teleport, fly, live in a house, go to clubs, take classes, make and view art, or just "hang out" in a virtual space on a computer screen. SL spans more than 42,000 acres in real-world scale. From press conferences and convention plenary sessions (Arrington, 2006; NYLC, 2006) to political speeches (Mistral, 2006), and live musical performances (Campbell, 2007), to film debuts (Meyers, 2007), SL is a second home to over 10 million "residents," who collaboratively create, purchase, and comment upon its content.

SL is a fully user-created virtual world and not a game, although it shares many of the same characteristics that define MMOG (massive-multiplayer online games). White (2007) argued SL "is a game, in the same way that Sims On-Line or World of Warcraft is, whereas others would argue that SL is too open ended and without any artificially imposed goals to be classified as a game" (p. 5). In essence, White (2007) contended that defining SL "boils down to your own definition of what constitutes work, leisure, and play and how you choose to approach SL" (p. 5). For what it is worth, SL is not a game, according to its CEO and founder, Philip Rosedale, aka Philip Linden, in SL:

> I'm not a gamer, and SL isn't a game. From the start, we/LL [Linden Labs] observed that something like SL would have its first uses in entertainment, and then grow beyond those uses and people became more confident in the capabilities of the new platform/OS/whatever-we-want-to-call-it. So we focused on making SL very exciting and visceral and inspirational, but not on making it a game.
>
> The future that we are all most passionate about is creating a new version of the world with a fundamentally different and better set of capabilities, and then see what happens when we all move there. This means we want SL to be able to reach everyone in the world, to be able to scale to 100s of millions of users and millions of servers, and to remain an open decentralized system in which creativity rules. (Linden, 2006)

The question of whether SL is a game or not may suggest the consideration of such art criticism issues as artist intent (Linden Labs), viewer or participant approach (avatar), and/or the place or institution in which the "object" is housed (virtuality, World Wide Web, Internet).

SL provides numerous opportunities to create with a defined space by its inhabitants. In fact, in SL, the method of building or making is the method of living (Rosedale & Ondrejka, 2006). Exploring, playing, making, researching, communicating, and brainstorming are but a few of the activities engaging a growing number of educators from around the world in this virtual community. Such virtual immersion is filled with seemingly limitless possibilities for invention and reinvention of physical appearance, spaces, relationship, and identities. Within the emerging discourses of social networking through such online virtual worlds as SL, digital visual culture facilitates and encourages collaborative interactions among users, viewers, consumers, producers, learners, and educators. As such emerging technologies continue to grow and take shape in forms unimaginable a few years ago, commonly held ideas of what art education is or should be are now altered and repositioned. How do examples of digital visual culture such as SL affect what it means to teach and learn? What constitutes an educational space and the identities of teachers and learners in digitally mediated visual contexts?

Brooke spends the majority of her time alone and making things. She is an intense green being whose pulsing fingers stay busy with terraforming[2] the land mass of eLASTIC arts island, setting up prims[3] to make walkways and stairs, constructing sky galleries and exhibitions, and/or twisting textural shapes into virtual sculpture. In 2007-2008, Brooke conducted two university classes partially in SL with 10 students in one class and 17 in another. Her students were hesitant to join the virtual world, but most of them quickly became fluent in its modus operandi; so much so that the plans Brooke had for the class were quickly expanded to include tasks and experiences she never imagined. For example, one student built his own island directly above eLASTIC arts. He built it so high that each member of the class had to don a special altitude feather to get there. Another student created a hovering artwalk that required each visitor to walk through images of works of art. Virtual discussions took place as avatars sat on temporary student-created objects that were made, purchased, gifted, or stolen by the students.

Rain spends much of her time visiting exhibitions, events, and lectures that explore social justice and identity development, as well as attending events and group meetings. Rain also likes to design her clothing and coordinate her shape. She constantly manipulates her visual representation and monitors other avatars' responses. Rain teaches courses that explore identity, race, sexual orientation, and gender. In one course, her students document and analyze their avatar development in SL. As Rain lectured to the students in in-world, she gave a quick demonstration of avatar development, and asked her students to record each decision, from type of avatar to eye color. She asked them to explain how close their decisions were based on their real appearances. They continued to journal as they proceeded through Orientation Island[4] and met other new avatars. Rain encouraged her students to talk to other avatars particularly about their avatar construction process. Once the students joined SL, Rain took them on field trips to places that specialized in exhibiting race, gender, and sexually oriented visual culture.

Rain Winkler

Through interactive spaces and film presentations, they explored such recreated concepts as stereotyping in SL. Interestingly, discussions in SL seemed to flow more freely and openly than in real life. After only one week in SL, students felt comfortable enough to explore difficult diversity issues that would typically take almost 6 weeks for students to feel safe enough to discuss in a real life classroom.

Metaphor enjoys attending art exhibitions, cultural events, and lectures. He is a member of several in-world groups and receives notices about events. He also enjoys improving his building skills, zooming around empty streets on his roller skates, and listening to jazz. Metaphor is currently working on a virtual interpretation of a real world social justice project that requires knowledge of the scripting language that enables objects to move and perform other interactive tasks. In the fall of 2007, Metaphor served as a teaching assistant for a course entitled Contemporary Visual Culture that was partially taught in SL. Eight students enrolled in the course and their avatars met with Metaphor during virtual office hours and field trips. For one assignment, the students located magazine advertisements that featured the human figure as the primary subject matter and then wrote interpretations. The advertisements were exhibited in the Teaching, Learning, and Visual Culture House, Metaphor's in-world residence. The interpretations were translated to notecards and inserted into the advertisements where they were available for downloading. Metaphor also invited three colleagues from other universities to appear as guest speakers in the class where they spoke to students and answered questions about teaching and learning in a virtual world. Similarly, Metaphor conducted two talks for university students on other campuses as a guest speaker.

AVATARS: DIGITAL VISUAL SELVES

Probably the most time-consuming, enjoyable, and indeed, liberating aspects of engaging in the virtual world of SL is the creation and constant re-creation of our appearance/identity as an avatar. It could be said that our avatars, like self-portraits (Taylor, Ballengee-Morris, & Carpenter, 2008), are cultural constructs and therefore extensions of our own bodies. In SL, our physical real world bodies are replaced with a digital body image that is a product of our decisions and possibly resonates with our fantasies, desires, or aesthetic choices that are not available to us in RL. Theorists such as Massumi (2002) argue there is a virtual/physical binary sliding scale; one is always present in the other. While others such as Suler (2002) view virtual worlds as providing opportunities to transcend beyond the human flesh through customization that may create a temptation to build an ideal body that becomes the preferred essence of self. Suler wrote that identity embodies multiplicity and cyberspace offers a place for deconstructing the self online. For some, this virtual working out of identity may be a healthy interaction. For others, it can be dangerous if fragmentation is already a problematic feature of their real world (Hillis, 1999).

Nakamura (2008) used the framework of "visual culture studies to focus on the ways that users of the Internet collaboratively produce digital images of the body... in the context of racial and gender identity formation" (p. 5). Further, Nakamura urged scholars to consider the Internet "as a popular environment for representations of identity" (p. 5). The social, cultural, racial, gender, sexual, and other contexts through which identity is constructed, interpreted, and negotiated all find new territory and renewed relevance within virtual worlds such as SL.

Brooke's look has not changed very much since November 2006 when she was born. She was deliberately made taller than her creator's RL personae and given a skin color that is not associated with any particular race (green). Although her inventory (closet) is packed full of outfits, shoes, wigs, and accessories she accumulates throughout her travels in SL, she usually wears the same types of clothes most of the time—jeans and a t-shirt with some kind of funky shoes. Her hair is magenta and spiked.

Rain's creator spends up to 6 hours designing clothes, hair, makeup, and shoes. Rain has been 8 shades of skin and eyes and 60 hairstyles. She changes her makeup frequently depending upon her outfit and hair color. She collected a variety of clothing and shoes that reflect activities such as swimming, ballroom dancing, disco, political activities, and casual look to attending the movies and wild inventions that have yet to find the right event, but she wears them anyway. From Rain's Prada-like red shoes to a red tiara, she is always slightly over the top and always looking for new couture.

Metaphor has a black beard and moustache and brown skin similar in tone to that of his creator. He is of average height for an avatar with a slightly muscular build. Although he changed his clothes quite often during his first few months of existence, for the past year he has limited his wardrobe to blue jeans, a black t-shirt, sunglasses, and a black Kangol hat. Occasionally, he will wear a red and black Ché Guevara t-shirt and khaki cargo pants. Most of the time he is barefoot, but sometimes wears black flip flops or roller skates.

Metaphor Voom

SL provides opportunities for participants to create new identities that are free from societal and physical limitations of ethnicity, gender, geography, sexual orientation or status. The virtual body becomes a part of the participant's identity. When referring to her avatar, author Taylor uses the pronoun "I." Author Carpenter refers to his avatar by name—"Metaphor," whereas author Ballengee-Morris moves back and forth between first and second person associations with her avatar Rain. The three different relationships the authors have with their avatars reflect the complex discourse of identity and the relationships faced by all users and their avatars in virtual worlds.

According to social networking consultant Jill Hurst-Wahl (2008), "Some people do take great pains to make their avatars look exactly like themselves. Other people like to experiment with a totally different look. And while some may not have tried to make their avatars look like themselves, they may have taken names in SL that were meaningful to them. So although we see this as a different world, we do take "our selves" there in many ways" (para. 2).

SO WHAT DOES SL HAVE TO DO WITH ART EDUCATION?

Simply, SL encourages the kinds of learning we believe are most meaningful in art education—interactive, collaborative, inquiry-based, constructive, connected, interdisciplinary, and relevantly provocative (Taylor, Carpenter, Ballengee-Morris, & Sessions, 2006)! Similar to some of the most meaningful learning experiences we have had as educators and learners in art education, SL and other virtual worlds promote collaborative interactions, the social construction of meaning, and situated learning (Hayes, 2006). The students in Rain's classes critically analyzed SL avatar construction as a means of exploring the construction of identity and community. Doing this in and through SL gave them both a freedom and sense of security that enabled them to interact more quickly and honestly than in their RL classroom. Meeting new people, sharing ideas, lecture, presentation, and just the down-to-earth conversations that characterize social networking are tantamount in Metaphor's SL existence. In addition to bringing multiple speakers into his classroom in a matter of minutes (10 minutes each speaker), Metaphor, whose RL personae travels extensively for speaking engagements, teleports to a number of SL spaces to guest lecture. According to Brooke:

> My favorite part of my SL existence is the lack of some of the real life physical boundaries that tend to inhibit my artmaking. As an artist, I know and have learned that respecting materials is important, but when I am feverishly trying to say something with my art, I don't want such limitations as gravity to weigh me down! In SL, I can make bricks and mortar float. I've dreamed of a space or state of being that placed no boundaries on imagination. SL is the closest yet.

In conclusion, we believe that such virtual worlds as SL have an important place in art education because of the cognitive and creative challenges and possibilities inherent in their seemingly limitless technology (Bentkowska-Kafel, Cashen, & Gardiner, 2007; Bitter & Legacy, 2006; Hansen 2004; Jenkins, 2006). As the basic structure of SL is based on real life metaphors (i.e., gravity, land, sky, water), initial immersion is not as intimidating as some virtual reality experiences that require external equipment and/or knowledge of coding and key-strokes. As in some[5] of the real life people who they may represent, SL avatars are varied. They exist in differing communities, and constantly deal with identity issues that relate to their environment, culture, and ideologies, as well as their appearance. SL avatars may also experience the volatile and, to most of us, inconceivable edges of society such as slavery (Meadows, 2008). As such, engaging with SL challenges educators and learners with different sorts of questions and experiments that, in addition to being more relevant to today's digitally literate students, trigger meaningful, critically reflective teaching and learning practices such as issues related to identity, community, and social justice. For example, virtual worlds offer rich possibilities for working through questions about the role of artists and artistic intentions of digital works of art and cultural productions when those works are generated collaboratively and asynchronously with multiple artists/avatars over time; questions about ownership of digitally produced works especially when those works are the result of combined participation of multiple viewers and their avatars; and questions about the meanings and significance of virtual places, contexts, or institutions on interpretations of the "born digital" works of art or cultural objects. In other words, working in SL makes us constantly question, think, and imagine as we make meaning. And isn't that what art education is all about?

The authors meet in Second Life.

REFERENCES

Arrington, M. (2006). Dell to make announcement in Second Life. TechCrunch. Retrieved April 22, 2007, from www.techcrunch.com/2006/11/13/dell-to-make-announcement-in-second-life/

Bentkowska-Kafel, A., Cashen, T, & Gardiner, H. (2007). *Futures past: Thirty years of arts computing.* Bristol, UK: Intellect.

Bitter, G. G., & Legacy, J. M. (2006). *Using technology in the classroom.* Boston: Pearson.

Campbell, V. (2007). On the bleeding edge of performance: Second Life musicians. Retrieved April 8, 2007, from http://campbell.vertesi.com/blog/on_the_bleeding_edge_of_performance_second_life_musicians

Carr, P., & Pond, G. (2007). *The unofficial tourists' guide to Second Life: The essential guide to an amazing virtual world—with millions of users.* New York: St. Martin's Griffin.

Hayes, E. R. (2006). Situated learning in virtual worlds: The learning ecology of Second Life. AERC Conference Proceedings. Retrieved June 28, 2008, from www.adulterc.org/applications/classifiedlistingsmanager/inc_classifiedlistingsmanager.asp?CategoryID=128

Hansen, M. B. N. (2004). *New philosophy for new media.* Cambridge, MA: MIT Press.

Hillis, K. (1999). *Digital sensations: Space, identity and embodiment in virtual reality.* Minneapolis: University of Minnesota Press.

Hurst-Wahl, J. (2008). My avatar looks like she goes to the gym. eNetworking 101: The Blog. Retrieved June 15, 2008 from www.enetworking101.com/blog/2008/01/my-avatar-looks-like-she-goes-to-gym.html

Jenkins, H. (2006). *Convergence culture: Where old and new media collide.* New York University Press.

Jones, R. (2007). MetaTerror: The potential use of MMORPGs by Terrorists. Counterterrorism blog. Retrieved July 10, 2008, from http://counterterrorismblog.org/2007/03/metaterror_the_potential_use_o.php

Linden, P. (2006). SL is not a game. *Second Life Wikia.* Retrieved February 10, 2010, from http://secondlife.wikia.com/wiki/Timeline

Massumi, B. (2002). *Parables for the virtual: Movement, affect, sensation.* Durham: Duke University Press.

Meadows, M. S. (2008) *I, avatar: The culture and consequences of having a Second Life.* Berkeley, CA: New Riders.

Meyers, M. (2007). Sundance holds screening in 'Second Life' for first time. C/NetNews.com. Retrieved April 8, 2007, from http://news.com.com/Sundance+holds+screening+in+Second+Life+for+first+time/2100-1026_3-6153064.html

Mistral, P. (2006). Ex-governor Mark Warner reveals SL actions figures' identity. The Second Life Herald. Retrieved April 7, 2007, from www.secondlifeherald.com/slh/2006/08/exgovernor_mark.html

NYLC (National Youth Leadership Council). (2006). The 18th Annual National Service-Learning Conference Enters Second Life. NYLC. Retrieved April 22, 2007, from www.nylc.org/happening_newsarticle.cfm?oid=5497

Nakamura, L. (2008). *Digitizing race: Visual cultures of the internet.* Minneapolis: The University of Minnesota Press.

Ondrejka, C. (2004): Living on the edge—Digital worlds which embrace the real world. Retrieved July 2, 2008, from http://papers.ssrn.com/sol3/papers.cfm?abstract_id=555661

Rosedale, P., & Ondrejka, C. (2006). Glimpse Inside a Metaverse: The Virtual World of Second Life. Retrieved December 15, 2006, from www.opendemocracy.net/arts/alterego_4620.jsp

Stephenson, N. (1992). *Snow crash.* New York: Bantam Books.

Suler, J. R. (2002). Identity Management in Cyberspace. *Journal of Applied Psychoanalytic Studies, 4,* 455-460.

Taylor, P. G., Ballengee-Morris, C., & Carpenter, B. S. (2008). It's not easy being green: SecondLife.com, self-portraiture, and identity. Conference presentation at the National Art Education Association Convention in New Orleans.

Taylor, P. G., Carpenter, B. S., Ballengee-Morris, C., & Sessions, B. (2006). *Interdisciplinary issues and approaches in high school art education.* Reston, VA: National Art Education Association.

Tofts, (2003). Avatars of the tortoise: Life, longevity and simulation. *Digital Creativity, 14*(1), 54-63.

White, B. (2007). *Second Life: A guide to your virtual world.* Indianapolis: Que.

ENDNOTES

1 The word *avatar* has several ancient roots. Within the Sanskrit Hindu philosophy an avatar is an incarnation (bodily manifestation) of a god that descends into the land of mortals to help address evil (Tofts, 2003). In 1992, Neal Stephenson was credited as the first person to describe an online environment that was real to its participants in his novel, *Snow Crash*. He created the idea of a cyberspace where people used audio-visual bodies to communicate with each other in a world called *Metaverse* (virtual reality) (Jones, 2007).

2 The term "terraforming" refers to the manipulation of areas that reflect the ground in SL, i.e., earth, rocks, mountains, sand, water, etc.

3 The term "prims" is short for primitives and refers to the basic shapes/forms that make up all objects in SL. For example, a hat may be made from a cone shape and a doughnut shape put together.

4 Orientation Island is where all new avatars go to learn how to walk, script, use tools, fly, and other needed skills in a safe space.

5 Second Life users may have multiple avatars and they may clone their avatars. Avatars may also be run by scripts, be robots, and/or be computer operated.

About the Authors

MEL ALEXENBERG is former Professor of Art and Education at Columbia University, head of the art department at Pratt Institute, research fellow at MIT's Center for Advanced Visual Studies, and dean of visual arts at New World School of the Arts in Miami. In Israel, he is creating a new School of Art and Multimedia at Netanya College and is former professor of art and Jewish thought at Bar Ilan University, Emunah College, and Ariel University Center of Samaria. His artworks exploring digital technologies and global systems are in the collections of more than forty museums worldwide. He is author of *The Future of Art in a Digital Age: From Hellenistic to Hebraic Consciousness* and editor of *Educating Artists for the Future: Learning at the Intersections of Art, Science, Technology, and Culture*. His blogs can be accessed through links at www.melalexenberg.com

LIÁN AMARIS is an interdisciplinary performance theorist and artist who focuses on gender, media, technology, and popular culture. She is currently the Robert and Ruby Priddy Professor of Performance Studies and Digital Media at Colorado College. Along with several forthcoming journal articles including an article in *TDR: The Drama Review*, Amaris has a forthcoming chapter on Madame Tussaud's Wax response to 9/11 to be included in the book *9/11 in Popular Culture*. The feature film and architectural installation of her performance project Fashionably Late for the Relationship (covered by the *New York Times*, *The New York Post*, and Reuters in July 2007) are currently touring throughout the United States.

SANDRA SUTTON ANDREWS is Research Director within the Applied Learning Technologies Institute at Arizona State University. She also teaches technology research courses in the Mary Lou Fulton College of Education at ASU. Her research interests center on the identification of emerging technologies and on investigations into their uses in education. Further research interests include participatory action research, grassroots community organizing, social justice issues such as the digital divide, and accessibility to persons with disabilities, all with respect to technology use. She has worked in the Yaqui and Pima communities in Arizona; with Mixtecans in Mexico; with mobile/disenfranchised populations; and with a variety of populations online.

CHRISTINE BALLENGEE-MORRIS is Associate Professor in the Art Education Department and the American Indian Studies Coordinator for The Ohio State University. She was the founding director of The Multicultural Center at OSU. This unit changed how diversity was defined, represented, and supported for and by students, faculty and community. Ballengee-Morris is past president of the United States Society for Teaching through Art. She has received numerous awards including the 2008 National Art Education Higher Education Western Division Award; the 2007 Ziegfeld Award for Diversity; the 2006 National Art Education Grigsby Award (research in and commitment to diversity); 2000 OSU-Newark research and service award; and NAACP Licking County, Ohio's Young Native American Woman leadership award.

MELANIE BUFFINGTON is Assistant Professor of Art Education at Virginia Commonwealth University. Her research interests include emerging technologies, museum education, multicultural art education, teacher preparation, and contemporary art. She previously taught middle school art and holds a BS from Penn State University and a MA and PhD from The Ohio State University.

B. STEPHEN CARPENTER, II is Associate Professor in the Department of Teaching, Learning and Culture, College of Education and Human Development, Texas A&M University in College Station. Carpenter's research explores art education and visual culture, hypertext curriculum theory and design, cultural studies through visual inquiry, and ceramics criticism. He co-edited *Curriculum for a Progressive, Provocative, Poetic, and Public Pedagogy* and coauthored *Interdisciplinary Approaches to Teaching Art in High School.* His research is published in such journals as *Art & Antiques, Art Education, Ceramics: Art and Perception, Educational Leadership, The Journal of Cultural Research in Art Education, The Journal of Curriculum and Pedagogy, The Journal of Educational Multimedia and Hypermedia, Studies in Art Education, Studio Potter,* and *Terracotta.* Carpenter earned his PhD from Penn State in 1996 and served as Editor of *Art Education* from 2004-2006.

JUAN CARLOS CASTRO is Assistant Professor of Art Education at Concordia University. His research focuses on the dynamics and qualities of knowing, learning and teaching art through new and social media as understood through complexity thinking, network theory, hermeneutics and phenomenology. He is also a practicing artist whose current inquiry explores place, ecology, and learning. Prior to joining the faculty at Concordia University, Juan taught at the University of Illinois, University of British Columbia, Johns Hopkins University, Maryland Institute College of Art, and the Burren College of Art. Juan is a National Board Certified Teacher and taught at Towson High School in Maryland. As a high school teacher, Juan's teaching and curriculum was awarded a Coca-Cola Foundation Distinguished Teacher in the Arts from the National Foundation for the Advancement in the Arts and twice awarded with a U.S. Presidential Scholars Teacher Recognition Award.

SHENG KUAN CHUNG is Associate Professor and Graduate Program Director of Art Education at the University of Houston, Texas. He has a BEd from National Hsinchu Teachers College, Taiwan; an MA from New York University; and a doctorate from the University of Illinois, Urbana-Champaign, all in Art Education. Chung has shown his art in over 20 juried exhibitions. He has written over 30 papers published in scholarly journals in Taiwan, UK, and the United States. His research interests include social reconstructionist art education (multiculturalism, visual/media culture, and social issues), computer-mediated art education, and Asian aesthetics. He is currently on the editorial board of *Art Education* journal.

DAVID DARTS is Assistant Professor of Art and Media Education and Co-Director of the Venice Studio Art MA program in the NYU Steinhardt School of Culture, Education and Human Development. His work focuses on the relationship between contemporary art and media, education and democracy. Through his research, he examines how contemporary art and media education can contribute to the preparation of literate, creative, and critically engaged citizens. His writings have been published in a number of prominent journals and books. He is chair of the Arts Based Educational Research Special Interest Group of the American Educational Research Association.

MARA JEVERA FULMER is Graphic Design Program Coordinator and Associate Professor at Mott Community College in Flint, Michigan. She holds an MFA in Studio Art/Graphic Design from Michigan State University, MA in Advertising Design from Syracuse University, and a BA in Photography and Journalism from SUNY/Albany. She previously was Art Director for the University of the South Pacific in Suva, Fiji, and SUNY/Albany, has clients in the US and abroad, and is a Fulbright Senior Specialist candidate. As an artist/educator, Fulmer focuses on cross-cultural design, using art as a catalyst for social change. She works in all media from print and Web, to book arts and video, and has exhibited in the US, Australia and Fiji.

CHARLES GAROIAN is Director, School of Visual Arts and Professor of Art Education at Penn State University. He is the author of numerous scholarly articles, book chapters, and books including *Spectacle Pedagogy: Art, Politics, and Visual Culture* (2008) with Yvonne Gaudelius, and *Performing Pedagogy: Toward an Art of Politics* (1999). Garoian has performed and lectured in colleges and universities, galleries and museums nationally and internationally, and received significant awards for his research and creative accomplishments. He has served on the Editorial Review boards of the *International Journal of Education and Art (IJEA), Studies in Art Education: A Journal of Issues and Research in Art Education, Qualitative Inquiry* journal, and the *Journal of Social Research in Art Education.*

DAVID GILL, an Illinois native, completed a BFA in Painting and studied aviation while at University of Illinois in 1989. Returning to UIUC, he finished a Master's in Art Education in 1995 before teaching for 4 years in several Illinois public schools. Gill later completed an Educational Doctorate under the mentorship of Kerry Freedman at Northern Illinois University. His dissertation was successfully defended in 2008; it explored digital technology through a case study of one public high school classroom where students used 3-D modeling and animation software to create narrative animations. Presently, Gill is serving as Assistant Professor of Art Education at Youngstown State University in Ohio, while residing in nearby Boardman with his wife and two stepchildren.

KIT GRAUER is actively involved in art education organizations at the local, national, and international levels. She has held executive positions in the BC Art Teachers Association, Canadian Society for Education through Art, National Art Education Association as Director in Higher Education, and the Chair of the NAEA Teacher Education Research Task Force and numerous executive positions in the International Society for Education through Art including President. She is also very involved with art education publications and has been on the Editorial Board of the *Canadian Review of Research and Issues in Art Education, The Canadian Art Teacher, Art Education, Cat's Cradle, Journal of Aesthetic Education* and is the former Editor of *InSEA News.*

KATIE HELMS is Program Coordinator and Lead Teacher at Bright Horizon-Pinnacle Drive in McLean, Virginia. She is currently studying for a Master's in Applied Healing Arts at Tai Sophia Institute. Her pre-K through middle school students' work focuses on bookmaking, painting, and printmaking. She holds a BA from New College of Florida and a MAE from Virginia Commonwealth University.

NICHOLAS HOSTERT is a practicing art educator and artist who resides in Chicago. He received his Master's of Arts in Art Education from The School of the Art Institute of Chicago in 2008, and his Bachelor of Science in Art Education from Illinois State University in 2003. He is currently investigating the artistic and educational impact of digital visual media, critical art theory, and collaborative digital communication. He has taught high school since 2004 in the Chicago area and currently serves on the Illinois Art Education Association Board of Directors.

JAN JOHNSTON is currently an adjunct instructor in the Department of Art Education in the School of the Arts at Virginia Commonwealth University in Richmond, Virginia. She holds a Master's of Art Education from VCU and is also pursuing certification in Instructional Technology. Johnston taught both high school and middle school for 7 years and received National Board certification in 2003. She has been a University Supervisor and a guest instructor for the Summer Intensive Program for Virginia Commonwealth University Qatar. She has presented at the local and national level at both NAEA and National Service-Learning Conferences. Johnston has long been involved with arts-based service-learning and, most recently began her 4th year with the Mayan Arts Program, an international service-learning program.

KAREN KEIFER-BOYD, Professor of Art Education and Affiliate Professor of Women's Studies at The Pennsylvania State University, co-authored *Engaging Visual Culture* (Davis, 2007) and *InCITE, InSIGHT, InSITE* (NAEA, 2008), co-edited *Real-World Readings in Art Education: Things Your Professors Never Told You* (Falmer, 2000), and served as editor of the *Journal of Social Theory in Art Education* and guest editor for *Visual Arts Research*. She is co-editor of *Visual Culture & Gender*. Her research on feminist pedagogy, inclusion, and cyberactivism is published in more than 40 peer-reviewed research publications and translated into several languages. Keifer-Boyd has been honored with several teaching, arts administration, and research awards including a Fulbright (2006).

MATTHEW KENYON is an Assistant Professor of New Media at Penn State where he teaches courses in Video Game Development, Physical Computing, 3-D Animation and Video Art. He is a founding member of the art group S.W.A.M.P.(Studies of Work Atmospheres and Mass Production), whose primary goal is to find creative expression within elements of culture that are inherently counter-creative. Kenyon's art has been exhibited at numerous galleries and museums in the US, Europe, South America, and Asia in such venues as SIGGRAPH 2005-Emerging Technologies in Los Angeles, The International Symposium of Electronic Language in Sao Paolo Brazil, Nicograph International, The Society for Art and Science in Seoul, South Korea, Bilbao Arte in Bilbao Spain, Forest City Gallery in London, Ontario, among others.

CHRISTINE L. LIAO is a doctoral candidate in art education in the School of Visual Arts at Penn State University. Her research focuses on new media, technology and society, contemporary art, pedagogy, identity, and the body. She has presented papers at the NAEA National Convention, the InSEA international conference, and the educators program at the 2007 SIGGRAPH international conference. Her article "Avatars, Second Life®, and New Media Art: The Challenge for Contemporary Art Education" was published in the March 2008 *Art Education* special issue on creativity.

MARISSA MCCLURE is Assistant Professor of Art and Visual Culture Education at the University of Arizona. She has taught at the elementary and preschool levels in urban and rural schools and museums as an art teacher, a reading teacher, and a general classroom teacher. As a researcher and teacher, she is interested in contemporary and historical theories of child art; constructions of childhood; children and visual and media culture; children as individual and group learners; relationships between art, play, learning, and teaching; critical theory in art education theory and practice; early childhood education; and pedagogical documentation as research methodology.

SELIN OZGUZER studied graphic design receiving her BFA degree in Turkey. She received her MFA from Bilkent University (1998) and University of Florida (2003). Since 2004 she has been teaching graphic design, Web design and interactive media at Jacksonville University. Her research interests are focused on use of flash interactivity in interactive story telling and graphic design education. She presented her paper on "Interactive Manga: A Prototype for Multi-Linear Visual Narrative" in the 5th International Symposium of Interactive Media Design that was held at Yeditepe University in 2007. Her poster and Flash portfolio designs received first and second place awards respectively in 2008.

CARLETON PALMER, PhD, NYU, 1978, is a veteran of more than 30 years' college and secondary school teaching of art and art education. A photographer of art, and former Museum photographer, his commercial work has appeared widely in books, catalogs, and magazines.

RYAN PATTON is a PhD candidate in Art Education at Penn State University. His research focuses on New Media education, specifically in the K-12 environment. He is co-author of a chapter in the forthcoming book *Digital Cityscapes: Merging Digital and Urban Playspaces*, and has presented on his work in new media education nationally and internationally. Prior to returning to Penn State, Patton taught art at Jane Addams High School for Academics and Careers, a part of the New York City Public Schools. He continues to teach Flash animation and game development with the Smithsonian Associates in Washington, DC.

RYAN SHIN is Assistant Professor in the School of Art at the University of Arizona. He received his PhD in Art Education from Florida State University in 2002, and taught at the University of Wisconsin at La Crosse from 2002 to 2007. His research has focused on Asian folk art and performance art, Asian visual culture, and digital media technology in art education. His articles have appeared in *Visual Arts Research* and *Journal of Cross-Cultural Research in Art Education*, and *NAEA Advisory*. He also has authored several book chapters, and has given presentations at national and international levels.

JAMES W. SHURTER is Instructor of Graphic Design at Mott Community College in Flint, Michigan. He holds an MFA in Studio Art/Graphic Design from Michigan State University, a BFA in Theatre Performance from the University of Michigan/Flint, and an AAS in Graphic Design from Mott. Shurter has worked in the educational field since 2003. He worked professionally as an Art Director/Prepress Manager and continues to work as a freelance designer for clients including the UM/F, Oakland University, and MSU to name a few. As an educator/artist/designer, Shurter is highly influenced by the theatre of life. His work strives to increase awareness of the unseen, to create new dialogues and perceptions, using varying media including print, Web, and video.

ANITA SINNER is an Assistant Professor in the Department of Art Education at Concordia University. Her research interests include arts research methods, life writing, teacher culture, and digital media. She is also a research collaborator exploring the arts and community-based new media programs. Her research focuses on arts-based research and life writing in teacher education and curriculum studies, and her dissertation has been recognized with the CASWE Dissertation Award, CATE Dissertation Award, and Penny Gouldstone Art Education Award. Her co-edited anthology with Christine Lowther, *Writing the West Coast*, was recently published by Ronsdale Press.

MARY STOKROCKI, Professor of Art, Arizona State University, is a World Councilor and former Vice-President of the International Society for Education Through Art. She is the recipient of the 2007 College of Arts & Architecture Alumni Award, Pennsylvania State University. She is a Distinguished Fellow of the National Art Education Association (NAEA), 2007 recipient of the Women's Caucus June King McFee Award; 2005 Lowenfeld Award; and 1995 Manuel Barkan Award for research. Her qualitative research focused on multicultural teaching/learning in inner-city Cleveland; Rotterdam, Holland; Ankara, Turkey; Sao Paulo, Brazil; Warsaw, Poland; Barcelona, Spain; Evora, Portugal; and the Yaqui, Pima/Maricopa, Ak-Chin, Apache, and Navajo Reservations in Arizona.

ROBERT W. SWEENY is Associate Professor and Coordinator of Art Education at Indiana University of Pennsylvania. He received his MFA from Maryland Institute, College of Art, and his BS and PhD from Pennsylvania State University. He has published numerous papers and book chapters dealing with the topics of digital visual culture, new media art, locative media, video games, and the relationship between surveillance technologies and visuality. He serves on the editorial boards of *The Journal for Cultural Studies in Art Education* and *Studies in Art Education*, and is the co-editor of *Performance, New Media, and Surveillance: Special Issue of the Journal of Surveillance and Society.*

KEVIN TAVIN is Associate Professor in the Department of Art Education at The Ohio State University. He holds a BFA, MEd, and a PhD in Art Education and has taught K-12 and post-secondary courses since 1990. Tavin's research focuses on visual culture, critical pedagogy, cultural studies, and art education. His work is published in numerous journals including *Art Education; InSEA News, The Journal of Cultural Research in Art Education; The Journal of Social Theory in Art Education; NAEA News; Studies in Art Education;* and *Visual Arts Research.* Tavin has presented papers and keynotes at international conferences and symposia in Sweden, Germany, South Korea, Japan, Finland, Denmark, Brazil, Czech Republic, Spain, and Belgium. Most importantly, Tavin has participated in an all-night karaoke session with Bob Sweeny.

PAMELA G. TAYLOR is Chair and Associate Professor in the Department of Art Education, School of the Arts, Virginia Commonwealth University in Richmond. Taylor's research explores service-learning, interactive digital technology, emerging media, visual culture, curriculum, and criticism. She authored *Amazing Grace: The Lithographs of Joseph Norman* and coauthored *Interdisciplinary Approaches to Teaching Art in High School.* Her research is published in such journals as *Art Education, Studies in Art Education, Journal of Cultural Research, International Journal of Education & the Arts, Computers in Schools, Journal of Educational Multimedia and Hypermedia,* and *FATE in Review.* Taylor earned her PhD from Penn State in 1999 receiving a J. Paul Getty Doctoral Dissertation Fellowship. Taylor served as Editor of *Art Education* from 2007-2008.

MICHELLE TILLANDER completed her PhD in 2008 from Pennsylvania State University and is currently Assistant Professor of Art at the University of Florida. Her research activities include engaging art education, technology, and culture as an integrated process to expand art educational technology practice. She presents at state and national conferences, most recently the International Conference on

Qualitative Research (QI2008) in Illinois. She currently serves on the *Art Education* journal editorial board. From 1985 to 1991, she helped implement the first Virginia's Governors School for the Arts, returning in 1998-2002 to serve as Chair of the Visual Arts Department.

SHEI-CHAU WANG is Associate Professor of Art Education at Northern Illinois University, DeKalb, Illinois. His research interests include teaching visual culture at the college level, e-learning in art and design, and electronic portfolio development and assessment. Before joining the NIU School of Art in Fall 2006, Wang taught art and design in several universities in Taiwan. He has published articles in both English and Chinese and presented numerous papers at both national and international conferences. He currently serves on the editorial board for the *International Journal of Education through Art* (InSEA) and the *Journal of Aesthetic Education* (Taiwan).

SARA WILSON MCKAY is Assistant Professor of Art Education at Virginia Commonwealth University. Since writing her dissertation on the politics of vision and visuality at The Pennsylvania State University, Wilson McKay has extended her research to include the ways in which works of art create new seeing, how looking can be a dialogic process, and the possibilities of seeing more of the educational process in and through art. Employing critical and new media theory in her work, her publications range from practical pedagogical models for teachers of art to theoretical essays considering art and education in a broader purview. Recent publications include: "Seeking Policies for Cultural Democracy: Examining the Past, Present, and Future of U.S. Nonprofit Arts" in *Studies in Art Education* (Summer, 2008 with L. Lewis); "Education as Installation Art and Other Useful Ideas from the Contemporary Art World: Conversations with Artist Annette Lawrence" in *Art Education* (March, 2008); and "Cultivating a Vision of Students Who Can Think and Act for Themselves: How Meaningful Art Education can Help Undo *Homo Systematicus*" in *Journal of Cultural Research in Art Education* (2007).

SOHHYOUN YOON is a graduate student in Art Education at Virginia Commonwealth University. She was born in Seoul, Korea and received BFA in Printmaking at Hongik University in Seoul. After graduating, she worked as a motion graphic designer at a broadcasting company for several years in Korea. Her experiences using technology led to interest in incorporating technology in art education. She is working on her thesis, Second Life in Art Education, and teaches 2nd- through 6th-grade students in art camp during summer.